Epistemology:
The Key Thinkers

Continuum *Key Thinkers*

The *Key Thinkers* series is aimed at undergraduate students and offers clear, concise and accessible edited guides to the key thinkers in each of the central topics in philosophy. Each book offers a comprehensive overview of the major thinkers who have contributed to the historical development of a key area of philosophy, providing a survey of their major works and the evolution of the central ideas in that area.

***Key Thinkers* in Philosophy available now from Continuum:**

Aesthetics, edited by Alessandro Giovannelli
Ethics, edited by Tom Angier
Philosophy of Religion, edited by Jeffrey J. Jordan
Philosophy of Science, edited by James Robert Brown

Epistemology:
The Key Thinkers

Edited by
Stephen Hetherington

continuum

Continuum International Publishing Group

The Tower Building
11 York Road
London SE1 7NX

80 Maiden Lane
Suite 704
New York NY 10038

www.continuumbooks.com

British Library Cataloguing-in-Publication Data
A catalogue record for this book is available from the British Library.

ISBN: HB: 978-1-4411-0345-1
       PB: 978-1-4411-5396-8

Library of Congress Cataloging-in-Publication Data
Epistemology : the key thinkers / [compiled by] Stephen Hetherington.
  p. cm. – (Key thinkers)
Includes bibliographical references and index.
ISBN 978-1-4411-0345-1 (hardcover : alk. paper) – ISBN 978-1-4411-5396-8 (pbk. : alk. paper) – ISBN 978-1-4411-1783-0 (ebook pdf: alk. paper) – ISBN 978-1-4411-9435-0 (ebook epub: alk. paper)
1. Knowledge, Theory of – History. 2. Philosophers – Biography. I. Hetherington, Stephen Cade. II. Title. III. Series.

BD161.E64 2012
121.09–dc23
                                                    2011031388

Typeset Newgen Imaging Systems Pvt Ltd, Chennai, India
Printed and bound in India

Contents

Notes on Contributors

Robert Bolton, Professor of Philosophy, Rutgers University, USA

Desmond M. Clarke, Member of the Royal Irish Academy, and Professor (Emeritus) of Philosophy, University College, Cork, Ireland

Alan Code, Professor of Philosophy, Stanford University, USA

Stephen Hetherington, Professor of Philosophy, University of New South Wales, Australia

Christopher Hookway, Professor of Philosophy, University of Sheffield, UK

P. J. E. Kail, University Lecturer in the History of Modern Philosophy, St Peter's College, University of Oxford, UK

Melissa McBay Merritt, Lecturer in Philosophy, University of New South Wales, Australia

Ram Neta, Associate Professor of Philosophy, University of North Carolina, Chapel Hill, USA

Nicholas D. Smith, James F. Miller Professor of Humanities, Lewis and Clark College, USA

Paul Snowdon, Grote Professor of Mind and Logic, University College London, UK

Gisela Striker, Walter C. Klein Professor (Emerita) of Philosophy and of the Classics, Harvard University, USA

John Turri, Assistant Professor of Philosophy, University of Waterloo, Canada

Markos Valaris, Lecturer in Philosophy, University of New South Wales, Australia

CHAPTER 1

EPISTEMOLOGY'S PAST HERE AND NOW
Stephen Hetherington

1. Key components

Epistemology's history is one of . . . what? Thinkers? Yes, at least that: hence this book's title. And then, through those thinkers, what other keys will unlock epistemology's past? Should we conceive of that history as a sequence, possibly a progression, of important ideas or concepts? What of pivotal theses and theories? Arguments and objections? Might notable problems and challenges have been driving epistemology from at least some times to other times? Must general traditions and overarching ways of thinking also be mentioned? Possibly all of these have mattered. But which thinkers – and which ideas, concepts, theses, etc. – have mattered most? Who and what have been epistemology's most influential forces? This book will help to clarify and answer that question.

2. Knowledge: epistemology's subject matter?

What have those ideas, concepts, theses, and so on – the tools used by epistemology's key thinkers – been *about*? What has been epistemology's subject matter? Has it stayed constant over the centuries? Or have there been shifts of focus and emphasis?

There has been at least some professed continuity. Probably the most consistently discussed topic within epistemology, from the beginning until now, is said to be knowledge. Etymologically, that is perfectly apt, with the term 'epistemology' hearkening back to the ancient Greek words *episteme* (knowledge) and *logos* (account). An account – a theory, an understanding, a grasp – of knowledge: is that, *most* centrally, what philosophers have long sought within epistemology?

Often it has been. Often it still is. Yet care is needed even here. Much epistemology has long been receptive to the possibility that its thinking will lead to *sceptical* conclusions, especially about people's chances of having knowledge. Imagine believing yourself to know a lot about the world. But imagine, next, your starting to question whether you really do have all of that knowledge: 'Surely I know. . . . Well, *do* I?' You proceed to think hard about this. *Then* imagine concluding that what had seemed to you to be so much knowledge on your part is not actually knowledge at all. With that conclusion, you would be embracing (even if reluctantly) a sceptical assessment of yourself as a knower. This could well constitute a problem for how you *wish* to view yourself. Sceptical results are challenges to initially favoured ideas and theses, such as the comforting presumption that one is a knower.

Indeed, such challenges can have a far wider reach. Sceptical conclusions within epistemology typically talk more generally – about people as a whole, not merely some unfortunate individual. For example, a sceptical conclusion could be universal in intent, proclaiming that there is *no* knowledge (even that there *cannot* be any). Or it might be less-than-universal but worrying nonetheless – by denying that the world does (or even could) include some notably important *kind* of knowledge.

And once an epistemological story does become sceptical, there is a sense in which it should not regard itself as ever having been about knowledge. It could not be claiming to tell us about knowledge-the-real-phenomenon-within-the-real-world – because it is denying that there *is* any such knowledge. Instead, the story would now be seen to have been a tale only of knowledge-as-it-*would*-be-if-any-really-existed. It is thus not about knowledge-actually. It is about knowledge-hypothetically.

That difference is important because an epistemological story only about knowledge-hypothetically, we may well feel, is about just an *idea* or *concept* of knowledge. It is not about knowledge, at any rate not if it is right to deny that any knowledge exists for the story to *be* about. The story would be about knowledge only as something we might *wish* to have, or as something we would – if not for the story – *believe* ourselves to have. (It would be about knowledge in somewhat the way that a fairy story is about wicked witches.)

And this is a potentially disturbing prospect to bear in mind as we study some of epistemology's history. Even when epistemological stories seem to be about knowledge, are they really so? We face at least the possibility of sceptical theses from epistemology's history being true. But *if* they are, have epistemology's stories ever really been about knowledge (as against merely seeming to be so)? The alternative would be epistemology's only ever having been about ideas or concepts of knowledge – knowledge-hypothetically – only knowledge as it *would* be if we had some. This book will contain many epistemological ideas, theories, arguments and so on – parts or wholes of epistemological stories. If we already know right now, *before* we engage with these, that knowledge exists, then we may read the book with a confidence that its focus will be upon knowledge itself.[1] We would know already, for instance, that when we fashion a concept of knowledge, this concept is answerable to the reality of what the knowledge 'out there' in the world is actually like.

But *do* we know that much, in advance of doing epistemology? Not clearly; and so we have an epistemological challenge *about* epistemology. We do epistemology, partly in order to find out *whether* we have knowledge. Our doing epistemology is not itself a guarantee of there being knowledge. The history of epistemology has often involved people writing as if they are telling us, somehow directly and unproblematically, about knowledge. Not always, though; more cautiously, some epistemologists acknowledge their writing first and foremost about a concept or idea of knowledge, rather than directly about the phenomenon of knowledge.[2] This is a delicate issue, threaded throughout epistemology's history. We have ideas as to what knowledge is, if it exists; do we want *more* than ideas? Yes: we also wish for them to be *accurate* ideas, *correct* in what they say about knowledge. And again, that desire is our hoping for epistemology to reveal something about knowledge the phenomenon, not only about our ideas or concepts of knowledge (even if these are intended in turn to be about knowledge). How is epistemology to accomplish this?

On the face of it, most epistemologists discussed in this book have *aimed* to be discussing knowledge itself (or something related), not only an idea or concept of it. They *say* that knowledge, or something related, is their topic. Ostensibly, they will talk of knowledge. But epistemology's practices or methods are discursive – discussing, proposing, reflecting. And these are not guaranteed in advance to be accurate. They *do* develop or fashion a concept (at least one; maybe more) of knowledge. However, discussion then continues, leading to criticisms and refinements of those concepts. In all of this, the goal remains that of accuracy. How is that outcome sought in practice? The concepts are subjected to strict and searching philosophical testing. Time and again, epistemologists ask whether a particular theorist's concept of knowledge is consistent and coherent, explanatory and illuminating. As the book proceeds, we will come to appreciate the efforts by some of history's outstanding epistemological thinkers to satisfy that sort of standard – hopefully so that their concepts are really *informing* us about knowledge and related phenomena.

3. Problems and progress

If such epistemological informing has occurred, it has done so over time; and not always smoothly so. Problems have arisen, repeatedly. How has this happened? Do concepts beget problems? Or do concepts arise from problems? Both of these occur, it appears, within epistemology as elsewhere. This book will display many instances of that reciprocal fecundity. The perennial desire, of course, is that the problems also beget solutions. But epistemologists have long been aware of the possibility that we will *never* reach solutions.[3] In that way, problems within epistemology could become a problem *for* epistemology – for its ultimate capacity to be informative, via its concepts, about knowledge as a phenomenon.

Of course, we will not know whether epistemology has such a problem, until we have surveyed its attempts to solve the problems it poses for itself. At the very least, we must bear in mind that talk of problems need not be an admission of defeat.[4] Epistemologists often speak of the problem of knowledge (and of associated problems such as scepticism).[5] This is usually meant to designate a cluster of problems for our *understanding* knowledge, for our gaining a philosophically adequate concept of knowledge. Yet there is also an epistemological *virtue* in confronting these problems. They are problems of which we might never even have thought prior to pursuing epistemology. Philosophical reflection on knowledge often reveals previously unsuspected problems for the would-be consistency, coherence, and explanatory power of what might have been our *pre*-philosophical concepts of knowledge. So, even if there is a problem for epistemology in not yet having solved these problems, there is a different sort of problem for non-philosophers if they have not even *noticed* the failings within their concepts of knowledge. Even the problem of not having solved a problem can be a piece of progress – an advance not made by those, such as non-philosophers, who remain unaware of the unsolved problem in the first place. Epistemology struggles; this is a problem for it. Even so, this problem could be progress, albeit not all the progress we might seek.

How much epistemological progress, if any, *is* guaranteed? Or might we never entirely solve the problems noticed by epistemologists? Perhaps knowledge is somehow not fully understandable by the likes of us, no matter that it is our knowledge. Maybe our best epistemological thinkers are those who are intelligent and insightful enough to notice philosophical *problems* within our concepts of knowledge, even when they cannot proceed to solve those problems.

Here, too, we must be careful: there is also the possibility of misleading ourselves into 'seeing' problems where there need not be any. We could be *creating* what we will deem problems, simply as part of creating the concepts. An epistemological problem-for-us might not be an epistemological problem-unavoidably. What will feel to us like an epistemological problem may emerge only *as* we fashion a concept – a problem, indeed, being shaped *by* our shaping of the concept. In short, the question here is this: Are these problems of our own epistemological making as we try to understand knowledge? In other words, the problem might not be 'out there', part of the reality constituted within the world by the phenomenon of knowledge. A particular problem might be a feature only of the concept with which, mistakenly, we believe ourselves to be describing knowledge as it really is. How do we know whether an apparent epistemological problem about knowledge is really about knowledge?

These are perplexing questions. But we will best answer them by considering epistemological *exemplars* – by having in front of us philosophy's most apparently powerful and incisive attempts, over the centuries, to understand knowledge. Those attempts, contemplated as a whole, suggest some patterns in this part of philosophical history; only some, though. Epistemology has unfolded irregularly over time. There have been starts and stops and starts and stops and . . . There has been discipline and originality. All of this happens in real time, as philosophically reflective lives unfold, chancily and possibly as may be. Epistemology is human-made (and it could be human-destroyed, if we are careless). Epistemology is and has long been alive, from then until when, from thenever until whenever. I mention all of this because epistemologists sometimes proceed as if they take themselves to be engaging with *timeless* philosophical problems – ones that should, once noticed and until solved, be of perpetual philosophical concern. In contrast, *if* epistemological problems reflect ways of conceiving, hopefully but not necessarily, of an independently real phenomenon of knowledge, then such problems are *not* necessarily of aptly perpetual philosophical concern. I am not saying that none merit such continuing attention. Many of the problems highlighted in this book have *long* held epistemologists' gazes. I am noting a possibility, though, one that renders even more problematic philosophy's attempts to understand knowledge by building upon *previous* attempts to understand it.

Here is a correlative note of caution. Also popular, it sometimes seems, is the idea that epistemological problems confronting us now are more philosophically *advanced* problems than those which faced previous epistemological generations – as if we face our particular epistemological problems only because we have learned all that needs to have been learned from our epistemological forebears. On that way of thinking, any epistemological progress by a thinker now, relative to other *current* thinkers, is automatically epistemological progress beyond all *previous* thinkers. If so, that would lower any pressure upon us, when pondering those ideas currently focussing epistemological minds, to take seriously epistemology's history. It could also be reassuring to believe that prior epistemological foci have *only rationally* given way to our present ones. According to that sort of optimism, epistemology as a whole could never be *re*gressing fundamentally in its best thinking at a time.

But surely that picture is *too* optimistic. Humility is needed here. We could be walking, even as groups of epistemologists, along paths soon to leave us stranded within an enveloping forest. For a start, we might not have learned all that we should have done from our epistemological ancestors. We could be misunderstanding them. We could be overlooking what was most important in their thinking. So, this book is doubly valuable. It tells us about previous epistemological forays, which are philosophically interesting in themselves. This also helps us to enrich contemporary epistemology, even as we seek to reflect *now* on knowledge and its kin. What should we have learned – what should we still learn – from epistemology's past? What *mistakes*, if any, might we be making now which were not made by our epistemological predecessors?

4. Theorizing and science

Whatever else epistemological thinkers do, they do it via claims and counter-claims, questioning and answering. And the point of all this is to theorize, at least a little; or to react to theories, by criticizing and moulding and replacing. This might be done stumblingly, tentatively, incompletely; sometimes inspiredly and brilliantly. However it transpires, an epistemologist is nothing without such theoretically attuned efforts. And epistemological influence (although it can be increased by the power of a personality) is most likely to *persist* only through the results of those efforts – the intellectual power of the questions, the answers, the theories, the . . . whatever else is needed for good philosophizing.

Then what else *is* needed? This book's essays will assist us in answering that question. At times, epistemological (like some other philosophical) thinking is compared to *scientific* thinking. Many epistemologists have wanted to be more rather than less scientific, in what they try to say about knowledge and in how they seek to theorize about it at all.

After all, in trying to understand knowledge, it helps to have in mind examples of knowledge. And some of the clearest examples come from science. Has there been scientific progress? If we are to talk of the growth of human knowledge over the centuries, we cannot ignore, it seems, what scientific progress has given us. It has given us much scientific knowledge.

Not only that; some epistemologists have wanted to do philosophy *by* theorizing as scientifically as possible. This can mean their consulting scientific observations and experiments, reflecting the science of the day. There can also be a more general scientific influence, a methodological one. How does scientific inquiry flow? Can philosophical inquiry flow similarly? Thus, epistemological theories (even when not scientific in content) are to be proposed – and then genuinely tested, so as perhaps to be refined, reshaped or replaced, tested anew and so on. In that sense, a scientific *method* has sometimes seemed attractive to philosophers trying to understand knowledge's nature and availability.

Should epistemology therefore become *part* of science? Would that ensure our understanding knowledge? Most epistemologists do not want to *subsume* epistemology within science.[6] This is because there are questions which most epistemologists ask about knowledge but which scientists ignore: scientists have generally not reflected so philosophically upon phenomena or ideas of knowledge. To seek and even to gain knowledge is one thing; to understand philosophically *what* one has sought and gained might well be something else – something not attempted, let alone achieved, by scientists. Epistemologists have long thought of science as a central test case for their theorizing about what knowledge is. But usually they have not thereby *ceded* their theorizing to science. This theme will be present in some of the book's chapters.

5. Beyond knowledge

Is knowledge the only phenomenon about which epistemologists have sought to think? Far from it, as this book will demonstrate.

Reasoning and evidence, truth and representation, and much more have mattered greatly within various epistemological arguments and theories. Sometimes, this is because these are thought to be part of knowledge; sometimes not.

For example, knowledge has often been assumed to admit of a kind of conceptual analysis: we understand the phenomenon of knowledge by fashioning a concept which talks relevantly of various further phenomena. The idea is that, once we reflect upon how the world might 'put together' an instance of knowledge, we find ourselves talking of opinions or beliefs, truth or correctness, evidence, perception and reason, etc. Hence we will also, at times, be trying to understand these in themselves, as a prelude to deciding whether knowledge can be obtained by 'putting them together'.

Even if we decide that (as was contemplated earlier) nothing *can* be 'put together' to constitute knowledge, because there is no knowledge, we may still conclude that there could be knowledge-*like* phenomena. There might be something else which is available and which, although not quite knowledge, is not so far from being knowledge. Having it could be as *close* as we ever come to having knowledge; and it might be welcome, too. What might such an attainment be? This sort of question will underlie some of the book's chapters. Discussing these ideas or phenomena other than knowledge might help us to answer it.

6. Plato

Systematic – extensive, ambitious, and written – Western philosophy began in the fourth century BCE with Plato's justly influential dialogues. That is also when systematic Western epistemology began:[7] a few of those dialogues have distinctive epistemological components, as Nicholas Smith makes apparent in Chapter 2.

Epistemological problems and challenges were thus introduced to an Athenian audience; now they are arrayed before us. Some of Plato's questions about knowledge are still among philosophy's central epistemological challenges. In most of those dialogues, Plato's teacher Socrates speaks – sometimes giving voice to his own views, at other times to Plato's. The results are always mind-catching.

For example, the question was posed, What *is* knowledge? Answers were proposed; arguments flowered; puzzlement bloomed. Many answers and questions; much puzzlement. Famously, Socrates wondered not only what knowledge is, but whether he knew much at all. He noticed, too, there possibly being different kinds of knowledge, such as would arrive through perception, or by way of reason. These epistemological themes – the nature of knowledge, its availability, and methods for obtaining it (if it is available) – would recur over subsequent centuries.

What was also notable about Plato's epistemological thinking was the way in which, when perusing possible answers to those questions, it speedily became *metaphysical*. In thinking about knowledge, he advanced theses about the world's underlying nature. This need not be surprising: as we will find throughout the book, epistemologists have often done this sort of thing; and aptly so, because when we know we are knowing parts *of* the world and we are doing *as* part of the world. What was surprising in Plato's case were his *specific* metaphysical conclusions. For instance, he portrayed Socrates as linking what we know now with what we knew in a *previous* life. If all knowledge is recollection (as he avers), at least some of it was not gained in this life: it was gained in an earlier one, able now to be recalled and thereby known. Well, *did* we have earlier lives? If Plato's epistemological story about knowledge is right, maybe we did; in which case, a great deal *more* than epistemology – even a metaphysical understanding of ourselves – could depend upon epistemology.

Probably the most famous Platonic mix of epistemology and metaphysics was his later discussion of knowledge as somehow being related to *Forms*; for the concept of a Form has itself been Plato's most celebrated albeit controversial metaphysical idea. Forms – if they exist – are abstract and universal properties, perfect 'models' existing somehow nowhere and everywhere at once and forever. Suppose you observe a particular red object – present here and now, specific in its spatio-temporal location. What *makes* it red? Plato's answer: There is a Form of redness, the *general* property of redness; and the particular object is red only by imitating, or participating in, that general Form of redness. Do we know by *reason*, though (and not by observation), that the Form exists? We observe the particular redness, thereby knowing it. Do we also know the Form of redness, even if not by observing it? *How?*

Those metaphysical thoughts are rather dramatic. Perhaps Plato's most lasting epistemological idea has been something a little less metaphysical – his distinction between knowledge and *correct opinion* (or true belief, as contemporary epistemologists call it). Is there more to knowing than being correct? Epistemology is still trying to say exactly *what* more is needed – while acknowledging Plato's as the initial philosophical formulation of the distinction.[8]

7. Aristotle

How often could there exist a teacher–student pairing as dynamic and influential as was that of Plato and his protégé Aristotle? Quite possibly, only once in the lifetime of a tradition; and in saying this I am thinking of philosophy in general, not only of epistemology. Like Plato, Aristotle's impacts were deep and vast, spread thickly throughout philosophy; this has included epistemology. Many ideas now taken for granted by epistemologists were first and most powerfully grasped, before being systematized, by Aristotle. His epistemological contribution was that of an insightful analyser and arranger. He discovered complexities within his physical and conceptual surroundings, without ever being overwhelmed by the resulting pictures. Robert Bolton and Alan Code convey this in Chapter 3.

Like Plato, Aristotle sought to understand not only the observable world, but also the process of gaining such understanding. What is the world like? How do we know what it is like? The latter question has always been central to epistemology. Unlike Plato, though, Aristotle's answer did not involve his talking of transcendent Forms, thinking of them as what ultimately explains the nature of the world's observable features. Aristotle searched *within* the observable world, not beyond it, for his explanations. These were to be formulated in terms of the observable world's essential characteristics. And the latter were to be described by explanatorily organizing principles. Aristotle recognized that, while there can be knowledge that something is so, beyond that there might also be knowledge of *why* it is so. But he did not regard that 'beyond' as short for 'beyond the observable world'. His goal was what we would now deem some explanatory *science*.

Of course, scientific explanations require not only observations; reasoning is no less vital. And we may view Aristotle as having initiated epistemology's continuing respect for attempts to understand reasoning in its various forms. As he realized, there is both deduction and induction, categories each with their own inner epistemological complexities. For example, can even deductive reasoning produce knowledge from non-knowledge? Or must knowledge always, when inferential, emerge from knowledge? What of the possibility of non-inferential knowledge? Aristotle asked whether some statements are not inferred from others,

while yet amounting to knowledge. Is there knowledge which is immediate and basic, *prior* in the order of explanation and evidential support to all other knowledge? This is a question about how a body of
knowledge – either all knowledge, or all science, or all within some
narrower part of science – is to be inferentially structured. It is a kind
of question which is still part of standard epistemological perplexity.
And Aristotle's seems to have been its first version. The question is one
of whether there are *foundations* to knowing, and of whether, if there
are, they would be notably secure, able to be established conclusively
or demonstratively.

   So many epistemic phenomena were discussed by Aristotle, as epistemology continued its process of beginning even to exist. Here are just
a few: appearances, observation, reasoning, scientific inquiry, scientific
knowledge of essences, empirical knowledge more generally, explanation, knowledge-that and knowledge-why, understanding, regress,
hypotheses, first principles, demonstrative knowledge. First with Plato;
then through Aristotle: epistemology was starting to find a language
of its own.

8. Ancient scepticism

So Plato and Aristotle, especially, helped to launch philosophy in general;
and epistemology was a vibrant part of that. Once epistemology enters
the philosophical tale, however, can sceptical thoughts be far behind?
Subsequent philosophical history suggests not; so did early Greek philosophy. And thus we must attend carefully to what, these days, are called
the ancient sceptics. Gisela Striker, in Chapter 4, describes their respective histories, influences and styles of argument. This is where epistemological scepticism began, at least in any systematic and sustained form.

   When contemporary epistemologists refer to scepticism, typically
they speak of two forms, blends, or eras – ancient scepticism and modern scepticism. The latter is generally traced to some of René Descartes'
seventeenth-century writings (see the following section); in some ways,
ancient scepticism is a quite different creature. There are overlapping features, naturally – such as a concern with what a serious desire for *truth*
means for people as inquirers. But there are substantial differences, no
less, between the two. For instance, there is an ancient emphasis upon

unsettling people's tendencies to believe or assent, as against a modern sceptical focus more upon denying that people have knowledge even when confident of doing so.

Who were the key ancient sceptics? Pyrrho (365–275 BCE) is the thinker most standardly mentioned, both for his personal and his intellectual impact upon others. Still, he was not the only one engaged in sceptical skirmishes at the time. Between his death and the renewal of interest in Pyrrhonism around two hundred years later, Plato's Academy included some philosophers – notably, Arcesilaus, Carneades and Philo – who honed a sceptical bent of mind when responding vigorously to the cognitive optimism of various Stoics. Could a person be misled (wondered these sceptics), so as to form an apparently correct and powerful 'impression' of how the world is in some respect – where in fact there is *no* such respect? Is that sort of mistake possible, slipping stealthily into our cognitive lives, present in spite of our being unaware of it? If so, then claims to *certainty* are unwise; should *fallibilism* therefore prevail? We could approach with some caution and humility the business of believing.

Yet even that way of weakening our expectations as knowers would have seemed unwarrantedly optimistic to a Pyrrhonist. Sextus Empiricus is our main source for Pyrrho's ideas; and a systematic and extensive source he was. To read him is to meet a cavalcade of competing viewpoints: of doubts about so much; doubts, though, reflecting so much also of what people already think. There are claims; but counter-claims too; impressions jostling with alternative impressions; perspectives face to face with dissenting perspectives; can such tensions ever be resolved impartially and non-dogmatically? Or is a kind of undecidability forever inherent in our claims as to what is really true, what the world really is? Pyrrhonism's probing inquiries stirred up some fundamental issues about what we can ever accomplish *rationally* as the believers we will most likely continue to be.

9. Descartes

From ancient to modern epistemology: contemporary epistemologists generally think of Descartes as being the father of modern epistemology; which, in a sense, he was. But in another sense, possibly he should not have been. Have epistemologists always taken from Descartes what *he* took himself to be doing as an epistemologist?

His epistemological influence has been due mainly to the way in which he formulated and engaged with some *sceptical* arguments about people having various kinds of knowledge. Not only he ever did this, of course. Nor (as Desmond Clarke makes clear in Chapter 5) was this all that Descartes did when reflecting upon knowledge. For a start, he did not regard *scientific* knowledge as answerable to sceptical worries: there, probability or plausibility (moral certainty) would suffice. What he did influentially do, however, was to convey vividly how attempts to gain *metaphysical* knowledge of the world would be vulnerable to some traditional sceptical doubts (Pyrrhonist doubts; as to which, see Chapter 4). He also captured, it seemed, what that vulnerability might feel like 'from within' a first-person perspective of inquiry. (It *feels* different to ask of oneself, 'As I seek knowledge of God, and thereby of the world, how can I overcome sceptical doubts?', rather than to ask of another, 'As she seeks knowledge of God and thereby of the world, how can she overcome sceptical doubts?') Here, metaphysical certainty was needed.

So, sceptical arguments were indeed important to Descartes, but perhaps (as Clarke explains) not as much so as contemporary epistemologists usually assume. Such arguments did help to fashion Descartes' famous *Cogito* ('I think, therefore I am') and his mind/body dualism (usually interpreted as each person's being a composite of non-physical mind and physical body). Yet these famous ideas were metaphysical, and not therefore – even if known – representative of all possible objects of knowledge. What mattered to Descartes, no less, was scientific knowledge (an interest which can be overlooked if we discuss just his *Meditations*). His reflections on scientific knowledge did not concern themselves to any marked extent with those famous sceptical arguments.

This matters, if we wish to do justice to Descartes' own epistemological emphases and challenges. It also matters more generally to the history of epistemology. It reminds us that Descartes – like the empirical-minded Aristotle before him (Chapter 3), and like the empiricists Berkeley, Locke, and Hume after him (Chapter 6) – regarded epistemology as having implications for how we should understand science and its hopes of progress. Accordingly, he was trying to balance both scientific and metaphysical concerns. The world around one could be examined from both of those perspectives. And would knowledge even of this single world, for example, be the same sort of thing within the two settings of scientific inquiry and of metaphysical inquiry? It need not be; and maybe, for Descartes, it was not. Thus, we may wonder whether people are answerable to disparate standards as, respectively, would-be scientific knowers and would-be metaphysical knowers. Descartes is often described by epistemologists as if he was talking just about knowledge *simpliciter*, with its involving a kind of certainty that resolves those sceptical doubts. But that story might be misleading about Descartes; and needlessly simplifying in its epistemological ramifications, its sense of what epistemological options await us as we reflect upon knowledge. Was Descartes a fallibilist about scientific knowledge but an infallibilist about metaphysical knowledge? Epistemologists often talk as if he was an infallibilist about all knowledge.[9] Clarke ends Chapter 5 with a suggestion as to why they make that mistake, if it is one.[10]

10. Locke, Berkeley, Hume

And so to British Empiricism – or at least its most historically significant initiators: John Locke, George Berkeley and David Hume, from the seventeenth and eighteenth centuries. As we noted a moment ago, Descartes' overall epistemology was very respectful of science, its needs and accomplishments. Contemporary epistemologists do not always think of Descartes in quite that way. Still, there is no such hesitation when they consider Locke's epistemology. It was tailored expressly to the scientific insights of his time. And great thinkers inspire great thinkers: Berkeley and Hume enveloped themselves partially in – even while being goaded to move beyond – some of those imaginative Lockean concerns, ideas, and lines of thought. In Chapter 6, Peter Kail guides us along the dominant paths in the philosophical territory opened up by these three philosophers.

As Kail acknowledges at the outset, an epistemological concern with experience – with empirical observation – as being important to knowing did not emerge only with these thinkers. Nor did it end with them. Just as people have always used their senses when trying to know the world, philosophers – most, at any rate – have always *noticed* their doing so. But some philosophers have *especially* noticed that happening. For these philosophers, empirical observation is the content and the engine of knowing: the latter begins, traverses, and ends with experience. And the most famous such philosophers were indeed Locke, Berkeley and Hume. They presented us with clarity, vision, and challenges. Actually, they presented us with what some may well feel are *inescapable* challenges – both epistemological and metaphysical – to be confronted by any ambitious version of empiricism.

In particular, are we fundamentally *limited* by our sensory powers – helped by them, yet limited too, as would-be knowers? Are we limited by them in what ideas we can think, in what meanings we can express with those ideas, and in which of those expressed meanings can constitute knowledge for us? We – our senses, our powers – are complex; what kinds and strengths of knowledge are possible for us anyway? Locke asked all of this forcefully. How should philosophers respond? In section 9 we noticed Descartes' use of a notion of probability. Such a notion is at the heart of empiricism. Do our sensory powers reveal sometimes what is, but also sometimes what *probably* is? Caution and humility could suggest that we will be safer – less likely to be mistaken – if we talk of how the world probably functions, rather than of how it does function. Yet Hume, most notoriously, bequeathed to us some influential reflections on epistemological aspects of probability. *Is* it so easy – is it always even possible – to understand the world probabilistically? We wish to understand the world's normal causal processes and, if possible, any miraculous exceptions to these. Does the concept of probable reasoning help us to do so? This is not clear, thought Hume, at least as he has traditionally been interpreted on this issue.

It could depend on what the world even *is*. Here we confront Berkeley, who laid before us a vision not only of all knowledge as sensory but of all matter as sensed. The world, argued Berkeley, is inherently sensed. It is an actual object of sensing – often by us, though always by God. Berkeley took this to be a commonsensical view, an assessment of his not widely shared by contemporary philosophers. In any case, perhaps the equally striking alternative was to bow before some form of *scepticism* – conceding that we do not know the world's matter, given that it is not always being sensed. Locke was aware of this danger within empiricism: in trying to know the world, we rely upon apparently sensory ideas; and we hope that they accurately reflect the world around us. But do they?

Hume was no less aware than Berkeley of sceptical ideas; and maybe he was, or maybe he was not, a sceptic himself. He seemed to glean from potentially sceptical reasoning a sense of how we *naturally* function as thinkers.[11] He did not repeat Berkeley's response; which was that the world is knowable through ideas because it *is* ideas – the alternative to accepting so being, again, a possibly unwelcome scepticism about our ever really knowing the world's matter.

For these empiricists as for so many other epistemologists, then, much in our thinking about knowledge and the world reflects how we react to sceptical challenges. These most influential of all empiricists also sharpened those challenges in the first place. Sceptics or not, still they appreciated the potential epistemological power in sceptical thoughts.

11. Kant

Later in the eighteenth century, Immanuel Kant followed those pivotal British empiricists, especially Hume, in reflecting on the nature of experience. He did so to markedly different effect, though. On those empiricists' shared metaphysical picture of how we know the world via experience, content comes to us from the world. In observing, we experience what, in being experienced, becomes mental content for us; then our minds can use that content in various ways. But Kant gave to epistemology a fundamentally new metaphysical picture of how we know the world via experiences. In effect, our minds *contribute* some essential content even to simple observations. And, strikingly, this contributed content helps us to know the world (rather than making us mere imaginers as to what it might be). What we contribute reflects a shared human way of 'shaping' and organizing – of giving needed form to – the sensory data coming to us.

In Chapter 7, Melissa Merritt and Markos Valaris explain this picture of Kant's, focussing on *Critique of Pure Reason* – his most epistemologically famous book. He began by arguing that observations of objects are of things located in space and time – but that the space and time being observed are *forms within* the observations. Our minds contribute a spatio-temporal structure within which fit those appearances of objects, presented to us in experience by the world. An observational experience is a combination of what comes from without – sensory matter presented to us – and what is already within us – a way of spatio-temporally accommodating that sensory matter or content.

Something similar happens when we proceed to think about these objects, beyond simply observing them. There are general concepts already within us, such as of substance and causality, with which we organize into thoughts the spatio-temporally constrained observations of objects. Such concepts are categories, in terms of which we understand what we observe. They are inescapably part of how we know truths about the world's objects.

Moreover, in knowing even these objects we have some self-knowledge. We know our own organizing selves. Not in every respect, perhaps; but at least *as* a continuing organizer 'within'. This is a *self*-reflective experience, yet part also of knowing the world outside.

Those remarks hint at the subtlety and complexity in Kant's epistemological thinking. Yet even great thinkers can at times receive less than their due. Merritt and Valaris remind us that this happened to Kant early in the twentieth century, but that in the century's second half his ideas were again at the centre of epistemological discussion due to the writings of Wilfrid Sellars and P. F. Strawson – important philosophers themselves, imaginative Kantians in some respects.

Sellars gained epistemological prominence in the 1950s with his questioning of what he called 'the Myth of the Given'. This was the empiricist confidence in there being epistemically *basic* observational experiences – epistemically basic, in the sense of amounting to knowledge without requiring further knowledge to support them, thereby *making* them knowledge. Sellars argued that, always, reflection upon how trustworthy an experience is remains possible. Kant would have welcomed this picture of somehow needing to reflect upon one's experience before it is to be knowledge.

Strawson was even more manifestly Kantian in his reflections upon the nature of experience. He highlighted what he took to be conceptually necessary aspects of experience. In particular, whenever we have an experience, must it always incorporate some general categorial accuracy about the world? And if that application of Kant's idea of our employing categories in experiencing the world is correct, are sceptical arguments misplaced from the outset (when supposing, as they often do, that a person could have a stream of experience that does *not* at all reflect the world)?

12. Pragmatism

Certainly the pragmatist tradition within epistemology sought, from its inception, not to succumb to what it viewed as the illusion of sceptical doubts. That tradition (discussed by Christopher Hookway in Chapter 8) is America's most distinctive contribution to epistemology's history. In their individual ways, its three most celebrated figures – C. S. Peirce, William James and John Dewey, in the late nineteenth and early twentieth centuries – advised all of us, then and since, never to allow philosophy to become distracted and defined by such insubstantialities as sceptical ideas. It is one thing to describe a supposed sceptical possibility; as a pragmatist epistemologist would point out, it is quite another thing for that possibility (if such it even be) to constitute a genuine challenge to inquirers and would-be knowers. Equally, of course, it is one thing to deny that we are genuinely susceptible or at least answerable to sceptical challenges; it is quite another thing to say, with philosophical depth within a fuller philosophical picture, *why* we are free in that way from sceptical musings. But pragmatism brought one such form of explanation to epistemology.

A tale thereby emerged of people as purposive and accomplished inquirers, yet ever fallible ones. Doubts are not to be idle, mere intellectual availabilities. They are to be pressing in practical and urgent ways, as we move inquiringly within an observable and manipulable world. Whatever beliefs we have, we have for reasons. So, we need not – and therefore should not – toss aside the beliefs simply on intellectual whimsy. Whenever we do replace a belief, we should do so as part of a progression towards a settled end – fixed belief, consequent truth, consequent reality. A settled end for one inquirer might not constitute certainty: it might not be settled for all inquirers. And even when it *is* settled for all of them, it still might not be certain relative to anything beyond the standards of those many, even if these are genuine inquirers. In that way, fallibility is forever present. Yet that is not a concern as such. It is a *feature*. It Just *Is*. Nor is it a barrier of principle to our having knowledge, including scientific knowledge. At any rate, it is not, unless sceptical doubts are real. Again, however, for pragmatists those doubts are not real.

Challenges do arise, naturally. We will wonder which moves are productive ones within well-ordered inquiries. When is it right to move from one belief to another? Which apparent tensions within a context of inquiry are real ones, deserving of respect? And what *is* knowledge if it need not be understood as what we have once we answer sceptical questions? Such questions, and more, will be touched upon in the chapters following Hookway's – a pattern which is testament in part to pragmatism's more or less overt continuing importance within twentieth century epistemology.[12] Its emphasis upon the conceptual centrality of inquiry and the associated emptiness of sceptical questions has been directly influential (Chapter 9). It has had subtle ramifications for empiricist conceptions of knowledge and evidence (Chapter 10). And its emphasis upon fallibility has been a theme underlying some recent not-necessarily-empiricist examinations of knowledge and evidence (Chapter 11). Finally, we should note that pragmatism has helped to shape some striking *challenges* to paradigmatic epistemological ideas.[13] All in all, it has been a suggestive and fertile way of thinking within epistemology.

13. Wittgenstein

One of the twentieth-century's most distinctive yet puzzling philosophical voices was Ludwig Wittgenstein's; and Paul Snowdon in chapter 9 helps us to hear and understand that voice's epistemological musings and mutterings. In spite of striving at times almost not to be philosophical, Wittgenstein could not help but be philosophical. Partly he did this by showing how philosophy could be unlike what it had previously been, how it might be pursued anew. Certainly his epistemological thoughts offered some original possibilities for further philosophical reflection.

Take his joust of sorts with his Cambridge colleague G. E. Moore. At stake was the right to walk away unscathed from the clutches of external world sceptical reasoning. Could this be done? If so, how? Moore famously replied to the sceptical reasoning with a show of hands – two of them, his own. This was argument in action. It was supposed to defeat, and manifestly so, the sceptical view that we cannot know there to be an external world with its external elements. Wittgenstein began (the notes which became posthumously) his *On Certainty* suitably bemused, allowing that *if* Moore could know his hands to be there, scepticism would indeed have been defeated.

Moore thought that he had done enough to undermine the sceptical reasoning; Wittgenstein disagreed. He paid even *more* attention to argument in action. He examined how Moore had – *and* had not – really done enough. My use of 'had not' reflects the sense in which Wittgenstein would find himself, unlike Moore, not attributing knowledge within such a circumstance. But I also said 'had' because in effect Wittgenstein regarded Moore as drawing to our notice something that does not need to be knowledge; it can be enough *like* knowledge for an inquirer's purposes. Even in some situations where Wittgenstein would (like Moore) set aside the sceptical reasoning as lacking power over us, he might not (unlike Moore) accord knowledge correlatively. How is that combination possible? It is bold; is it also coherent? How does it evade giving aid to sceptical reasoning?

That Wittgensteinian blend was contextualist.[14] Pragmatists can find it congenial. Its emphasis is upon contexts of inquiry, in line with Wittgenstein's earlier ruminations on what he called *criteria* – meaningfully decisive yet non-deductive and possibly defeasible evidence. Wittgenstein was particularly concerned with the nature of our evidence for other people's mental aspects – the traditional epistemological challenge of knowing 'other minds'. And is ascertaining whether another person has some particular knowledge a special case of that? In other words, if knowing is a mental state, does the challenge of knowing whether another person has a specific piece of knowledge amount to a challenge of 'other *epistemic* minds'? Or is knowledge's presence not quite like that? Is this especially so when the putative knowledge would be of something we could not sensibly doubt? Are we equally unable sensibly to claim knowledge in such a circumstance? Think (thought Wittgenstein) of how some claims are presumed, never actually made, within a given context of inquiry. This can be fruitful, guiding us, breathing life into our inquiring – initiating it even while rendering some doubts as sensible. Never in these settings, however, do doubts sensibly arise in turn about these presumed claims. The latter are thereby what Wittgenstein called hinge propositions: fixed for now, allowing so much else within inquiry to function and to flower, not themselves known but also not needing to have been known. What Moore showed us, it could seem, were some such propositions.

Is that possible? Even if rational, it is (notes Snowdon) not rationalist. How are hinge propositions not known, yet still for us enough *like* objects of our knowledge? Perhaps we are being given a picture of people as knowing *how* to inquire sensibly on the basis of hinge

propositions, instead of knowing *that* these are true. If there is a kind
of certainty in this (as Wittgenstein apparently believed), it takes more a
pragmatist's than a rationalist's form. It would be certainty in cognitive
action, not a cognitive or mental state of certainty.[15]

14. Quine and Goldman

One theme recurring throughout the book is that of the various ways
in which science enters epistemology. Manifestly, there have long been
questions about the nature and availability of scientific knowledge. But
sometimes too, particularly in the past fifty or so years, questions have
arisen about whether knowledge – not only scientific knowledge, but
all knowledge – is *understandable* partly via science. In order to understand frogs, say, we would observe relevant aspects of the world – individual frogs alive or dead, their habitats, etc. Years could pass; these
observations may coalesce; and science can benefit: there would be a
systematized accumulation of knowledge about frogs. Now, is *knowledge* at all like frogs in that respect? To what extent, if any, can we
understand knowledge scientifically? That could be determined by the
extent to which people, when knowing, are functioning as scientifically
describable elements in 'the natural world'. We do not inhabit just *any*
world. We are here, in this world of instincts and reactions, patterns
and regularities; and do we exemplify these, when knowing our world,
fundamentally as other animals do so? Those themes and questions are
central to Chapter 10, where Ram Neta introduces us to W. V. Quine
and Alvin Goldman. They have been philosophy's two most influential advocates, during the twentieth-century's second half, of one or
another version of the idea that no theory of evidence, justification, and
knowledge is complete without recognizing and reflecting that how we
gain evidence and how we know are accomplishments which to some
significant extent are describable scientifically. Quine gave us the term
'naturalized epistemology' and Goldman the term 'reliabilism' – evoca-
tive notions, both.

    For example, are there psychological regularities in how we perceive,
in how we organize our perceptions, even in how we form theoretical beliefs? And if there are, then in describing such regularities with

a scientist's eye would we be describing the substance of what it is to know? Is knowing a matter, most notably, of how reliably one is perceiving and reasoning ('reliably', in the sense of believing more and more truths, fewer and fewer falsehoods)?

In their respective ways (carefully described by Neta's Chapter 10), each of Quine and Goldman does argue that epistemology can be refined in scientific terms, especially ones from cognitive psychology. Must individual observers or reasoners therefore be *aware* of themselves in those same psychological terms? Not at all. Knowers are not being expected to be scientists about themselves. The naturalistic epistemological point is that to be a knower is at least largely to be functioning in ways that would be fit objects of study for a scientist.[16]

Quine sketched his program with broad strokes; Goldman's epistemological drawings have been more extensive and detailed. But each portrayal has been suggestive and influential.

15. Gettier's challenging legacy

Perhaps the most *surprisingly* influential contribution to epistemology's development has been a brief 1963 paper by Edmund Gettier (in response to which, indeed, Goldman began his own epistemological enterprise). Gettier did not then continue as an epistemologist. But he had already sowed the seeds of his notable ongoing impact. John Turri, in Chapter 11, describes that impact upon large parts of contemporary epistemology.

The dominant question posed by Gettier's legacy has been, 'What is knowledge?' Varying theories of knowledge's nature have been proposed as answers, often sparked by reflection directly upon the thought experiments in Gettier's paper (and upon similar ones that have appeared subsequently). Post-Gettier, theories of knowledge have standardly been held accountable to those thought experiments, the latter generally being regarded as decisive or near-decisive tests of any particular theory's accuracy.

We could think of much of this epistemological activity as exemplifying a form of epistemological *rationalism*: imagined situations are offered as sufficient tests of the theories in question, with *intuition* supposedly being called upon to adjudicate such confrontations. Distinguish that methodological predilection from what could, roughly speaking, be called the epistemological *empiricism* that animated Quine clearly, and Goldman to some extent. Still speaking roughly, this distinction divides the epistemology in Chapter 10 from that in Chapter 11.[17]

The impetus for this segment of epistemology's history was Gettier's succinct challenge to an apparently widely entrenched conceptual hypothesis as to what it is for something to be knowledge. According to that hypothesis, any instance of knowledge is a belief which is true and which is well supported by good evidence (or by something comparable) bearing favourably upon its chances of being true. But Gettier described, picturesquely, two possible situations where a belief would be like that *without* – he claimed – being knowledge. And most epistemologists have since agreed with that assessment of his. What *is* knowledge, then, if it need not be a well justified true belief?

Turri describes the main sorts of suggestion to arise as epistemologists have striven to answer that question. He also, significantly for our purposes, charts how this debate brings us starkly face to face with a most fundamental choice confronting anyone at any time trying to understand knowledge's nature. This choice is about standards for knowing; and thereby about how optimistic we should be, regarding our prospects for knowing. How demanding an achievement or state is that of knowing? In particular, can knowledge be achieved or present *fallibly*? If not – such as if fallibility on a question is inherently a failing incompatible with knowing the question's answer – then perhaps knowledge is never realistically within our reach. Or is that a needlessly pessimistic thought? Should we instead be more optimistic about our capacity to gain knowledge, sometimes at any rate? If so – with knowledge-scepticism thereby set aside – then perhaps we may conceive of knowledge as able to incorporate rather than preclude fallibility, so that fallibility can characterize *how* one knows a particular truth.

These themes – in one form or another, these questions – have long been with epistemologists. Plato introduced versions of them; they have remained with us. The Gettier problem – the challenge of rebounding from Gettier's challenge with an understanding of knowledge's nature – has sharpened the questions and reinforced the themes. Can we understand ourselves as knowing fallibly? That is the central question with which Gettier has left us.[18] Rightly, several of the book's chapters engage with aspects of fallibilism. It is at the heart of what makes epistemology pressing and important.

16. The book's structure

Sections 6 through 15 have said a little about what each chapter will discuss. Let us also approach the book with a sense of how its chapters are organized. Broadly speaking, there are three groupings of chapters:

Ancient epistemology: Plato: first epistemology (Chapter 2)

    Aristotle: empiricism and science (Chapter 3)

    Sceptical doubts (Chapter 4)

Modern epistemology: Descartes: metaphysics and science (Chapter 5)

    Locke, Berkeley, Hume: observation and its limits (Chapter 6)

    Kant: experience and categories of thought (Chapter 7)

Recent epistemology: American pragmatism: inquiry and fallibilism (Chapter 8)

    Wittgenstein: sense and certainty (Chapter 9)

    Quine and Goldman: naturalism and science (Chapter 10)

    Gettier: fallibility and defining knowledge (Chapter 11).

That listing is not the only reasonable way of conceiving of even just the main stages in epistemology's development over the past two-and-a-half millennia. Nor does it exhaust epistemology's potentially significant ideas.[19] Nonetheless, these chapters will provide a solid philosophical base from which to explore whatever else within epistemology likewise deserves further attention.[20]

Notes

1 Or upon whatever *related* phenomena the world is held to include, such as kinds of rational thinking (see Section 5). Different chapters will touch upon a variety of such phenomena – if, that is, the phenomena do exist.

2 For more on the epistemological choice between discussing knowledge and discussing a concept of knowledge, see Kornblith (2006).

3 Kekes (1980: 42) raises a contrary possibility, that 'insofar as philosophical arguments are perennial, they deal with problems that need to be solved again and again'.

4 For instance, on how progress within science, along with some non-science, is built upon problems and research traditions, see Laudan (1977).

5 See, for example, Ayer (1956) – an influential book – and Williams (2001) – so titled out of respect for Ayer's book and *its* title.

6 Still, some do. And in recent times those who have wished to do so, such as Kornblith (2002), tend to cite Quine (1969) especially as their inspiration. Chapter 10 will discuss this (and see Section 14 below). For doubts as to how effective such a subsumption could be, see Stroud (1984: ch. VI).

7 The key word here is 'systematic'. There was also what we call pre-Socratic philosophy, some of which was – or at least some of the surviving fragments of which are – intermittently epistemological. On this, see Gerson (2009: ch. 2).

8 The current way of discussing this is to ask what *value* there is in knowing which is not present merely in being correct. See, for example, Kvanvig (2003). In any case, see Chapter 11 also on contemporary answers to the question, 'What is knowledge?'

9 For just a few of the standard contemporary epistemological accounts of Descartes on knowledge, see BonJour (2002: ch. 2), Feldman (2003: 52–5), Popkin and Maia Neto (2007: 145) and Zagzebski (2009: 39). For a view which appreciates the potential epistemological unnaturalness in that account of Descartes, yet which retains the account even so, see Williams (2010).

10 Fallibilism about knowledge in general has been a focus of study within comparatively recent epistemology: see Chapter 11. If Clarke is right, then Descartes-on-scientific-knowledge may also have welcomed the fallibilist ideas and clarifications developed as part of this more recent focus.

11 On Hume's not really being so sceptical after all, see Hetherington (2008).

12 The chapter on Kant (Chapter 7) also reveals this, through its discussions of Strawson and Sellars.

13 Notably, Rorty (1979) criticized post-Cartesian epistemology's mistake, as he viewed it, of having relied upon the idea of knowledge as accurate in its *representing* a world 'already there'. Brandom (1994; 2000) develops that theme further. And in a similar spirit, Allen (2004) argues for knowledge's being *artifactual*: we make it; we thereby use it; we thereupon make it anew; which is to say that we use it anew; and so on. For a version, in part, of pragmatism, see Hetherington (2011).

14 Indeed, until recently, the term 'contextualism' was used by epistemologists to designate something like this Wittgensteinian view of justification and knowledge (e.g. Annis, 1978). The term is now being used differently within epistemology: see section 2.4 of Chapter 12.

15 For more on Wittgenstein on knowledge-how and certainty, see Moyal-Sharrock (2005) and Hetherington (2011: secs. 2.3, 6.6).

16 Naturalistic epistemology thereby tends to apply an epistemic *externalism* to knowers: when knowing on the basis of good eyesight or even good evidence, say, one need not be able to be *aware* of how these are functioning and of how they are being so helpful. Quine and Goldman are paradigmatic epistemic externalists. Descartes, in contrast, is a paradigmatic epistemic internalist, since he did regard at least metaphysical knowing as requiring that sort of awareness of how the knowing is being constituted. For more on the difference between epistemic externalism and epistemic internalism, see Hetherington (1996: chs. 14, 15) and Kornblith (2001).

17 Can the two methodologies be linked? Goldman could be regarded as seeking to blend the potentials strengths of each of these methodological approaches. He consults empirical research into the actual reliabilities of this, that, and the other belief-forming process or method. But when he constructs correlative theories of knowledge, he also tests these against apparent intuitions.

18 For an argument, though, to the effect that Gettier never really escaped *in*fallibilism's conceptual grip, and hence failed to challenge fallibilism 'from within', see Hetherington (forthcoming).

19 Might the book have included, for example, a chapter on mediaeval epistemology? It does not, only because epistemology from that period did not clearly have so much *influence* upon subsequent thinkers. For some discussion of mediaeval epistemology, see Zupko (1993). For a sense of such epistemology's historical setting, see Floridi (2010).

20 Chapter 12 will have some suggestions as to what else (within contemporary epistemology, at any rate) you might wish to explore.

References

Allen, B. (2004), *Knowledge and Civilization*. Boulder, CO: Westview Press.

Annis, D. B. (1978), 'A contextualist theory of epistemic justification', *American Philosophical Quarterly*, 15, 213–19.

Ayer, A. J. (1956), *The Problem of Knowledge*. London: Macmillan.

BonJour, L. (2002), *Epistemology: Classic Problems and Contemporary Responses*. Lanham, MD: Rowman & Littlefield.

Brandom, R. B. (1994), *Making It Explicit: Reasoning, Representing, and Discursive Commitment*. Cambridge, MA: Harvard University Press.

—(2000), *Articulating Reasons: An Introduction to Inferentialism*. Cambridge, MA: Harvard University Press.

Feldman, R. (2003), *Epistemology*. Upper Saddle River, NJ: Prentice Hall.

Floridi, L. (2010), 'The rediscovery and posthumous influence of scepticism', in R. Bett (ed.), *The Cambridge Companion to Ancient Scepticism*. Cambridge: Cambridge University Press, pp. 267–87.

Gerson, L. P. (2009), *Ancient Epistemology*. Cambridge: Cambridge University Press.

Hetherington, S. (1996), *Knowledge Puzzles: An Introduction to Epistemology*. Boulder, CO: Westview Press.

—(2008), 'Not actually Hume's problem: On induction and knowing-how', *Philosophy*, 83, 459–81.

—(2011), *How To Know: A Practicalist Conception of Knowledge*. Malden, MA: Wiley-Blackwell.

— (forthcoming), 'The Gettier-illusion: Gettier-partialism and infallibilism', *Synthese*.

Kekes, J. (1980), *The Nature of Philosophy*. Totowa, NJ: Rowman & Littlefield.

Kornblith, H. (ed.) (2001), *Epistemology: Internalism and Externalism*. Malden, MA: Blackwell.

—(2002), *Knowledge and Its Place in Nature*. Oxford: Clarendon Press.

—(2006), 'Appeals to intuition and the ambition of epistemology', in S. Hetherington (ed.), *Epistemology Futures*. Oxford: Clarendon Press, pp. 10–25.

Kvanvig, J. L. (2003), *The Value of Knowledge and the Pursuit of Understanding*. Cambridge: Cambridge University Press.

Laudan, L. (1977), *Progress and Its Problems: Towards a Theory of Scientific Growth*. London: Routledge & Kegan Paul.

Moyal-Sharrock, D. (2005), *Understanding Wittgenstein's On Certainty*. Basingstoke: Palgrave Macmillan.

Popkin, R. H. and Maia Neto, J. R. (eds) (2007), *Skepticism: An Anthology*. Amherst, NY: Prometheus Books.

Quine, W. V. (1969), 'Epistemology naturalized', in *Ontological Relativity and Other Essays*. New York: Columbia University Press, pp. 69–90.

Rorty, R. (1979), *Philosophy and the Mirror of Nature*. Princeton: Princeton University Press.

Stroud, B. (1984), *The Significance of Philosophical Scepticism*. Oxford: Clarendon Press.

Williams, M. (2001), *Problems of Knowledge: A Critical Introduction to Epistemology*. New York: Oxford University Press.

—(2010), 'Descartes' transformation of the sceptical tradition', in R. Bett (ed.), *The Cambridge Companion to Ancient Scepticism*. Cambridge: Cambridge University Press, pp. 288–313.

Zagzebski, L. (2009), *On Epistemology*. Belmont, CA: Wadsworth.

Zupko, J. (1993), 'Buridan and skepticism', *Journal of the History of Philosophy*, 31, 191–221.

CHAPTER 2

PLATO'S EPISTEMOLOGY

Nicholas D. Smith

1. Introduction

Plato scholars continue to debate which general approach to interpreting his dialogues is the most reliable. Included among these interpretive strategies are several versions of what has been called the 'Unitarian' approach, which holds that Plato's philosophical views remained fully stable throughout his career, and the dialogues, rightly understood, will show no deviation in these settled views. Contrasted to the Unitarian approach is the 'Developmentalist' view, which holds that Plato's views changed over time, though remaining consistent within certain periods of his career. Contrasting to both of these interpretive positions is what might be called a 'Particularist' approach (scholars have not yet agreed on what this approach should be called, however), which holds that each dialogue should be read as a single whole, and that there is no reason to expect Plato to maintain philosophical consistency between any two dialogues.

In this chapter, I will show that Plato's epistemology is best understood from a Developmentalist perspective, though because much of what I will discuss regarding the changes in Plato's epistemological views will be based on evidence from individual dialogues, much of what I will say will be compatible with a Particularist approach, as well. At any rate, I will show that the dialogues do not support the idea that Plato's views about knowledge and belief remained the same throughout his lifetime.

2. Plato's early epistemology

Developmentalists have generally regarded the dialogues of what is generally known as Plato's 'early' period[1] to reflect Plato's philosophical portrait of Socrates; hence, the early dialogues are sometimes also called the 'Socratic' dialogues. Although no sustained exposition of epistemology is provided in these dialogues, several general epistemic commitments may be found expressed and repeated by Socrates. The most ubiquitous of these has come to be known as the Socratic 'profession of ignorance' or 'disclaimer of knowledge'.[2] Recent scholarship has divided over the best way to characterize this disclaimer, but some aspects of it are uncontroversial. First, Socrates uses 'knowledge' (*epistēmē*) in his disclaimers interchangeably with 'wisdom' (*sophia*), and not just any kind of wisdom, but specifically, wisdom about what he calls 'the most important things' (*Apology* 22d7–8). In claiming not to have knowledge, accordingly, Socrates is not committing himself to global scepticism. Moreover, several passages may be found in which Socrates either claims to have knowledge of some sort, or credits others as having some knowledge[3] or even wisdom.[4] Second, the sort of knowledge that Socrates claims not to have is not simply or purely informational, but also involves something like technical skill.[5] Third, the sort of knowledge that Socrates lacks is definitional knowledge of ethical terms, without which one cannot explain what makes some ethical judgement correct or incorrect.[6] Finally, the knowledge that Socrates lacks is also lacked by all other human beings. This is why, as Socrates puts it in the *Apology*, when the oracle at Delphi told Chaerephon that no one was wiser than Socrates,

> he means that human wisdom is of little or no value. And he appears to mean that such a person is Socrates and to have used my name, taking me as an example, as if to say, 'This one of you, O human beings, is wisest who – as Socrates does – knows that he's in truth worthless with respect to wisdom. (*Apology* 23a6–b4; trans. Brickhouse and Smith, 2002)

Socrates has what some scholars have called 'non-expert knowledge';[7] he and all other human beings lack 'expert knowledge' of 'the most important things', by which he seems to mean knowing how best to live, which would include at least having a complete understanding and possession of all of the virtues. This latter sort of knowledge, it seems, is available only to the gods.

But even if only the gods could know in the expert sense, Socrates plainly believed that we were capable of and would reasonably pursue epistemic improvement. Inherent to what has come to be known as 'the Socratic method' of questioning is a form of what might be called 'epistemic optimism'. By this, I mean a form of optimism about the epistemic value of what we do when inconsistencies in our views are revealed to us. In response to Socratic questioning, interlocutors are encouraged to jettison one of their views in order to eliminate an inconsistency in their cognitive system. A pessimist might contend that the decision an interlocutor makes is as likely or more likely to be incorrect than correct, but Socrates seems to hold that whatever decision the interlocutor makes is likely to be an improvement in the interlocutor's cognitive system. He never clearly explains why he thinks this is the case, but the improvement seems to derive from cognitions innately held by all of us, which is why we find Socrates sometimes attributing what he regards as the correct beliefs to others, even as these others vigorously deny holding those beliefs.[8] Whatever its theoretical basis, it is Socrates' epistemic optimism, we may suppose, that led him to claim that 'the unexamined life is not worth living for a human being' (*Apology* 38a5–6). However, because no one is wiser than Socrates, as the oracle stated, Socratic epistemic optimism did not provide any significant hope that any human being could come to possess the knowledge that Socrates lacked. Socratic epistemic optimism, accordingly, was severely limited by a considerable degree of epistemic pessimism about just how much progress even the most earnest inquirer could possibly achieve.

3. The *Meno*

In Plato's *Meno* we get an explanation of how and why epistemic optimism would be supported: all knowledge, we discover in that dialogue, derives from what was learned in a former life, and so epistemic improvement may be achieved in our present life through recollection (*Meno* 81c5–9). The reason that epistemic optimism is sustained, accordingly, is that when faced with inconsistencies in their beliefs, interlocutors are more likely to engage in (accurate) recollection than when they wrongly imagine their cognitive systems to be consistent. Already in the *Meno*, then, we see that what I have called Socratic epistemic pessimism begins to give way to a much greater optimism. However, the *Meno* leaves open the question central to Socratic pessimism, namely, whether human beings can ever know 'the most important things'.

The main question of this dialogue is whether virtue can be taught. The discussion stalls, however, when Socrates challenges Meno to give a definition of virtue (71d5), and after Socrates shows that Meno's attempts to give a definition have failed, Meno accuses Socrates of being like a 'torpedo fish', which numbs its victims (79e7–80b7). Socrates exhorts Meno to continue the search, but Meno responds with what has come to be known as 'the paradox of inquiry':

> Meno: How will you look for it, Socrates, when you do not know at all what it is? How will you aim to search for something you do not know at all? If you should meet with it, how will you know that this is the thing that you did not know? (80d5–8; Grube trans. in Cooper, 1997)

In response to this challenge, Socrates introduces his theory of knowledge as recollection, and Socrates seems to assume that the definitional knowledge of virtue is one of the things we can recollect, which is why Socrates returns to this search after his demonstration with the slave (at 86c4–6). Meno, however, insists on returning to the question of whether or not virtue can be taught, instead (86c7–d2). Socrates objects to this procedure, contending that the definitional question is prior to the question of teachability (86d3–6), but then agrees to continue the discussion by working 'by means of a hypothesis', namely, that virtue is a kind of knowledge (86e1–87c6).

Socrates provides a dramatic example of the process of recollection at work by questioning Meno's slave about how to draw a square twice the size of a given square (82b9–86b5). The slave first guesses that such a square could be constructed by doubling the lengths of each side, but Socrates quickly shows that this would result in a square four times as large as the original. By careful questioning, Socrates leads the boy to the correct answer, which is to construct a square whose sides are equal to the diagonal of the first square. Socrates concludes this part of the argument by getting Meno to agree that the boy's 'recollections' are now true opinions, but these could become knowledge if the boy were asked more such questions in various ways over a longer period of time (85c6–d2).

What is recollected in the *Meno* account is plainly informational: Meno's slave boy is shown to have begun the process of recollecting certain truths about geometry. But the information is also the basis of a kind of expertise or know-how – in this case, the ability to do geo-metrical constructions.

As we will soon see, the theory of recollection (and the cycle of reincarnation that allows recollection from former lives) will be revisited but also revised in later dialogues. But later in their discussion, Socrates and Meno add a new element to their theory – and this addition is one that Plato will later abandon. Contemporary epistemology texts typi-cally begin their analyses of knowledge by considering the claim that knowledge is justified true belief. This account has its *locus classicus* in Plato's *Meno*.

When Socrates and Meno appear to reach another impasse in their discussion – the result of finding no reliable teachers of virtue – Socrates indicates that he wants to revise something they had agreed to earlier. Whereas earlier they agreed that no benefit can come without knowl-edge (88e4–89a1), Socrates now reconsiders:

> Socrates: But that one cannot guide correctly if one does not have knowledge; to this our agreement is likely to be incorrect.
>
> Meno: How do you mean?
>
> Socrates: I will tell you. A man who knew the way to Larissa, or anywhere else you like, and went there and guided others would surely lead them well and correctly?
>
> Meno: Certainly.
>
> Socrates: What if someone had had a correct opinion as to which was the way but had not gone there nor indeed had knowledge of it, would he not also lead correctly? (*Meno* 97a6–b3; Grube trans. in Cooper, 1997)

Meno and Socrates conclude that true opinion is just as beneficial as knowledge, and that one with true opinion will be just as successful as one with knowledge in every case. This leads Meno to wonder what the difference between knowledge and true opinion might be, and Socrates responds to Meno's puzzlement by comparing true opinions to the statues of Daedalus: like the famous statues, true opinions tend to 'run away and escape if one does not tie them down' (97d9–10). Knowledge, he concludes, is nothing other than true opinion 'tied down' with an explanatory account (98a3–8).

The theory of knowledge that Plato has Socrates give here, while never explicitly given in the early dialogues, appears to be consistent with what we do find there, for the distinction between knowledge and belief here is given in terms of what would *explain* the truth in each case. In the early dialogues, the explanation would be in the form of a definition (see especially *Euthyphro* 6d9–e7). Although more restrictive than what contemporary epistemologists have in mind as justification, we can see the basis for contemporary theory of knowledge in this text. As I will soon show, however, Plato later abandons this view, and came to regard the distinction between knowledge and belief in very different terms.

4. The *Phaedo*

The *Phaedo* retains the doctrine of recollection (and thus the epistemic optimism) from the *Meno*, but modifies significantly the nature of what is known. For the first time in the *Phaedo* the famous but problematic conception of Platonic Forms is introduced. The context of the dialogue is Socrates' last day in jail, and the work ends with the death of Socrates from hemlock poison. The main arguments of the dialogue are intended to show that the soul is immortal, and thus that Socrates' friends need not worry about his fate, for his soul will survive his death. Recollection, accordingly, is not introduced in this dialogue as an answer to the paradox of inquiry, but rather as a ground for optimism about an afterlife.

The Forms are first introduced in the dialogue at 65d4:

> What about the following Simmias? Do we say that there is such a thing as the Just itself, or not?
>
> We do say so, by Zeus.
>
> And the Beautiful, and the Good?
>
> Of course.
>
> And have you seen any of these things with your eyes?
>
> In no way, he said.

Or have you ever grasped them with any of your bodily senses? I am speaking of all such things such as Size, Health, Strength and, in a word, the reality of all other things, that which each of them essentially is. Is what is most true in them contemplated through the body, or is this the position: whoever of us prepares himself best and most accurately to grasp that thing itself which he is investigating will come closest to the knowledge of it?

Obviously. (65d4–e6; Grube trans. in Cooper, 1997)

Socrates' strategy here is to lead to the point where 'escape from the body' (66e4–5) is the only way one can ever hope to have pure knowledge of the Forms. Although Simmias seemed satisfied with this argument, another character, Cebes, balks. In effect, Cebes does not share Simmias's epistemic optimism: even if escape from the body would be the only way to have knowledge, why should we believe that the soul would survive the death of the body? In other words, if escape from the body is a necessary condition of knowledge, perhaps all that proves is that knowledge is impossible. So Cebes challenges Socrates to give some reason for being optimistic about the survival of death and the possibility of knowledge (69e5–70b4).

Socrates' response to this challenge is another argument, the general principle of which is that things come into being from their opposites. Giving several examples of this (the smaller coming to be from the larger; the weaker coming to be from the stronger; the worse from the better; the more from the less just; separation from combination; cooler from hotter, and so on – 70e10–71b10), Socrates then applies it to living and dying: the dead come from the living, but also the living come from the dead (71c1–72a8); but also this process must continue in a balanced way, lest either opposite be wholly absent from the world (72b8–d3).

Cebes immediately sees the connection between this argument and Socrates' theory that learning is recollection (72e1–73a3). But now Simmias interjects and wants the details of this theory. Cebes replies on behalf of Socrates,

There is one excellent argument, said Cebes, namely that when men are interrogated in the right manner, they always give the right answer of their own accord, and they could not do this if they did not possess the knowledge and the right explanation inside them. Then if one shows them a diagram or something else of that kind, this will show most clearly that such is the case. (73a7–75c4; Grube trans. in Cooper, 1997)

Socrates then supplies Simmias with what is supposed to be direct evidence of this phenomenon of recollecting, showing that Simmias can judge the relative equality of sticks and stones he observes, but does not observe Equality Itself through perception. But if Equality cannot be observed through perception, how did it become available to Simmias for judging perceivable equalities and inequalities? The answer Socrates supplies is that Simmias possessed knowledge of the Equal Itself *prior to* any perception of more or less equal perceivable things, which means that his soul must have lived prior to his current life as a perceiver (74a5–75b8), and the same must also be true of other qualities that Simmias and other human beings are able to judge, without having ever encountered a perfect example of it in perception (75c6–d5).

5. Taking stock

We have seen a number of threads of Plato's epistemology running through various arguments he gives to Socrates in several different dialogues. One such thread is what I have called Plato's 'epistemic optimism', by which I mean that Plato characterizes Socrates as thinking that reflection and philosophical inquiry are likely to lead to improvements in one's cognitive condition. If we ask what grounds this optimism, we have found some evidence for thinking that Plato held some version of an innateness hypothesis, which by the time we get to the *Meno* is explained by the theory of recollection. It is not difficult to see several problems with this account, however. For one, the ground for epistemic optimism we are given in this theory is that we already know what we seek to know, because we had that knowledge in a former life. But, we might naturally now ask, how did we get that knowledge in the former life? The only answer Plato gives to Socrates seems to consist in the balance of the process of life coming from death and death coming from life, which would seem to assure that the process leads us on an infinite regress of former lives – so the question, 'When did we first learn all these things?' never arises. Such an answer obviously contradicts the evidence of cosmogeny, as well as that of biological evolution, which would take us back to a time when our evolutionary predecessors could hardly be described as having all cognitive capacities and states available to human beings. Of course, there is no reason to think that Plato would recognize these problems, but we might wonder just how comfortable he would be with the implied regress. Another problem concerns the excessiveness of the theory – it appears to require that all people are in some way in possession of all possible knowledge at all times. This theory makes true ignorance impossible: Ignorance must now be understood only in terms of failure to recollect what one actually does latently know. But evidence of ignorance is unfortunately ubiquitous, and the phenomenology of learning is not (or at any rate not *always*) that of recovering what one already had. Genuine discovery seems also to be a real source of knowledge.

Contemporary epistemologists plainly have very different ways of grounding epistemic optimism, but few now accept anything like Plato's theory of innate *content*. Obviously, epistemic optimism can also be supported by a theory of innate *capacity*. If our cognitive capacities are such as to be more likely to yield truth than falsehood (when used in appropriate ways), then we have no need to saddle ourselves with the great burden of cognitive content that the theory of recollection in the *Meno* would require. Of course, different epistemologists have very different opinions about whether we have good reason for thinking that our capacities are reliably truth-conducive,[9] and sceptics will contend that we do not have a good enough reason for thinking that they are. But it is enough for our purposes now to recognize that a commitment to innate cognitive *content* is not required to sustain epistemic optimism. As I will show in the next section, even if he failed to recognize this in his early career, Plato became aware of it later on, grounding epistemic optimism on the basis of a new theory, in this case, one of innate capacity, rather than innate content.

The *Phaedo* actually marks a transition to this new theory, without actually announcing it explicitly. Though it continues the commitment to recollection, the account Plato gives to Socrates in the *Phaedo* actually provides a way out of the regress implied by the theory of recollection in the *Meno*. Our judgement of things in this world is the result of knowing the Forms before our birth. Rather than relying on a cycle of rebirth, however, this theory requires (at most) only a single prior discarnate existence when cognitive encounter with the Forms occurred. Indeed, given the non-sensible nature of the Forms (and thus the non-sensible means of coming to know them), the theory unveiled in the

Phaedo actually excludes the possibility that the knowledge we might acquire in this life can be recollected from some former *embodied* life. Rather, all knowledge (in any of our embodied lives) must rely on a disembodied encounter with the Forms, and this encounter does not seem to require previous encounters of the same sort to establish a basis for recollection in an embodied existence. One might now raise the question of whether or not the cognitive capacity engaged in the encounter with Forms is one we continue to have (or at least could have, under the right conditions) in effective condition in our (current) embodied life. If it is, the entire theory of recollection can be set aside, for the requirements of epistemic optimism can be met simply by engaging this cognitive capacity in a reliable way. This is precisely the theory Plato supplies in the *Republic*, where all talk of innate content vanishes, and a theory of innate capacity is provided in its stead.

Finally, with the appearance of the theory of Forms, and with such Forms as The Beautiful and The Good at least in principle accessible to human cognitive capacities, what I noted earlier as Socratic epistemic pessimism seems now to have all but disappeared. Even if knowledge of the 'most important things' remains extremely difficult for a human being to acquire, there no longer seems to be any reason to think that its acquisition is humanly impossible. From this point on in his philosophical career, Socratic epistemic pessimism will never again reappear in Plato's epistemology.

6. The *Republic*

Interpretations of the epistemology Plato provides in Book V of the *Republic* have too often been flawed by scholars' attempts to assimilate what Plato says too much to their own (contemporary) epistemological preconceptions. But this assimilation comes at a very high cost, for it makes nonsense out of the most explicit features of Plato's epistemology, namely, that knowledge and belief in this passage are described not as cognitive states, but as cognitive *capacities* (*dunameis*). Accordingly, knowledge is plainly *not* characterized as a species of belief (as it is in contemporary epistemology), but rather as a different capacity, and also the objects of knowledge and belief (the *known* or *believed*) are not facts or propositions or information, as they are variously conceived in contemporary epistemology, but are individual objects characterized by the predicates they bear. The capacity of knowledge is said to be in relation to, or set over (*epi*) the Forms; belief is said to be in relation to, or set over, the sorts of things that may be said to be both beautiful and ugly, just and unjust, double and half, big and small, light and heavy *at the same time* (*hama* – 478d5). This is Plato's classic and standard description of sensible particular things (such as the more or less equal sticks and stones we found at *Phaedo* 74a–75b8). Plainly, the Form of Justice is not some fact, statement, proposition or information about justice, but is rather the proper referent of the word, 'Justice'. So, too, more or less equal sticks and stones are not facts, statements, propositions or information *about* sticks and stones; they are, rather, the very things that such statements or whatever are *about*.

The first error of much scholarship on this passage – failing to recognize adequately that Plato is talking about capacities rather than states[10] – led scholars to conceive of the relationships between knowledge and belief and their distinct objects as an *intentional* relation, such as we find in contemporary accounts. Briefly (and at the risk of begging some questions that are regarded as important ones in contemporary epistemology, about whether it is propositions or information that is known or believed) knowledge and belief, in contemporary accounts, are propositional attitudes that are *of* or *about* the subject-terms of the propositions they encode. So, when contemporary accounts provide analyses of knowledge, we attempt to give the necessary and jointly sufficient conditions required for '*S* knows that *p*' to be true, where *S* is the cognizer and *p* is some proposition (or information) we can represent with the form '*x* is *F*' (e.g. 'Pluto is an asteroid'). My belief that Pluto is an asteroid is a belief *about* the object, Pluto – it is a belief *about* what sort of object Pluto is: an asteroid, rather than a planet. But this intentional relation is not the same as the one Plato established between his cognitive capacities and their objects. Here is what Plato has Socrates say about capacities:

> Capacities are a class of the things that are that enable us – or anything else for that matter – to do whatever we are capable of doing. Sight, for example, and hearing are among the capacities, if you understand the kind of thing I'm referring to. (477c1–4; Grube/Reeve trans. [modified] in Cooper, 1997)

A moment's reflection on Plato's first two examples of capacities will show that the relations between capacities and their objects is not an intentional one; rather, the capacity's relation to its proper objects will produce a *state* that will then bear an intentional relation to its objects. Sight (the capacity) acts on visible things in such a way as to produce a seeing *of* something; hearing (the capacity) acts on audible things in such a way as to produce a hearing *of* something. But sight (the capacity) sees what it sees, but is not *of* what it sees, and hearing (the capacity) hears what it hears but is not *of* what it hears. So, too, Plato's capacities of knowledge and belief are not *of* what they know or believe, but are what allow knowing or believing to happen. But even putting it this way risks too much assimilation to our contemporary epistemology of cognitive *states*.

Plato distinguishes his cognitive capacities by an appeal to two criteria: to what the capacity is naturally related and what the capacity produces (*eph' hō te esti kai hō apergazetai* – 477d1). Let us call these two conditions 'the relata condition' and 'the production condition', respectively. As I have already said, the bearer of the relata condition, for knowledge, is the Forms: the knower's knowledge is related to Forms, whereas the believer's belief is related to sensible particular things. But what do these cognitive capacities produce?

I have suggested that the cognitive capacities will operate on their objects in such a way as to produce states, and it is the states produced that bear intentional relations to their objects. But are the states produced by Plato's cognitive capacities the sort of cognitive states one finds as the focus of contemporary analyses? I used to think they were,[11] but I am now sure they are *not*. Let us consider more carefully the operations of Plato's cognitive capacities.

Knowledge, Plato tells us, will operate on a Form. Let us consider, for example, how this works with the Form of Justice. For the actual nature of the operation, Plato offers a number of (not always clear or helpful!) metaphors: Knowledge *grasps* the Form of Justice, or *sees* it. I have been saying that knowledge *knows* the Form, but I hope by now I have cautioned my readers well enough against trying to understand my use of this verb in the way contemporary epistemology does. Since the Form is not a proposition, in knowing the Form, one would not either *produce* a propositional attitude, for there is just the character of the Form under cognitive review here. Instead, we should understand the operations of Plato's cognitive capacity of knowledge as achieving the best possible *conception* or *conceptualization* of justice – of what justice is. The visual similes that Plato provides throughout his discussion are particularly useful here. One who sees the very thing itself has a better conception of the thing than one who sees only an image of that thing. Mirror images, for example, reverse the features of the thing left-to-right; hence, seeing a mirror image of a thing will fail to provide an entirely accurate representation of the thing. If the operations of the intellect are like the operations of perception, then, what is produced by a cognitive encounter with an original (the Form) will be a more accurate representation – a more accurate conception, we might say – of that thing than we can achieve via a cognitive encounter with something that is but an image of that thing. Propositional attitudes, however, have not (yet) made their appearance in the epistemology of the *Republic*, accordingly. Instead, the epistemology of Book V is that of concept-formation, rather than that of propositional or informational states.

This epistemology is provided by Plato in support of his thesis that properly trained philosophers will make better rulers than those who lack philosophical training – the former and not the latter, Plato says, will employ the capacity of knowledge (480a6–8). But the actual operations of ruling certainly will require the application of the ruler's conceptions to the business of making judgements. The philosophical ruler, then, will apply her conceptions of Justice in making judgements *about* whether a certain rule or decree will be the most just one possible in what Plato has Socrates call the 'noble city' (*kallipolis*) he envisions in the *Republic*. These judgements, then, will be the sorts of propositional attitudes we normally focus on in contemporary epistemology.

Several results follow from this very brief review of the epistemology of the *Republic*. First, one problem that has plagued scholarship about Plato's account may now be dissolved entirely. Scholars have worried that what is called Plato's 'two world ontology' (including the world of the Forms and the world of particulars) created an intractable problem for his epistemology: since knowledge could only be *of* Forms, philosophers could not apply knowledge in ruling, since the judgements in ruling are judgements that are of or about particular affairs of state. But the employment of knowledge was supposed to be the very reason why they would be better rulers! We can now see why this is a nonproblem for Plato. Knowledge is not *of* or *about* the Forms; it operates *on* the Forms to generate conceptions. In making judgements about the affairs of state, Plato's rulers could perfectly well apply the conception of justice they gained through cognitive contact with The Just Itself; this conception, moreover, being far more accurate and undistorted, relative to a conception engendered by cognitive contact only with images of Justice, would explain why the philosopher's judgements will be far more reliable. This is why Plato later talks of a *single* capacity of judgement – the 'eye of the soul' (see 508d4–9) – which can 'turn its gaze' upward to the realm of truth, or downward to the realm of opinion, and can be habituated to see clearly what is in the (invisible) world of the Forms, and then apply what it has seen in that higher realm in judging the shadows in 'the cave' of politics. That capacity of judgement, I claim, can make use of the products of knowledge, or the products of opinion – and which products it uses will make all the difference.

Secondly, we can see in this account a very different ground than Plato had earlier provided for epistemic optimism – one that now does not require all the burdensome and implausible baggage of innate *content*. The account of cognition given in the *Republic* gives us reason to think that cognitive improvement is possible in virtue of a reliable innate capacity (knowledge), which functions reliably when properly habituated and trained, since it is well-adapted to the environment (the realm of Forms) to which it is naturally applied.[12] The products of this capacity can then be applied in judgements about the world, which will never go wrong (see Plato's claim that knowledge is infallible [*anamartēton*] at 477e4) insofar as the conceptions it generates are as flawless as the objects that gave rise to them.

Moreover, once we complete the picture of the epistemology of concept-formation we are given in Book V with the operations of judgement Plato describes in Books VI and VII, we can now find in Plato's complete account much that would be congenial to contemporary epistemologists. Like contemporary foundationalists, Plato does regard the relation between knowledge and the Forms as epistemically basic in some sense – though plainly not in the sense of being self-justifying. Like coherentists, Plato's Socrates examines candidates for knowledge and finds them lacking in knowledge if they cannot maintain a coherent account of what they claim to know. But the coherence of the knower's cognitive system is actually an artifact of that system's generation: the system is coherent because it relies only on the conceptions provided by the operations of the infallible capacity of knowledge. Plato's account most closely aligns, I claim, with proper functionalist accounts of knowledge: The philosopher-ruler's knowledge of justice is caused by Justice, and her judgements of just things are reliable for the same reason. Moreover, her capacity of knowledge functions properly because it is well-adapted to the world of Forms. Plato does not, in the *Republic*, at any rate, explain just how this capacity came to be so well-adapted. An evolutionary account seems not to have been available to him, but neither does he explicitly provide a supernatural explanation for the reliability of knowledge.

7. The *Theaetetus*

The *Theaetetus* is the only one of Plato's dialogues devoted entirely to the question of what knowledge is. The dialogue itself can be frustrating to contemporary readers because so many of the arguments seem to turn on obvious fallacies, especially false alternatives. But at least most of these problems are the product of the method Plato has Socrates put on display in the dialogue. Repeated in this dialogue is the familiar Socratic disclaimer of knowledge, but here the disclaimer is applied to a very new context: It now seems that Socrates' own lack of knowledge is not universalizable – others, he now claims, may have the knowledge he lacks. His familiar role as questioner has now become what he calls his 'midwifery', as he helps others to 'give birth' to the knowledge that is within them (149a1 ff.). In the early dialogues, recall, Socrates was the wisest of men because he alone recognized his own lack of wisdom. This aspect of the dialogue, then, seems simply to affirm what I have called 'epistemic optimism', but the remainder of the dialogue provides nothing to explain or even to sustain this optimism, since the dialogue itself ends up with the disappointing result that Theaetetus did not actually give birth to any knowledge. The problem with Socratic midwifery is thus exemplified in the dialogue with Theaetetus: interlocutors may be 'pregnant' with phantoms, rather than real knowledge, and it is also part of Socrates' job as midwife to distinguish the true from the false offspring (150a8–b4). Even so, no indication is ever made that Theaetetus's failure is something we should expect from *every* 'pregnancy'.

Theaetetus makes several attempts to say what knowledge is. The first of these is that knowledge is perception (151e2–3). This theory is shown to fail after a lengthy discussion, roughly on the ground that one can perceive things one doesn't know – for example, one can hear a foreign language being spoken (or see it written), but not know what one perceives (163b1–7), and also because if knowledge just is perception, then there could be no knowledge where there is no perception (so, for example, there could be no knowledge from memory of an earlier perception – the knowledge would disappear as soon as the knower closed his eyes [164b1–12]). After a long argument involving puzzles about false judgement, Socrates and Theaetetus then try out the idea that knowledge might be something more like memory: In this model, the soul is likened to a wax tablet that receives impressions from the outside world through perception, but only those that leave an adequate and lasting impression count as knowledge (191c8 ff.). This theory is quickly shown to fail on the ground that it would seem to make false judgement impossible for non-perceptual cases (the case given involved errors in arithmetic), since the 'impressions' of simple numbers would seem both adequate and lasting, in which case errors involving them seem inexplicable (195e1–196c9). In reaction to this failure, Socrates next proposes that the soul be conceived as being something like an aviary, where the 'birds' in the aviary are knowledge, but these can sometimes escape, and at other times, even when someone has a bird in his aviary, he may not actually have that bird in his grasp. Things learned but not cognitively now available would be like ungrasped birds in the aviary (197d5 ff.) – in this way, Socrates introduces the distinction between what is now called dispositional and occurrent knowledge. The problem of false judgement arises again here, however, for it would seem to require identifying one bird with another, where the ground for the identity could only be another (true) bird (199d1–8), which leads Theaetetus absurdly to suggest that perhaps the birds in the aviary should include positive bits of ignorance, as well. Once Socrates shows how unhelpful this suggestion is, Theaetetus more promisingly proposes that knowledge is true judgement (*doxa*, which can also be translated as 'belief' – 200e4–6). The argument here is one contemporary philosophers will find more satisfying, if also predictable: The problem now is that people can be led to hold true beliefs via the wrong reasons (the example Socrates gives is that of jurors being led to hold the correct beliefs about a case, but on the basis of distortions or only partial truths offered by the advocates who argued the case – 201a7–c6). Theaetetus reacts to this objection by adding something like a justification condition: knowledge, he now claims, is true judgement with an account (*logos*, which may also be translated as 'reason') provided (201c7–d3). But now Socrates and Theaetetus must decide exactly what is required for something to be an 'account'. The problem here is similar to what is now called the regress of justification: either the basic terms of the account (Socrates calls these 'elements' – *stoicheia*) cannot be known, because they cannot be accounted for, or they can be known, but are then counterexamples to the analysis of knowledge as true judgement with an account. Socrates and Theaetetus consider other possible accounts of what an account might be. The first of these is speaking or saying one's thoughts, which we might conceive of as actually providing one's justification for one's belief, but this fails because anyone with a true belief can explain why he believes what he does (206c7–e3). The next possibility is that an account would be an enumeration of all of the component parts of the thing, but (to avoid infinite regress) this leads to unanalysable elements of the sort that created the problem in the first place (207a3–208b10). The last possibility they consider is that an account might consist in the providing of a distinguishing mark (what we could call a 'criterion' – Socrates gives as an example, accounting for the sun by saying that it is the brightest of the heavenly bodies (208d1–3). This suggestion wrecks on the ground that the criterion must itself be known, and so adds knowledge to the definiens, rendering the definition circular (209d8–210b3). Knowledge of compounds, in this version, would be defined in terms of knowledge of the distinguishing mark. But now we need a definition of *that* sort of knowledge. At this point, Theaetetus simply gives up, whereupon Socrates declares the boy to have delivered only 'wind-eggs . . . not worth bringing up' (210b8–9).

It is tempting to see Plato's Forms in Socrates' unanalysable elements in the final argument of the dialogue (though they are never named as such), in which case perhaps a different kind of knowledge of these elements could be invoked to avoid the circularity that lead to the final impasse.[13] But the theory of Forms seems itself to have been under some modification by Plato by this time in his career, as it is subjected to extensive criticism in the *Parmenides*, so precisely how we should assume Plato sought to fit his epistemology to his metaphysics when he wrote the *Theaetetus* is less clear than we might like it to be. As it stands, the dialogue ends in puzzlement, and the reader is thus invited to continue the search, by reading the *Sophist* and *Statesman*, where knowledge is attached first to a new metaphysical picture (see e.g. *Sophist* 248c10–d3, and esp. 253b9–e8), and then applied again in the figure of an ideal ruler (see *Statesman* 259d4–6). However, the exact nature of knowledge is never stipulated in these dialogues, nor is epistemology as such ever again a primary focus in Plato's later work.

8. Concluding remarks

In this review of what Plato has to say about knowledge and belief in his dialogues, it should be clear that Plato's own views (or at least the views he represents in his dialogues) did not remain stable throughout his writings. I have argued that the dialogues that are the most pessimistic about our ability to attain knowledge are those normally associated with Plato's early or 'Socratic' period. By the time Plato wrote the *Phaedo* and *Republic*, his mood was more optimistic, and in the latter work, he describes philosopher-rulers who have in fully realized form an epistemic capacity Plato identifies as infallible. But Plato's optimism on behalf of the philosopher-rulers was grounded in the metaphysical stability of Forms, and as his thoughts about the metaphysical grounding of knowledge began to change, his conception of knowledge had to undergo complementary change, as well. In still later dialogues, however, the possibility of knowledge is reaffirmed, and associated again both with theoretical wisdom and also with the capacity to make practical judgements in the world. In what precise ways Plato has modified his conception of knowledge from the analysis he provided in the *Republic*, however, is never explicitly stipulated.

Notes

1 Several strategies have been offered for arranging the dialogues into different groups according to when Plato may have written them. Stylometric studies measure features of the writing itself (about which, see Brandwood, 1992);

content analysis (a famous example of which may be found in Vlastos, 1991) compares the views offered in different groups of dialogues and groups them according to their degree of consistency with each other (plainly, Unitarians would claim that the dialogues form just a single group). Other approaches have also been suggested, but none are uncontroversial. For my purposes in this chapter, I count among the early dialogues (in alphabetical order): *Apology*, *Charmides*, *Crito*, *Euthydemus*, *Euthyphro*, *Gorgias*, *Hippias Major*, *Hippias Minor*, *Ion*, *Laches*, *Lysis*, *Protagoras*, *Republic* I. The *Meno* contains some elements that are not anticipated in any of the early dialogues, but also lacks some of the distinctive features of the middle dialogues, and hence counts as transitional between the early and middle periods. The middle dialogues are (also in alphabetical order): *Cratylus*, *Phaedo*, *Republic* II–X, *Symposium*, *Phaedrus*. The *Parmenides* and *Theaetetus* appear to have been written later than the five middle period dialogues, and later still are the *Critias*, *Philebus*, *Sophist*, *Statesman* and *Timaeus*. The unfinished *Laws* is generally regarded as the last of Plato's works to have been written.

2 Examples may be found at *Apology* 20c1–3, 21d2–7, 23b2–4; *Charmides* 165b4–c2, 166c7–d6; *Euthyphro* 5a7–c5, 15c12, 15e5–16a4; *Laches* 186b8–c5, 186d8–e3, 200e2–5; *Lysis* 212a4–7, 223b4–8; *Hippias Major* 286c8–e2, 304d4–e5; *Gorgias* 509a4–6; *Republic* I.337e4–5.

3 *Apology* 23b2–4, 29b9, 32b8; *Euthydemus* 293b7–8, 296e8–297a1, *Gorgias* 511c4–5, 512b1–2; *Ion* 532d8–e3.

4 *Apology* 22c9–e1.

5 The association of knowledge with craft, skill, or expertise (*technē*) may be found at *Apology* 22c9–e1; *Euthydemus* 279d6–280b3; *Gorgias* 459b1–3, 464c6; *Protagoras* 361a5–c2.

6 See *Gorgias* 509a5. On the connection between definitional knowledge and reliable judgement, see *Euthyphro* 4e1–5d1, 6d9–e7; *Hippias Major* 304d5–e3; *Laches* 189e3–190b1; *Lysis* 223b4–8; *Protagoras* 312c1–4. For discussion of the implications of these passages, see Brickhouse and Smith (1994: 36–60).

7 See Woodruff (1990).

8 See, for example, *Gorgias* 474b2–8, 475e3–5.

9 So Kornblith (2000) argues that our evolutionary success supplies such a reason; Plantinga (1993: 216–37) argues that a supernatural explanation is required.

10 A vivid example of the sort of failure may be found in Gail Fine's (1990) widely cited paper on the epistemology of the *Republic*. Criticisms of Fine's view are provided in Gonzalez (1996) and Smith (2000).

11 See Smith (2000).

12 I provide a contemporary account of knowledge that is like this (without Forms, however) in Smith (2002).

13 For an example of this approach, see Lesher (1969).

Further reading

Brickhouse, T. C. and Smith, N. D. (2000), *The Philosophy of Socrates*. Boulder, Colorado: Westview Press.

Fine, G. (1979), 'Knowledge and *logos* in the *Theaetetus*', *The Philosophical Review*, 88, 366–97.

—(1990), 'Knowledge and belief in *Republic* V–VII', in S. Everson (ed.), *Companions to Ancient Thought 1: Epistemology*. Cambridge: Cambridge University Press, pp. 85–115.

Gonzalez, F. J. (1996), 'Propositions or objects? A critique of Gail Fine on knowledge and belief in *Republic* V', *Phronesis*, 41, 245–75.

Gulley, N. (1961), *Plato's Theory of Knowledge*. London: Methuen.

Smith, N. D. (1979), 'Knowledge by acquaintance and "knowing what" in Plato's *Republic*', *Dialogue*, 18, 281–8.

Stokes, M. (1992), 'Plato and the sightlovers of the *Republic*', in A. Barker and M. Warner (eds), *The Language of the Cave*. Edmonton: Academic Printing and Publishing, pp. 103–32.

Szaif, J. (2007), '*Doxa* and *epistēmē* as modes of acquaintance in *Republic* V', *Études platoniciennes*, 4, 253–72.

Vlastos, G. (1981), 'Degrees of reality in Plato', in G. Vlastos, *Platonic Studies* (2nd edn). Princeton: Princeton University Press, pp. 58–75.

—(1994), *Socratic Studies*. Cambridge: Cambridge University Press.

References

Brandwood, L. (1992), 'Stylometry and chronology', in R. Kraut (ed.), *The Cambridge Companion to Plato*. Cambridge: Cambridge University Press, pp. 90–120.

Brickhouse, T. C. and Smith, N. D. (1994), *Plato's Socrates*. New York: Oxford University Press.

—(eds) (2002), *The Trial and Execution of Socrates: Sources and Controversies*. New York: Oxford University Press.

Cooper, J. M. (ed.) (1997), *Plato: Complete Works*. Indianapolis: Hackett.

Kornblith, H. (2000), 'Knowledge in humans and other animals', *Philosophical Perspectives*, 13 (Epistemology). Suppl. to *Noûs*, 327–46.

Lesher, J. H. (1969), '*Gnōsis* and *epistēmē* in Socrates' dream in the *Theaetetus*', *Journal of Hellenic Studies*, 84, 72–8.

Plantinga, A. (1993), *Warrant and Proper Function*. New York: Oxford University Press.

Smith, N. D. (2000), 'Plato on knowledge as a power', *Journal of the History of Philosophy*, 38, 145–68.

—(2002), 'Generic knowledge', *American Philosophical Quarterly*, 39, 343–57.

Vlastos, G. (1991), *Socrates: Ironist and Moral Philosopher*. Cambridge: Cambridge University Press.

Woodruff, P. B. (1990), 'Plato's early theory of knowledge', in S. Everson (ed.), *Companions to Ancient Thought 1: Epistemology*. Cambridge: Cambridge University Press, pp. 60–84.

CHAPTER 3

ARISTOTLE ON KNOWLEDGE

Robert Bolton and Alan Code

1. Various forms of perceptual knowledge

What we know changes over time as we acquire new knowledge. According to Aristotle, one way in which this happens is that we make use of the senses to accumulate and retain perceptual knowledge of various sorts. A tremendous amount of our knowledge is due to the use of our perceptual faculty to acquire and retain information about the properties of substances such as plants and animals, earth and water, as well as celestial bodies such as the sun, moon and stars. In some cases Aristotle classifies the observable properties as perceptible *in themselves*. Some such properties are the *special* objects of the five special sense modalities. We see what colours things have, hear their sounds, taste their flavours, smell their odours, and through touch are aware of such qualities as heat, coldness, hardness, softness, wetness and dryness. For Aristotle, either it is impossible to be in error about these special sense objects, or at any rate we are least prone to falsehood concerning them.[1] We may be mistaken about just what object it is that has a certain colour, or is making a certain sound, and we may be mistaken about where that object is located, but we are not liable to be mistaken that there is a colour or that there is a sound. There are also *common* sensibles that are perceived in themselves, but are accessible through any one of the sense modalities. Through the perception of these common sensibles we are aware of how big things are, what shapes they have, how many of them there are, as well as their movements from place to place.[2] Additionally, there are all sorts of cases that he classifies as *incidental* perception. For instance there is incidental perception of the son of Diares when one perceives something that is pale, and the pale thing happens to be the son of Diares.[3] Although we are not prone to error as to whether what we perceive is pale, we may indeed be mistaken as to whether the pale thing that we see is in fact the son of Diares. In general, we are more liable to error about the incidental objects of perception than we ever are with regard to the special objects of the five senses, although there is even more room for error when it comes to the common sensibles.[4]

Although we perceive particulars, we perceive them *as* instantiating properties that are general and repeatable. We are capable of retaining appearances of them in memory, and capable also of grouping together our memories of similar things in such a way as to constitute experience (*empeiria*).[5] For instance, by frequently observing, and remembering, what kind of treatment helped particular people who were sick in a certain way we may acquire experience that is at once knowledge of particulars and also in some way general and applicable to new cases. We shall consider this more fully below.

Although this experience must be acquired and is not innate, our capacity for such knowledge is itself innate, and because we have such a capacity we are able to grasp collections of explicable, general facts. We know a great many such facts through experience, and these serve as the observational data that can provide us with the explanatory first principles for scientific knowledge, as well as for the various forms of art or craft expertise. He stresses this fundamental role that experience plays when he writes:

> it is the business of experience to give the principles which belong to each sub-ject. I mean for example that astronomical experience supplies the principles of astronomical science; for once the phenomena were adequately apprehended, the demonstrations of astronomy were discovered.[6]

Experience as such does not involve explanatory or causal knowledge, and unlike somebody in possession of craft knowledge or theoretical science, a person of experience does not as such grasp explanatory universal principles. However, Aristotle thinks that it was experience concerning the observational phenomena about the celestial bodies that enabled the ancient astronomers to grasp the principles of astronomy that explain those very observed facts. These perceptual facts were not, of course, attributable to the research activities of a single person, but rather drew upon the accumulated, recorded knowledge of generations of experts. As with other areas of scientific inquiry, here too there were individuals who observed and recorded facts that are available to the senses, and that involve connections and regularities that serve as explananda for causal inquiries. However, although the attainment of causal knowledge about the physical world depends upon general perceptual knowledge, scientific knowledge involves *reasoning* to and from explanatory principles and hence goes well beyond what the perceptual faculty itself can provide.

2. Reasoning and knowledge

This brings us to another way in which what we know changes over time. Aristotle holds that we apply deductive or inductive reasoning to what we already know in ways that enable us to acquire additional knowledge. According to the opening sentence of Aristotle's *Posterior Analytics*, 'All teaching and all intellectual learning come about from already existing knowledge' (I.1, 71a1–2). This includes the kind of thinking involved in productive arts, in the practical disciplines of ethics and political science, and in theoretical scientific thought. Scientific thinking involves being able to reason correctly about the consequences of what one takes to be the case. The more we reason and think clearly about some domain of investigation, the more firmly we grasp the systematic connections between what we already grasp and the further truths to which this leads. Ultimately it is by the use of reason that we are able to arrive at an understanding of the most basic and fundamental truths, the first principles of some subject of rational inquiry. Humans are by nature rational, and the highest expression of that rationality is the intellectual grasp of those principles that yield the systematic understanding of the intelligible features of the world. Although the use of our perceptual capacities provides a complex and rich array of perceptual and experiential knowledge of that world, this higher cognitive achievement requires the use and exercise of distinctly *intellectual* capacities, over and above what can be provided by the perceptual faculty alone.

Aristotle wrote two major treatises that describe in some detail methods for inquiry and investigation, his *Analytics* (consisting of what are today known as the *'Prior Analytics'* and the *'Posterior Analytics'*) and his *Topics*. The former treatise, as Aristotle tells us at the beginning, chiefly concerns procedures to be used for reaching what he called 'demonstrative *epistêmê*', and the latter concerns procedures (*Topics* VIII.5, 159a32ff.) for dialectical 'testing and investigation'. These treatises arguably contain some of Aristotle's most original work, for in connection with the topic of reasoning (*sullogizesthai*), which covers for him demonstrative as well as dialectical reasoning and proof, he states:

> Concerning *sullogizesthai* we had nothing at all from any earlier time to report, but simply were kept labouring, over a long time, in inquiries by trial and error.[7]

Since Aristotle offers two chief methods for *sullogizesthai*, a main question for scholars, in addition to the question as to what each of these methods itself amounts to, has been how Aristotle takes them to be related to each other. One dominant approach to this issue has been to assign these two methods to different stages in Aristotle's philosophical development. For instance, some[8] have argued that Aristotle first followed his master Plato in taking dialectic to be the method of choice for philosophy and science and then, later, broke from his teacher and developed analytics as his own preferred alternative. A major challenge to this kind of developmental account, and to the developmental approach to this issue altogether, came in the mid-twentieth century when G. E. L. Owen (himself no foe overall of developmental analyses of Aristotle's thought) argued (1961) that dialectic and analytics were not *successive* offerings as *the* method to use for the purposes of philosophy or science, but rather were two methods, codified and constructed in the main simultaneously and intended by Aristotle for different purposes. Owen's own extremely influential proposal was that generally speaking Aristotle's own method both for discovery and confirmation in his main systematic works (such as his *Physics*, *On the Soul*, *Metaphysics* and *Nicomachean Ethics*) was and remained some form of dialectic. On his view the proper use of analytics, by contrast, was simply to show how discoveries in these areas, once made and confirmed, ought to be organized and presented. This has led many scholars to treat the *Analytics* as offering us little or no guide to Aristotle's actual procedures of inquiry and confirmation in his main systematic works.

This kind of interpretation of Aristotle's views on the acquisition and presentation of knowledge carves out a position on method for Aristotle on which a sharp distinction is to be drawn between those areas of systematic inquiry that, as dialectical, are the province of what we should call philosophy, and those which, as empirical, are the province of science. To a large extent it is this interpretation that has served to set the terms for the later debate that continues to this day on the roles and uses of dialectic and of analytics for Aristotle.

3. The role of *phainomena* in philosophical argument

This is not the place to discuss at length either the details of Owen's account or its subsequent influence on contemporary work on Aristotle's epistemology, or our reasons for departing from it in various ways in what follows. We have singled out his contributions in part because his leading – and inspired – point of departure was an account of Aristotle's use of the term '*phainomena*', 'things that appear so'. Any adequate account of Aristotle's epistemology must address the roles of appearances in his treatment of inquiry, warrant and explanation. Owen noted, with earlier commentators, that Aristotle commonly uses this term to designate those strictly *empirical* or *perceptual* data from which scientific inquiry properly takes its start and by reference to which its theoretical results are to be ultimately tested and confirmed. In addition to the passage we have already cited from *Prior Analytics* I.30, there is a key methodological passage in *On the Heavens* (*de Caelo*) that provides additional detail:

> In fact their [i.e., Platonists'] explanation of the phenomena is not consistent with the phenomena. And the reason [for this failure] is that their ultimate principles are wrongly assumed: they had certain predetermined views, and were resolved to bring everything into line with them . . . In the confidence that the principles

are true they are ready to accept any consequence of their application. As though some principles did not require to be judged from their results, and particularly from their final issue! And that issue, which in the case of productive knowledge is the product, in the knowledge of nature is the phenomena always and properly given by perception [*to phainomenon aei kuriôs kata tên aisthêsin*].[9]

The principles of a science are to be judged by reference to their consequences, and if it is a science that deals with perceptual phenomena those consequences must be in agreement with what authoritatively appears to be the case from perception. It is the role of the collected perceptual *phainomena* that make up genuine *empeiria* to provide us with knowledge of principles in any science or any art whatsoever. This is because these principles are properly found and become known and confirmed *as* the things from which there is genuine demonstrative explanation of these very *phainomena*.

In a similar vein he writes in *On the Soul* (I.1, 402b22–25):

when we are able to give an account conformable to experience [*phantasia*] of all or most of the properties of a substance, we shall be in the most favourable position to say something worth saying about the essential nature [*ousia*] of that subject.

He is here presupposing the idea, discussed further below, that definitions of essential natures of objects specify causes of their explicable attributes, and function as first principles of scientific demonstrations. However, he is making the further point that knowing these attributes contributes to our knowledge of those very definitional principles that are used to explain the attributes. Scientific definitions and principles are of epistemic value precisely because and when they enable us to explain the perceptual data known through experience. This is a doctrine not only of the *Analytics*, but equally of *On the Heavens* and *On the Soul*, and we find main elements of the same doctrine in many places elsewhere.[10]

However (as Owen also noted), this use of the term '*phainomena*' to denote the collected perceptual data that make up genuine *empeiria* is not Aristotle's only important use of this term in methodological contexts. He not only uses this term for the empirical starting points and controlling data for reaching demonstrative knowledge, in any art or science, but also uses the term '*phainomena*' for the proper premises for all *dialectical* argument. In *Prior Analytics* I.1, for instance, Aristotle says:

> A dialectical premise (*protasis*) is, for the one who is putting questions, an asking [sc. an invitation to choose one] of a pair of contradictories. For the one who is reasoning to a conclusion it [a dialectical *protasis*] is something secured as apparent [*phainomenon*] and reputable [*endoxon*].[11]

Aristotle distinguishes two uses of the term translated '*protasis*' (literally, a putting forward) in dialectical contexts – one use for the question itself which is put forward by a questioner in expectation of a 'yes' or 'no' answer from an interlocutor, another use for the proposition which is secured by the answer of the interlocutor. Such a proposition must be, for proper dialectical argument, *phainomenon* – i.e. something that appears so – and *endoxon*, i.e. reputable, or noted and accredited. In general, the premises of a dialectical argument are reputable opinions. This same use of the term '*phainomena*' is also found elsewhere, as in *Topics* VIII.5 where, in giving his rules for an answerer in a dialectical encounter, Aristotle says, 'All of the *phainomena* should be conceded [as premises by an answerer]'.[12] In speaking of the *phainomena* in such passages Aristotle does not have in mind the same class of exclusively perceptual data that make up genuine *empeiria*. By way of contrast, any *endoxa* that count as genuine dialectical premises must count as *phainomena* in this second use. According to *Topics* I.10, such dialectical premises include any opinions held by all people, or by the preponderant majority; and any opinions held by all, or most or the most famous recognized experts (*sophoi*) providing that they do not conflict with common opinion.[13] Equally, many of the *phainomena* that are dialectical premises, or commonly accredited notions, are clearly not items of authoritative perceptual experience, or *empeiria*. So the two classes of *phainomena*, though they may overlap, are far from being identical.

Consequently, there are different ways in which appearances may figure into our reasoning. When the premises are *endoxa*, or reputable opinions, the reasoning is dialectical. Dialectical arguments are not, for Aristotle, scientific proofs because they do not explain *why* the conclusion is true, much less why it must be the case and could not possibly be other than it is. The failure to explain is not due to invalidity, but rather to the fact that its premises do not include the principles that are proper to the subject matter. Such arguments cannot account for the intrinsic connection that holds between a subject and its explicable attributes. A genuine dialectical deduction is every bit as valid as a scientific proof, but does not show what it is about a subject that accounts for an attribute belonging to it as such, as the subject that it is.[14] By way of contrast, a scientific demonstration is a deduction that accomplishes just that by proceeding from premises that are first principles of a particular science. As we have already seen, for natural sciences that deal with perceptible objects (general) perceptual appearances are conclusions of demonstrations, and the fact that the principles yield these conclusions is useful for the inquiry into principles.[15]

4. Syllogistic argument

Reasoning is central both to Aristotle's analysis of demonstrative knowledge and to his discussions of methods of inquiry and of extending our knowledge. For Aristotle, both dialectical argument and scientific demonstration employ a kind of discourse that he calls a 'syllogism'.[16] The concept of a syllogism is a wider notion than that of a demonstration (and certainly wider than that of a dialectical argument as well). Every demonstration is a syllogism, but it is not the case that every syllogism is a demonstration. In light of what has already been noted we may say that in order for a syllogism to count as a *demonstration* the premises must explain why the conclusion is true. It is because a syllogism need not be explanatory that not every syllogism is a demonstration.

Accordingly, although the subject matter of the *Analytics* is demonstration and demonstrative knowledge, he starts with a treatment of the more comprehensive notion of a syllogism. It is important to note that there are two different forms of inferential reasoning involved in his epistemology, the syllogism, or deduction, and induction. Consequently, he writes that 'every reasoned conviction comes either through deduction or from induction'.[17] Deduction is the form of reasoning in which conclusions follow *of necessity* from the premises that are laid down, whereas induction is a form of reasoning in which one infers something

universal from more particular statements. The former is characterized
in the following way (*Prior Analytics* I.1, 24b18–22):

> A deduction [*sullogismos*] is a discourse [*logos*] in which, certain things being
> stated, something other than what is stated follows of necessity from their being
> so. I mean by the last phrase that it follows because of them, and by this, that
> no further term is required from without in order to make the consequence
> necessary.

In order to specify the nature of syllogistic inference the *Prior Analytics*
contains an abstract characterization of those valid arguments that contain two simple statements as premises, have a single simple statement
as conclusion, and involve just three terms: the predicate of the conclusion (major term), the subject of the conclusion (minor term) and a middle
term. All demonstrations must contain a middle term that occurs in both
premises, but not the conclusion, and 'mediates' the connection between
the subject and the predicate in the conclusion. (The two terms in the
conclusion are also called 'extremes'.) As we shall see later, an important
feature of his approach to scientific knowledge is that definitions of essential natures are also expressions of explanatory causes of the conclusions of
explanatory demonstrations, and function as middle terms. The simplest,
most basic, syllogisms contain as premises a pair of simple statements, and
have a simple statement as the conclusion. Larger, more extended, pieces
of scientific reasoning are to be analysed as (possibly branching) sequences
of two premise syllogisms in which each premise is either a first principle
or is demonstrated by a previous syllogism.[18] When a premise in a scientific
proof is itself a theorem, not a first principle, it must be demonstrated by
another scientific proof that will itself have two premises, and so on.

The conclusion of a syllogism necessarily follows not because of the
truth of the premises (even when they are true), but because of the way
the subjects and predicates of those premises are assumed to be related
to each other, and the way that the conclusion that is drawn relates its
subject and predicate. What it is for the conclusion to follow of necessity from the premises is, he says, for it to follow 'because of them', and
for this to be the case no further term is required from without in order
to make the consequence necessary. No term not already present in one
of the premises is needed in order for the conclusion of the syllogism to
follow of necessity.

Despite its limitations this has a certain kind of generality in its scope in that it abstracts from the content and subject matter of the statements involved in a syllogism. Every syllogism is composed of statements with determinate subjects and predicates, and each statement is about something, and either affirms or denies something. Nonetheless, syllogistic reasoning takes place in *all* demonstrative sciences, and is not confined to any one subject matter, or any one set of attributes. If the relation of syllogistic consequence that holds between premises and a conclusion depended upon the subject matter, or upon what was being said about that subject matter, there would have to be some common content to all of the demonstrative sciences. However, on Aristotle's view there is no genus of being, and no one kind of thing that all valid reasoning is about. Different sciences study different genera, and these different genera cannot be subsumed under a single common genus. Nonetheless they all prove theorems by syllogistic arguments.

Both Aristotle's analysis of scientific reasoning and his treatment of dialectical argument rely on the notion of syllogistic inference. As already noted, scientific demonstrations prove their conclusions by showing how those conclusions necessarily follow from their explanatory principles. To know scientifically involves the ability to reason validly from indemonstrable starting points. In a similar manner, the logical expertise exemplified by a dialectician in two-person question and answer exchanges involves the production of valid inferences, and this ability is not confined to a single domain. In *Topics* I.1 dialectical skill is characterized as an ability both to reason syllogistically from reputable opinions to conclusions that necessarily follow from them, and to avoid being refuted by one's own concessions in argument.

Topics I.2 indicates that dialectic is useful for intellectual training, for persuading a general audience, and for philosophical knowledge. Among other things, it enables one to develop and examine the arguments on both sides of philosophical puzzles, thereby facilitating the discernment of truth. Furthermore, the dialectical scrutiny of credible opinions provides a path, or road, that leads to the first principles of the sciences.

Unlike scientific arguments that argue from first principles and are concerned with items within a single subject genus, dialectical argument is possible concerning any subject matter whatsoever. In this sense it is topic-neutral, and a general account of the way in which a dialectician

shows that reputable opinions and an interlocutor's concessions neces-
sitate further conclusions will require abstraction from subject matter. In
dialectical argument one asks questions, and produces syllogisms using
the answers as premises, and as already noted this does not result in
causal knowledge since the arguments do not reason from explanatory
premises already known by the respondent. Although credible opinions,
which can include commonly accepted views as well as the opinions of
the wise, must not be obvious falsehoods, they may in fact be false, and
certainly need not be explanatory first principles. Reasoning from them
is in any case no guarantee that the conclusions reached are true. Even
where the premises are true, they (typically) would not explain the truth
of the conclusion.

5. Appearances, inquiry and justification

There currently is no scholarly consensus as to the role that *phainomena*
play in inquiry or justification. To a large extent this is due to disagree-
ments about the extent to which dialectic is the method to be employed
in various contexts for these tasks. For instance, given that the first principles cannot be demonstrated by prior principles (more on that later),
many scholars have been attracted to the view that first principles are
either arrived at or justified by dialectical argument. Although dialectical
argument might not explain why the principles are true, this observation leaves it open whether argument from endoxic appearances could
enable one to discover what the principles are, or perhaps even provide
some kind of non-explanatory justification or defence of them once
arrived at, or at least could test claims to knowledge or expertise.

  As indicated above, there are texts that support the view that theoretical results are ultimately tested and confirmed by reference to empirical, perceptual data, and this is not dialectical argument from reputable
opinions or *endoxa*. Nonetheless, dialectic does have its own uses in
connection with the examination of claims to knowledge. For instance,
for Aristotle one type of dialectical argument is '*peirastic*'. Peirastic argument allows one who does not have scientific knowledge to examine
claims to scientific knowledge by using as premises answers accepted
by somebody who makes a claim to such knowledge, and it employs
premises that anybody claiming knowledge of the subject would have

to know.[19] One might (though we do not) hold a more extreme view according to which dialectic provides the only possible mode of discovery or justification possible for principles, or alternatively assign a more limited role to dialectic and maintain that non-dialectical arguments concerned with perceptual appearances play a central role in the search for and knowledge of principles. Regardless of where one comes down on this, it is one of Aristotle's great achievements to have clearly separated the two classes of *phainomena* and also to have insisted that items of genuine perceptual *empeiria* do not count merely as opinion, but rather are themselves items of knowledge.

The kind of interpretation we take to be most promising is one according to which perceptual phenomena constitute the final authority for the confirmation of results in natural science (*phusikê epistêmê*).[20] Accordingly, in what follows we will develop our account of his epistemology along these lines. This approach does not leave it open that it is the role primarily of *endoxa* to lead us to principles in some areas of science. Aristotle's claim is that it is the role of experience itself – of the collected authoritative perceptual *phainomena* that make up *empeiria*, and of nothing less – to do this. Thus, according to *Prior Analytics* I.30, no genuine *epistêmê* or *technê* or branch thereof, such as what we find in the *Physics*, has its principles discovered or confirmed primarily, much less exclusively, dialectically. In that text, at least, Aristotle is not concerned with how to present systematically and intelligibly results reached either by dialectical or by empirical means, but rather is commenting upon the procedure for discovery or confirmation.

6. Knowledge THAT and knowledge WHY

One finds a similar message conveyed when Aristotle says:

> It is the role of perceivers (*aisthêtikoi*) to know the *that* (*to hoti*), of mathematicians to know the *reason why* (*to dioti*).[21]

In this passage Aristotle attributes to *perceivers* the knowledge of the fact, or *to hoti* – which is his language[22] for what he takes to be the proper, initial, starting point in the search for demonstrative explanations. As the context shows, he has particularly in mind here the procedure actually used in the so-called mixed sciences such as astronomy, mechanics and harmonics. However, later passages in this work make the same kind of point in more general terms. For instance, he goes on to argue that the acquisition of all scientific knowledge depends on the prior possession of appropriate perceptual data since it is reached by demonstration from universal principles and such principles can become known only by induction starting from suitable strictly perceptual data.[23]

Furthermore, in the *Metaphysics* Aristotle says, now quite generally:

> For men of experience know that the thing is so, but do not know why, while the others [with scientific knowledge or art] know the 'why' and the cause . . . [The senses] do not tell us the 'why' of anything – e.g. why fire is hot; they only say that it is hot.[24]

Metaphysics A.1 closely parallels and amplifies for us the much more compressed account found in *Posterior Analytics* II.19, and offers us perhaps our best guide to the interpretation of that text as well.

The central difference between scientific knowledge and the kind of knowledge of empirical fact provided by the senses is that the former involves a grasp of the causes of those facts. This causal knowledge is unqualified *epistêmê*, and is the kind of knowledge we have when we know that the cause of some fact being the case is its cause, and that the fact could not possibly be other than it is.[25]

A theoretical science has as its subject matter either substances or items in non-substance categories such as geometrical shapes, and also the proper attributes of the objects that fall within its scope. The possessor of scientific knowledge is able to demonstrate why the objects of the science in question must have the intrinsic attributes that they do have. For instance, a triangle intrinsically possesses angles equal to two right angles (2R). This fact is a necessary truth and could not possibly be otherwise. One has scientific knowledge of this fact by possessing the proof that gives the reason why a triangle, as such, must have that property. *Posterior Analytics* I.4–5 introduces the idea that unqualified *epistêmê* is of universals, or of things that hold universally, in a very special sense. The relevant notion is introduced there as follows: 'I call universal whatever belongs to something both of every case and in itself [*kath' hauto*] and as such' (*Posterior Analytics* I.4, 73b26–27). One has knowledge of such universal connections by having demonstrations that show the reason why some general fact must be the case.

7. Scientific demonstration and first principles

Speaking generally, for Aristotle the explanatory structure of such a science is *demonstrative*. This project has often been thought to have affinities with foundationalist accounts of knowledge in that the first principles provide warrant for the theorems that they explain. Aristotle thinks that we know and rely upon what is posterior on the basis of principles that we know and rely upon even more (*Posterior Analytics* I.2, 72a30–7). When we are able to deduce a theorem from principles that explain it, that theorem is trustworthy or reliable precisely because the principles through which we know it are themselves trustworthy and reliable, and are so to an even greater extent. There is a way in which the principles confer epistemic warrant on the theorems given that they are themselves known and reliable.

A demonstration itself is a scientific syllogism, a syllogism by virtue of which we know, and its premises provide the epistemic warrant for the conclusion it demonstrates. The first principles involved in unqualified scientific understanding must be true, primary, immediate, and better known than, prior to, and explanatory of those things of which they are the principles (*Posterior Analytics* I.2, 71b19–22). Since a first principle is known through itself, and not through other things, there is no explanation as to why the principle is true. It is not explained or 'caused' by anything, and it cannot be known by tracing it back to causes. A first principle is indemonstrable, for it is both primary and immediate. To be immediate, it must be primary in the sense that there is nothing prior to it in terms of which it is understood or known. If it is a statement (such as a definition) with both a subject and a predicate, there is no middle term that explains or mediates the connection between its subject and its predicate. In general, a first principle is indemonstrable in that it cannot itself be explained by deducing it from prior principles. The other necessary truths of a science are explained or 'caused' by something other than themselves. They are known by tracing them back to principles and causes that are known through themselves.

Crucial to this account is the view that the first principles must be known without themselves being objects of demonstrative knowledge. *Posterior Analytics* I.3 shows Aristotle's firm commitment to the position that the principles, although known, are not known demonstratively. He there rejects two rival views according to which all knowledge is demonstrative. According to one view, if what is posterior is known through what is prior, then on pain of infinite regress there must be first principles. However, if the first principles are not demonstrated they are not known (since on this view all knowledge is demonstrative). However, in that case the things that depend upon them are also unknown, and so nothing is known *simpliciter*. According to the other rival view, which also accepts that all knowledge is demonstrative, it is possible for there to be *circular* demonstration, and hence nothing prevents there from being knowledge of everything. Aristotle, however, both accepts the possibility of demonstrative knowledge and at the same time rejects the idea that all knowledge is demonstrative. He grants that there cannot be an infinite series of propositions in an explanatory hierarchy, and hence accepts that at some point the premises of demonstration come to a stop with primitive principles. As principles they are prior and better known than what they explain, and for that reason cannot be *demonstrated* in a circular fashion. Circular demonstration would require that the demonstration of a principle A uses as a premise some other principle A* such that A is used in the demonstration of A*, and hence A would be prior to and better known than A*, and also A* would be prior to and better known than A.

He indicates, however, that although circular demonstration is impossible, it may be the case that principle A is prior without qualification to a demonstrated conclusion A* even though A* is prior to first principle A in some other way. A* may be one of things initially known *to us*, on the basis of which A is made known without qualification through induction (*Posterior Analytics* I.3, 72b27–30). In the case of empirical sciences, a variety of propositions about some subject S (and of the form 'S is P') are initially known to us through experience without being demonstrated. So, there is a way in which the principles in a demonstration confer warrant on theorems, and also a way in which those propositions that later serve as conclusions of demonstrations are initially known to us on the basis of experience, and as such are a basis for knowledge of the principles that in fact explain them. Furthermore, once they are demonstratively known through their principles the theorems are objects of unqualified knowledge. Since the principles are better known than the theorems, there must also be some way in which the principles are objects of unqualified knowledge, though not through being demonstrated by means of anything prior to or explanatory of them. In *Posterior Analytics* II.19 the name of this superior epistemic condition is *noûs*.

8. Different kinds of first principles

Aristotle holds not only that there must be some principles that are known in a non-demonstrative manner, but also that none of the principles of the various special sciences are themselves demonstrated by some higher science. In particular he rejects a Platonic conception of a general dialectical science of all being, or everything that there is. Aristotle has no room for a science that would prove the principles of the departmental sciences, and instead upholds the independence or autonomy of the departmental sciences. Building on his key insight that knowledge requires both an understanding of 'causes' and the necessity of what is known, the *Posterior Analytics* distinguishes different kinds of first principles, and takes the majority of principles of a science to be unique to just that science. The first principles of a science divide into axioms and theses, and the latter further divide into hypotheses and definitions. Unlike *theses*, axioms are common to all sciences. They are principles from which reasoning arises, and as such must be grasped by anybody who is going to learn or scientifically understand anything at all. Examples of axioms are the principle of non-contradiction, and the law of excluded middle.

Turning now to the special principles, those that are unique to a science, a definition is an account that states what something is, and a hypothesis is a postulate that states *that* something is or is not. A definition is an account signifying an essence. For instance, if the definition of man is 'rational animal', then being a rational animal is the essence of man. Definitions and hypotheses are proper (or unique) to a science that studies the things they define or assert to exist, and so any particular set of definitions and hypotheses is employed only in that branch of knowledge, and cannot be demonstrated by the principles of some other science.

His account of the demonstrative structure of a science is built around the concept of definitions that are indemonstrable statements of essences, and the associated notion of a 'middle term' that is employed in his analysis of syllogistic reasoning. Scientists know or understand things by knowing the essences signified by real definitions, and these essences are the causes that explain the intrinsic connections between the subjects and predicates in scientific theorems. As such the *definiens* functions as an explanatory middle term in a demonstration, and the essence expressed in the account of what something is also a cause of its having the scientifically explicable intrinsic features that belong to it universally in the way that 2R (having angles equal to two right angles) belongs to triangle.

9. Knowledge of essential natures and stages of inquiry

How is it that one arrives at knowledge of these essential natures? Earlier we saw that in connection with the explanation of perceptual data, at a minimum the analytical requirements of Aristotle's method introduce two stages for successful scientific inquiry. At the first stage one accumulates experience (*empeiria*), which comes to us primarily in the form of knowledge *that* concerning the genuine accidents of a subject. At a subsequent stage we then find the essence of that subject by finding the chief definitional principle that offers the basis for the best causal explanation of the possession of those accidents by that subject. That is one message of the *Analytics* itself and of many other related texts throughout the scientific works.

However, Aristotle provides more by way of detailed instruction for the working scientist than this, both in the *Analytics* and elsewhere. There are large stretches of the *Analytics* that also directly purport to address these matters. Aristotle begins *Posterior Analytics* II with the following remarks about procedures of inquiry and knowledge acquisition in science:

> The things we seek are equal in number to those we understand [know scientifically]. We seek four things: (i) the *that* [to hoti], (ii) the *reason why* [to dioti], (iii) if it exists [ei esti], (iv) what it is [ti esti]. . . . When we know the that we seek the reason why . . . and knowing that it exists we seek what it is.[26]

We inquire into facts, and when we know facts we also inquire into their causes. Additionally, we inquire into whether various things exist, and when we know that something exists we also inquire into what it is, into its essential nature. In keeping with the idea that the essence is the cause of a thing having its intrinsic, explicable attributes he adds that 'to know what it is is the same as to know why it is' (*Posterior Analytics* II.2, 90a31–32). The proper use of the procedures he advocates culminates in the knowledge of the ultimate cause and essence of a thing. He equates this with that knowledge of its *ti esti* and *dioti*.

Success at an initial or first stage of inquiry involves knowledge that S is P (the *hoti*) and knowledge that S exists, for a suitable range of subjects S and attributes P. A proper grasp of a nominal definition, or what Aristotle calls 'an account of what a name or phrase signifies' (93b30–31, our translation), counts for him as the achievement, in favourable cases at least, of a preliminary stage of scientific inquiry.[27] Such an account is not the definition of the ultimate essence of a thing, and does not express a cause, but it can serve as a suitable starting point for inquiry. Although the real definition, or account of the ultimate essence of thing, serves as the basis for a proper causal explanation of the other theoretically knowable features of a thing, knowledge of the nominal definition, or initial account of what a thing is, provides a basis for knowledge of the existence of the thing insofar as it picks it out through salient and presumptively explicable features. Causal inquiry can then uncover the real definition by finding the ultimate cause and best explanation of the features that figure in the nominal definition and other features on a par with it.

In *Posterior Analytics* II.19, for instance, where Aristotle describes the stages by which we come to knowledge of scientific principles and, thus, to knowledge of essence, he says:

> Thus from perception there comes memory [i.e. the retention of perceptual information], as we say, and from frequently repeated memory [i.e., frequently retained perceptual information] concerning the same thing there comes experience (*empeiria*), since many [such retained] memories constitute an item of experience which is one in number. But [then] from experience, or from the resting of all [such items] – of the universal (*katholou*) – in the soul, of the one item alongside (*para*) the many [memories] which is one and the same in respect of all of them, [there comes] a principle (*archê*) of art (*technê*) or science (*epistêmê*).[28]

His more expanded account of these stages in *Metaphysics* A.1 contrasts what comes to humans by nature (*phusei*) with what comes only

with the possession of art (*technê*) or science (*epistêmê*). Perception,
memory and experience come by nature. That is, they do not result
from the use of reason or from the use of any inferential or theoretically based mode of inquiry, but rather, as Aristotle puts it here, simply
by use of our sense faculties. He opposes experience (*empeiria*) to reason (*logos*), and in connection with the attainment of scientific knowledge assigns its origin to the natural unreasoned result of the repeated
perception of suitably similar things.[29] Nevertheless, despite its humble
origins, Aristotle here gives a very elevated status to *empeiria*. As we
have seen, *empeiria* is sufficient for, or simply is, knowledge of the
that (*to hoti*). However, this is his designation for knowledge that is
fully sufficient to enable an inquiring scientist to proceed to the search
for causes, or knowledge *why*. Nothing more is needed than genuine knowledge *that*, for Aristotle, to move to this final stage of causal
inquiry.

The grasp of a preliminary account of what something is, at least of
the sort that is captured in a nominal definition, is needed to have the
appropriate knowledge *that* which enables proper causal inquiry to
go forward. Such a grasp cannot come about after *empeiria* because
empeiria itself is already sufficient for, or simply is, knowledge *that*. To
illustrate this consider the example in *Metaphysics* A.1 of fire. *Empeiria*
provides us with knowledge *that* fire is hot, and somebody with such
knowledge, derived from suitable frequent experience, would clearly
seem to know in a preliminary way what fire is. Fire might be defined
nominally as a certain very hot flaming stuff. He could go on from this
kind of starting point to inquire why fire is such hot stuff and, by virtue of learning this, uncover the ultimate cause and essence of fire.[30]
We accumulate, independently of theoretical assumptions, *empeiria*
or knowledge that which concerns genuine natural kinds and their real
properties, and is sufficient to then permit successful causal inquiry
that is able to uncover the ultimate essences of those genuine kinds.
It is collected common experience, and continuing extensive observation, that itself, by nature, fixes on genuine kinds. Our preliminary
knowledge of what are in fact genuine kinds is further confirmed and
refined for us when we find the proper causal explanation of what
we know by virtue of having by nature this preliminary knowledge of
what they are.

Notes

1 *On the Soul (de Anima)*, II.6, 418a11–12; III.3, 428b18–19. Unless noted otherwise, translations are from Barnes (1984) – for short: *ROTA*. All bracketed material has been supplied by us.

2 *On the Soul* II.6, 418a17–19.

3 *On the Soul* II.6, 418a20–24.

4 *On the Soul* III.3, 428b18–25.

5 Aristotle's most extended treatments of experience are at *Posterior Analytics* II.19, 100a3–9, and *Metaphysics* A.1, 980b25–981b9 (discussed below).

6 *Prior Analytics* I.30, 46a17–21.

7 *Sophistical Refutations* 34, 184b1–3, our translation.

8 Friedrich Solmsen and W. D. Ross are influential examples. See Solmsen (1929) and Ross (1923: esp. pp. 57–9).

9 From *On the Heavens* III.7, 306a 5–17.

10 For instance, in *On Generation and Corruption* I.2 (316a5ff.), in *Parts of Animals* I.1 (639b5–10 with 640a13–15), in *Generation of Animals* III.10 (760b27–33), and in *History of Animals* I.6 (491a7–14).

11 *Prior Analytics* I.1, 24b10–12, based on Owen's translation.

12 *Topics* VIII.5, 159b21, our translation.

13 *Topics* I.10, 104a8–11.

14 Although Aristotle also countenances inductive dialectical arguments, his discussion of dialectic is largely confined to deduction.

15 Unlike dialectical argument, the premises of which are appearances, the premises of scientific proof need not be, though in some cases they might be. For instance, we can explain an eclipse of the moon by reference to the fact that the earth is interposed between the moon and the sun, its source of light, without ever having observed that interposition. *Posterior Analytics* II.2, 90a26–27, contrasts this with the hypothetical case of observers on the surface of the moon who would be able to observe this cause of the eclipse simultaneously with the observation of the eclipse.

16 In Greek, *sullogismos*. An alternative translation is 'deduction'.

17 *Prior Analytics* II.23, 68b13–14, with 'reasoned conviction' for ROTA's 'belief'.

18 *Prior Analytics* I.25 deals with extended deductions.

19 See *Sophistical Refutations* 2 with *Topics* VIII.5.

20 And even, according to *Prior Analytics* I.30, in any craft (*technê*) or *epistêmê* whatsoever.

21 *Posterior Analytics* I.13, 79a2–3. We depart from *ROTA* which has 'empirical scientists' where we have 'perceivers', and 'fact' where we have 'that'.

22 For instance, in *Posterior Analytics* II.1–2.

23 See *Posterior Analytics* I.18.

24 *Metaphysics* A1, 981a28–30; b11–13. Closely related points, if not the same point, are made in *Posterior Analytics* I.31 and II.19.
25 See *Posterior Analytics* I.2, 71b9–12.
26 These quotes are from *Posterior Analytics* II.1, 89b23–34. We here depart from ROTA both by translating *'to hoti'* as 'the that', rather than 'the fact', and by translating *'ei esti'* as 'if it exists', rather than 'if it is'.
27 In what follows we offer considerations in favour of the view that the grasp of nominal definitions already involves knowledge of the existence of a genuine kinds, but there is scholarly controversy as to whether this typically occurs at a prior stage. For a detailed discussion of the stages of inquiry, and arguments in favour of treating these as distinct stages, see Charles (2000).
28 *Posterior Analytics* II.19, 100a3–8, our translation. Both the translation and the interpretation of the details of this much-discussed text are highly controversial.
29 *Metaphysics* 981a5ff. Note that he attributes a share of *empeiria* to unreasoning animals at 980b26–27.
30 We would urge that this is how Aristotle thinks one could learn what fire is in this elevated sense, without already knowing this prior to causal inquiry, and avoid an assumption of Meno's paradox of inquiry (*Meno* 80e1–5).

Further reading

Barnes, J. (1994 [1975]), *Aristotle's 'Posterior Analytics'*, translation with commentary, 2nd edn. Oxford: Clarendon Press.
Bolton, R. (1990), 'The epistemological basis of Aristotelian dialectic', in D. Devereux and P. Pellegrin (eds), *Biologie, Logique et Métaphysique chez Aristote*. Paris: Editions du Centre National de la Recherche Scientifique, pp. 185–236.
—(2003), 'Aristotle: Epistemology and methodology', in C. Shields (ed.), *The Blackwell Guide to Ancient Philosophy*. Malden, Mass.: Blackwell, pp. 151–62.
Burnyeat, M. (1981), 'Aristotle on understanding knowledge', in E. Berti (ed.), *Aristotle on Science: 'The Posterior Analytics'* (Atti dell' VIII Symposium Aristotelicum). Padua: Editrice Antenore, pp. 97–139.
Code, A. (1986), 'Aristotle's investigation of a basic logical principle', *Canadian Journal of Philosophy*, 16, 341–57.
—(1999), 'Aristotle: Logic and metaphysics', in D. Furley (ed.), *Routledge History of Philosophy, Vol. II: From Aristotle to Augustine*. London: Routledge, pp. 40–75.
Everson, S. (1997), *Aristotle on Perception*. Oxford: Clarendon Press.
Frede, M. (1996), 'Aristotle's rationalism', in M. Frede and G. Striker (eds), *Rationality in Greek Thought*. Oxford: Clarendon Press, pp. 157–73.

Irwin, T. H. (1977), 'Aristotle's discovery of metaphysics', *Review of Metaphysics*, 31, 210–29.

—(1988), *Aristotle's First Principles*. Oxford: Clarendon Press.

Kahn, C. H. (1981), 'The role of *nous* in the cognition of first principles in *Posterior Analytics* II 19', in E. Berti (ed.), *Aristotle on Science: 'The Posterior Analytics'* (Atti dell' VIII Symposium Aristotelicum). Padua: Editrice Antenore, pp. 385–414.

Kosman, L. A. (1973), 'Understanding, explanation and insight in the *Posterior Analytics*', in E. N. Lee, A. P. D. Mourelatos and R. Rorty (eds), *Exegesis and Argument: Studies in Greek Philosophy Presented to Gregory Vlastos*. Assen: van Gorcum, pp. 374–92.

Long, A. A. (1981), 'Aristotle and the history of Greek scepticism', in D. J. O'Meara (ed.), *Studies in Aristotle*. Washington: Catholic University of America Press, pp. 79–106.

Modrak, D. K. W. (1987), *Aristotle: The Power of Perception*. Chicago: University of Chicago Press.

Reeve, C. D. C. (1998), 'Dialectic and philosophy in Aristotle', in J. Gentzler (ed.), *Method in Ancient Philosophy*. Oxford: Clarendon Press, pp. 227–52.

Smith, R. (1993), 'Aristotle on the uses of dialectic', *Synthese*, 96, 335–58.

Taylor, C. C. W. (1990), 'Aristotle's epistemology', in S. Everson (ed.), *Epistemology* (*Companions to Ancient Thought: 1*). Cambridge: Cambridge University Press, pp. 116–42.

References

Barnes, J. (ed.) (1984), *The Complete Works of Aristotle: The Revised Oxford Translation*, 2 vols. Princeton: Princeton University Press.

Charles, D. (2000), *Aristotle on Meaning and Essence*. Oxford: Clarendon Press.

Owen, G. E. L. (1961), 'Tithenai ta phainomena', in S. Mansion (ed.), *Aristote et les Problèmes de Méthode*. Louvain: Publications Universitaires de Louvain, pp. 83–103. Reprinted in Moravcsik, J. M. E. (ed.) (1967), *Aristotle: A Collection of Critical Essays*. Garden City, NY: Anchor Books, pp. 167–90. Also reprinted in J. Barnes, M. Schofield and R. Sorabji (eds), (1975), *Articles on Aristotle*, vol. 1. London: Duckworth, pp. 113–26.

Ross, W. D. (1923), *Aristotle*. London: Methuen & Co.

Solmsen, F. (1929), *Die Entwicklung der aristotelischen Logik und Rhetorik*. Berlin: Weidmann.

CHAPTER 4

ANCIENT SCEPTICISM

Gisela Striker

1. Introduction

'Scepticism' is a word derived from ancient Greek, but it has long become a part of ordinary modern English. To be sceptical about something is to have doubts – for instance, about the story somebody has told, or about the possible success of a project. This use of the word probably goes back to Descartes in the seventeenth century, who used some of the arguments of the ancient Sceptics – then newly rediscovered – in his famous method of doubting everything that could possibly be doubted. Descartes' aim was to find an indubitable truth – and this was something the ancient Sceptics would hardly have expected to find. The noun 'sceptic' literally means 'inquirer', and the ancient philosophers who are now referred to by this label were primarily known for the usual result of their inquiries, namely suspension of judgement. How did this philosophical attitude come about, and how did it differ from the modern versions of scepticism?

According to the ancient tradition, Scepticism began with Pyrrho of Elis (365–275 BCE), a man who seems to have been famous mainly for his lifestyle and his unshakeable equanimity. Pyrrho explained his attitude by the claim that there was no way of finding out whether any belief about the world around us is either true or false. He himself wrote nothing, but his pupil and admirer Timon of Phlius wrote glowing accounts of Pyrrho's life and teaching, as well as a large number of satirical verses in which he ridiculed all other philosophers. Only fragments of Timon's literary production survive. The most informative passage has been preserved in the work of the early church father Eusebius, who was in turn quoting from Aristocles, a Greek historian of philosophy:

> Pyrrho's pupil, Timon, says that anyone who is going to lead a happy life must take account of the following three things: first, what objects are like by nature; secondly, what our attitude to them should be; finally, what will result for those who take this attitude. Now he says that Pyrrho shows that objects are equally indifferent and unfathomable and undeterminable because neither our senses nor our judgements are true or false; so for that reason we should not trust in them but should be without judgement and without inclination and unmoved, saying about each thing that it no more is than is not or both is and is not or neither is or is not. And Timon says that for those who take this attitude the result will be first non-assertion, then tranquillity. (Aristocles in Eusebius, *Praeparatio Evangelica* XIV 18.2–4; tr. Annas and Barnes, 1985: 11)[1]

The passage begins and ends with a reference to happiness and tranquillity, the state of mind of the happy person. It presents an account of Pyrrho's prescription for a happy life that is based on an epistemological argument indicated only by its conclusion: neither our senses nor our judgements are either true or false. But given its context in Aristocles' book, it is clear that behind this conclusion stands the old argument from conflicting appearances: our senses present us with contradictory evidence about their objects. The wind that appears warm to one person appears cold to another; what seems round at a distance looks square from nearby; what tastes bitter to one person tastes sweet to another, and so on. Philosophers had used such examples from the Presocratics on to denounce the unreliability of the senses as sources of information. By the time of Pyrrho, the same sort of conflict could be observed in the endless disputes among philosophers who purported to rely on reason and argument rather than perception, and Pyrrho saw no way of resolving those conflicts. As his later followers would put it, both sides in each controversy have the same authority; arguments on both sides have the same strength; so there is no reason to prefer one view to another. This argument is encapsulated in the formula *ou mallon* – no more this than that – and the advice to suspend judgement on all matters. The result of giving up on any attempt to find the truth was then supposed to lead to Pyrrho's attitude of indifference to all questions and eventually to tranquillity.

Pyrrho was not the kind of person to found a school, and the history of his followers apart from Timon remains obscure until the revival of Pyrrhonism some two centuries later. Let me therefore set aside Pyrrho for the moment and take a look at the second ancient version of Scepticism that arose in Plato's Academy in the third century BCE.

2. Scepticism in the Academy

In 268 BCE, a man named Arcesilaus became head of the Academy. An older colleague had been elected first, but he stepped down immediately in favour of Arcesilaus, who was clearly already the most prominent member of the school. Plato's school had lost some of its appeal after the new doctrines of Epicurus and Zeno of Citium, the founder of the Stoa, had been introduced to Athens around the turn of the century. Arcesilaus had brought the Academy back to public attention by engaging in a lively debate with Zeno about the possibility of knowledge. He had gone back to the method of Socrates in Plato's early dialogues. Like Socrates, Arcesilaus would examine an interlocutor's views by adopting his opponent's thesis as a premise and then argue, adding more premises accepted by the opponent, that the opponent's beliefs would lead him to contradict his initial claim. The Stoics, following perhaps the model of Epicurus, had proposed a criterion of truth – an instrument of judgement that would allow one to attain the certain knowledge that Socrates had always been looking for. They said that the foundation of knowledge was what they called a cognitive impression, which they defined as 'an impression that comes from what is, is imprinted and sealed in exactly according to what is, and such that it could not arise from what is not' (DL 7.50). Impressions of this sort would enable one to grasp a truth without the need of proof. Distinguishing between impression and belief, they introduced the notion of assent, which may be given or withheld from an impression. The sense impressions of humans as rational beings can be articulated in language, and a belief or judgement is formed by assenting to an impression, thus accepting it as true. The Stoics held that one could achieve knowledge by assenting only to cognitive impressions, avoiding assent to unclear or false impressions that would result in mere opinion.

The definition of the cognitive impression was clearly formulated primarily with regard to sense impressions, even though 'what is' might be a fact – 'what is the case' – rather than simply a perceptible object. The Academic–Stoic debate was therefore conducted mainly in terms of sense impressions. In an anecdote that is no doubt too good to be true, Cicero reports that Zeno initially proposed a shorter definition that did not include the last clause. When Arcesilaus asked him how one could avoid error if faced with a false impression exactly like a cognitive one, Zeno added the last clause, 'such that it could not arise from what is not'. Zeno presumably thought that a true and precisely accurate impression of any object would fulfil this condition, but the Academics responded with a series of counterexamples to show that for any given true sense impression one could describe a situation in which an indistinguishable impression would be false. The conclusion of this line of argument was twofold: that knowledge (in the Stoic sense) is impossible, and that a wise person would have to suspend judgement on all matters. The debate between Stoics and Academics went on for two centuries, focused on this last clause.

The examples put forward by the Academics were of two sorts: very similar kinds of objects, and conditions in which one's judgement would be impaired. In the first group, they started with examples of eggs or coins from the same mint or imprints from the same seal. The Stoics would concede that things of these sorts could not easily be distinguished, but they insisted that even these were in principle distinguishable, as shown by the alleged example of a Delian poultry farmer who could tell the difference between two eggs laid by the same hen. A Stoic who did not have the farmer's expertise would simply suspend judgement in cases of this sort (see Cicero, *Luc.* 57). More difficult examples are illustrated by two anecdotes from the early Stoa: suppose that a man sends a slave to deposit a sum of money with a friend, and then has the deposit picked up later by the twin brother of the slave. If the friend did not know that the first slave had a twin brother, could he have detected the difference between the two? (DL 7.162). In the second example, king Ptolemy Philopator ordered wax pomegranates to be served at a dinner. When the Stoic Sphaerus reached for one of the pomegranates, the king triumphantly pointed out that he had not been able to distinguish the impression of a fake pomegranate from that of a real fruit (DL 7.177). In both these examples, the person who makes the mistake has no reason to suspect that he might be faced with one of a set of very similar objects so that he would suspend judgement. Since incidents of this kind are not predictable, someone who wanted to avoid error would have to exercise caution at all times, and even that would not guarantee success.

Nevertheless, the Stoics defended their view by appealing to the principle that no two different things can be indiscernible. After all, most people are not identical twins, and their mother could no doubt distinguish even the twins; also, a closer look at the pomegranates might have revealed that they were made of wax. But the metaphysical principle of the identity of indiscernibles, even if true, is not sufficient to guarantee that there would be *perceptible* differences between items that had, for example, a different history. So an impression might indeed be cognitive in the sense stipulated by the definition, and yet an observer would not be able to distinguish it from a false one.

The Stoics also maintained that cognitive impressions tended to be so clear and distinct that it was practically impossible to resist assenting to them. This led to the second kind of counterexamples: dreamers and madmen. People who are dreaming or insane will often believe wildly implausible things in their dreams, such as that they are seeing a friend who has long been dead or, as in the story of Heracles' madness, they might mistake their own children for those of an enemy. Heracles' actions proved that he could not distinguish between true and false impressions. Here the Stoics replied that they did not have to maintain that error could be avoided even in dreams or in states of mental derangement. They insisted that the impressions of dreamers and madmen are in fact different from those of sane and sober waking persons, as shown by the fact that dreamers easily recognize their errors once they wake up, and those who are seized by fits of madness often express bewilderment and hesitation about the situation in which they seem to find themselves (see Cicero, *Luc.* 51–3).

Apart from defending their own position, the Stoics also attacked the Academic stance of suspending judgement on everything by arguing that a life without assent or belief is impossible. As Aristotle had already pointed out, any action presupposes belief: if somebody avoids a ravine, this shows that she believes both that there is a ravine and that it would be bad to fall in. Philosophers who pretended to hold no beliefs were therefore mistaken about their own position, or else they would have to be paralyzed. This argument, labelled 'inactivity', eventually led the Academics to work out a detailed alternative to the Stoic theory of knowledge. But the first responses, attributed to Arcesilaus, followed the pattern of refuting an opponent's thesis without adopting a different position. Arcesilaus is said to have pointed out that assent, a notion only recently introduced by the Stoics, was not necessary for action. Animals, for instance, would act instinctively in response to certain impressions, as a lion would go after its prey as soon as he saw it, or a gazelle would take flight as soon as it saw the lion (see Plutarch, *adv. Col.* 1122b ff.).

This answer would not have satisfied the Stoics, who were arguing about human actions based on reasons and decisions, not unreflective instinct. When asked how a man who suspends judgement would decide what to do, Arcesilaus took his answer from the Stoics themselves (SE, M 7.158):

> He who suspends judgement on everything will regulate his choices and avoidances, and his actions in general, by the standard of the reasonable, and by proceeding in accordance with this criterion he will act rightly.

The suggestion that one should act in accordance with what is reasonable is taken over from the Stoics. Since even the wisest of men cannot foresee the future, a Stoic would do what he thinks it would be reasonable for a human being to do in any given situation, without assuming that his action would be successfully completed. They defined appropriate action as 'what, when done, can be given a reasonable justification' – and this description would be true even if one did not achieve what one set out to do, so that one would not have formed a false belief. Arcesilaus suggested that one could take this attitude with respect to all possible judgements, treating them as reasonable guesses rather than certain truths.

We have only a single report of this response. There is no indication that Arcesilaus explained, for example, what would count as a reasonable opinion for a person who suspends judgement, or why this would not involve assent. It seems most likely that Arcesilaus was content with a simple refutation of the Stoics' objection in their own terms and did not go beyond this.

In the second half of the third-century BCE, the Stoic school had recovered from the critical attacks of the Academy under the

leadership of Chrysippus of Soloi (c. 280–208 BCE), the most important and influential of the Stoic philosophers. He elaborated in detail
the doctrines of Zeno and also wrote extensively against the sceptical
arguments of the Academics. This renewed challenge was taken up
in the next century by Carneades of Cyrene (214–129 BCE). Though
Carneades belonged to Plato's school, he had carefully studied
Chrysippus' works, no doubt more widely known at his time than
those of Plato and Aristotle with which Arcesilaus had grown up.
Instead of replying to specific Stoic arguments in a piecemeal way,
Carneades, drawing on Chrysippus' own works, outlined a sceptical
alternative to the Stoic doctrine.

He began with a general argument to show that there was no infallible criterion of truth as had been postulated by the Stoics, since both
our cognitive faculties, perception and reason, can and do often lead us
into error. Knowledge or cognition in the Stoic sense would therefore
be impossible, but this did not mean that a philosopher who suspended
judgement would be left with no way of arriving at plausible views
about what might be the case or what one should do. Assuming, as
the Stoics did, that finding out about the world must begin with sense
perception, Carneades then explained how one might proceed in the
absence of certainty. Some of our sense impressions appear convincing, others murky and unconvincing. In most cases, we will be guided
by the convincing ones. But since those may sometimes be false, we
can test their reliability by considering whether they are consistent with
other impressions relevant to the situation, and also whether our sense
organs are in good order and the conditions for accurate perception are
favourable. Given that clear and convincing impressions tend to be true
for the most part, this will be sufficient for an agent to make reasonable
decisions (see SE, M 7.159–89).

Yet since one can never be certain to have found the truth, a philosopher who wants to avoid error will never assent to any impression
in the full Stoic sense of accepting it as true. In this sense, then, he
will continue to suspend judgement on everything. But there is also
a weaker sense of assent, namely approval, that consists in accepting
an impression as a kind of hypothesis or informed guess without committing oneself to its truth, and that would be enough to guide one's
actions (Cicero, *Luc.* 104).

Carneades' theory answered the inactivity argument while staying mainly within the Stoic framework. The most significant change was that he treated sense impressions as providing evidence rather than an immediate grasp of a fact. It seems that some Stoic contemporaries of Carneades later integrated parts of his theory into their own, saying, for example, that in order to receive a cognitive impression, one must not hold any background belief that might conflict with the impression and constitute an obstacle to assent (SE, M 7.253–7). The impressions that Carneades' theory described as most reliable though never conclusive evidence were in the end just those that the Stoics would have considered as cognitive.

After the death of Carneades, the controversy between Stoics and Academics did not end, but it seems that no new arguments were put forward. Some of Carneades' followers adopted his theory, which had probably been proposed not as a doctrine, but as an equally plausible alternative to the Stoic one, and made it the official position of the Academy. Some, like Metrodorus and Philo of Larissa, held that it was legitimate to assent to a convincing and tested impression, provided that one realized that this leads only to plausible opinion, not to knowledge. Others, like Carneades' successor Clitomachus, insisted that full assent could never be justified, so that an Academic philosopher would always suspend judgement. Finally, the last head of the Academy, Philo of Larissa, in a work written in Rome towards the end of his life, took one step beyond the sceptical stance: he recognized that one does not need to claim certainty to justify a knowledge claim, and advocated a version of fallibilism. He said that as far as the Stoic criterion was concerned, things cannot be known, but as far as the natures of things themselves are concerned, one can come to know them (SE, PH 1.235).

With the hindsight of many centuries, the dispute between Stoics and Academics about the possibility of knowledge that looked like an endless controversy to its contemporaries may appear more like cooperation than dispute: a discussion in which criticism and objections forced each side to revise and refine their position. The Stoics remained convinced that knowledge requires a self-evident and infallible foundation, while Philo chose the more modest position of fallibilism; but the framework of both epistemological theories remained the same.

3. Pyrrhonism revived

It must have been around the time of Philo, in the first century BCE, that a more radical form of scepticism was revived under the banner of Pyrrho. Almost nothing is known about the life of Aenesidemus, the founder of this movement, and his works are lost. All we have is a summary by the ninth-century Byzantine patriarch Photius and a few scattered references in earlier authors. Photius' report suggests that Aenesidemus was a member of the sceptical Academy who broke away from his school, disappointed by its turn towards a modest form of philosophical teaching. He described the Academics of his day as 'Stoics fighting with Stoics' and set out to re-establish a philosophical position of universal suspension of judgement. Most famous among his works was a collection of 'modes' (of bringing about suspension of judgement), arguments about various kinds of subjects designed to illustrate the ubiquitous confusion arising from conflicting appearances, perceptions as well as theoretical views, that would leave an inquirer unable to settle for any belief in the face of the equal strength of arguments on both sides of every question.

Pyrrhonism is represented for the modern reader primarily by Sextus Empiricus, a doctor who lived in the second century CE and most of whose works have survived. Though Sextus lived long after Aenesidemus, he was clearly drawing on his predecessors to compile his books, and it is difficult to determine whether his version of Pyrrhonism was in any important respect different from that of Aenesidemus.

Sextus begins his *Outlines of Pyrrhonism* with a classification of philosophies (PH 1.1–3):

> When people are investigating any subject, the likely result is either a discovery, or a denial of discovery and a confession of inapprehensibility, or else a continuation of the investigation. This, no doubt, is why in the case of philosophical investigations, too, some have said that they have discovered the truth, some have asserted that it cannot be apprehended, and others are still investigating.
>
> Those who are called dogmatists in the proper sense of the word think that they have discovered the truth – for example, the schools of Aristotle and Epicurus and the Stoics, and some others. The schools of Clitomachus and Carneades, and other Academics, have asserted that things cannot be apprehended. And the Sceptics are still investigating.

A few paragraphs further down, Sextus explains what Scepticism is (PH 1.8):

Scepticism is an ability to set out oppositions among things which appear and are thought of in any way at all, an ability by which, because of the equipollence in the opposed objects and accounts, we come first to suspension of judgement and afterwards to tranquillity.

The argumentative skills of Scepticism are displayed in the Ten Modes (PH 1.35–163). Sextus has assembled a vast number of examples of conflicting views under ten different headings: the same things appear different to humans than to other animals, to different humans, to different senses, in different circumstances, and so on, showing that there are conflicting opinions about every imaginable subject. He then goes on to argue that these conflicts cannot be solved: one cannot prefer one's own sense impressions to those of other animals or persons, since every observer has the same authority. Nor will it do to appeal to an expert, since experts notoriously disagree among themselves. Nor can one rely on a criterion of truth, because once again different criteria have been proposed by different philosophers. Given that the views of each side are equally well supported, whether by authority or by argument, the Sceptic finds himself unable to decide. The conclusion, in each case, is that one can only say how things appear, not what they are like by nature or in themselves, and one is therefore compelled to suspend judgement.

Many of the examples are less than convincing, such as the age-old case of the tower that appears round at a distance, square from nearby. Others raise more serious questions, such as the different views about right and wrong among different cultures. Yet the cumulative effect may well be overwhelming, and that probably explains why Aenesidemus made the collection, and why Sextus goes on at such great length.

The form of these undecidability arguments is the same in all the Modes, but there is one anomaly that points to a different tradition of dealing with conflicting appearances. In the introduction to the Modes, Sextus claims that all of them can be subsumed under the general heading of relativity. The subclasses are the modes from the subject judging, from the object judged, and from a combination of both. This accurately describes the types of argument he sets out in the following chapter, but relativity also appears in the third group, as the eighth Mode. Why would the genus also count as one of its species? In the chapter on relativity, Sextus again describes the structure of the preceding arguments, though the taxonomy is slightly different: he explains that 'everything appears relative' has two senses, 'relative to the subject judging' and 'relative to the things observed together with it', and adds that he has already shown that everything is relative. But then he adds another set of arguments, hopelessly fallacious as it happens, of the following sort (PH 1.137):

> Do relatives differ or not from things in virtue of a difference [i.e. absolute or non-relative things]? If they do not differ, then the latter are relatives too. But if they do differ, then, since everything which differs is relative (it is spoken of relative to what it differs from), things in virtue of a difference will be relative.

A look at the shorter summary of the Modes in Diogenes Laertius shows that Sextus has replaced an older, more specific set of examples by the general schema of the undecidability arguments. Here is Diogenes' version (DL 9.87–8; tr. Annas and Barnes, 1985: 174–5):

> Tenth is the mode based on things set alongside one another – e.g. light to heavy, strong to weak, bigger to smaller, up to down. Anything on the right, for instance, is not by nature on the right, but is thought of according to its relation to something else – if that is moved it will no longer be to the right. Similarly both father and brother are relative; day is relative to the sun; and everything is relative to thinking. So things that are relative cannot be known in themselves.

This is a version of the relativism, however crude, famously associated with Protagoras in Plato's *Theaetetus*, and exemplified there (151e–152c) by a conflict of appearances: the same wind appears warm to one person, cold to another; we cannot say that one or the other is wrong; rather, we should say that the wind is warm for one, cold for the other, but in itself neither warm nor cold. The general principle behind this type of argument is the premise that whatever holds of a thing only in relation to something else does not belong to it by nature or in itself. This is in fact the principle to which Sextus himself seems to appeal in the opening sentence of the chapter on relativity: 'The eighth mode is the one deriving from relativity, in which we conclude that, since everything is relative, we shall suspend judgement as to what things are independently and in their nature.' The general thesis that everything is relative in this sense is surely untenable, as Sextus' own subsequent arguments show: horses are different in relation to cows, but they are not horses relative to cows. However, relativity arguments were clearly parts of the sceptical tradition, and they could seem useful in many cases, since they lead to the same conclusion as the undecidability arguments: we cannot tell what things are like in their own nature. Sextus himself occasionally uses them in the *Outlines*, and they play a prominent role in his book *Against the Ethicists* (M 11), where they tend to have a more limited form: if anything is by nature F (e.g. good or bad), then it must be so for everybody. But the same things are F for some, not F for others; therefore, nothing is F in itself or by nature (see e.g. M 11.71). The problem with these arguments is, however, that they are not consistent with the official sceptical attitude of leaving every question open and refraining from judgement: the relativity arguments not only start from a dubious premise, but also lead to a straightforwardly negative conclusion. Relativism is a philosophical doctrine, even if it leads to the conclusion that nothing can be known about the nature of things.

It is not clear whether Sextus himself clearly recognized the difference between undecidability and relativism, but some of the Sceptics from the period between Sextus and Aenesidemus probably did. At some point, an otherwise unknown man named Agrippa, whose name appears only in Diogenes Laertius' *Life of Pyrrho* (DL 9.88), introduced a new set of five modes, this time explicitly epistemological arguments. Sextus lists them as: from disagreement, from infinite regression, from relativity, from a hypothesis and reciprocity (PH 1.164–9). Disagreement and relativity pick up the argument schemata from the earlier modes, and since relativity is explained in terms of the relations of an object to an observer or to other objects observed with it, they should probably coincide, though this is not immediately obvious because Sextus illustrates the first by a disagreement between philosophers, not conflicting impressions from the same object. But later on Sextus himself illustrates relativity with an example of the sort he used in arguing for general relativism (PH 1.177): 'objects of thought are relative too; they are called objects of thought relative to the thinker.' The other three represent a trilemma that can be used to argue against anyone who might try to arrive at a true judgement by offering a justification for her belief: if the person puts forward a warrant for her claim, the Sceptic will say that the warrant needs another warrant, which itself needs another, and so on ad infinitum. If the dogmatist begins with something she simply assumes without proof, the Sceptic may assume the contradictory without being less trustworthy. If the opponent then brings forward something that depends on the claim in question for justification, the Sceptic will suspend judgement about both, since neither thesis can be established by the other. In other words, any attempt at establishing the truth of a judgement will either begin with an unfounded claim, lead to an infinite regress, or involve a circular argument. Together, the three offer strong support for the undecidability argument by purporting to show that no attempt at deciding a question can ever succeed. Sextus is happy to use this device at the end of many of his surveys of different philosophical doctrines, and has in fact also used it a few times in his exposition of the old modes. The epistemological quandary encapsulated in this trilemma is still very much alive in epistemology today, and philosophers have proposed a variety of different solutions. Since both regress and circular argument have seemed unacceptable to ancient as well as early modern philosophers, their solutions have consisted mainly in trying to single out some self-evident truths as a foundation for knowledge. Only very recently, some have argued that circularity may not be avoidable, but some circles are very large and need not be vicious, especially since different theses will depend on different premises.

Agrippa's Five Modes are an attempt to integrate the trilemma into the Sceptical repertoire of arguments by using the general labels 'disagreement' and 'relativity' for the older argument-forms. He may have discovered the new ones in Aristotle's *Posterior Analytics* (I.3), as the school treatises of Aristotle were more widely read at his time than before. Agrippa's list is not intended to replace the old modes, as Sextus notes, but just to add variety to the refutations of dogmatic rashness.

But in the next chapter, Sextus tells us that the younger Sceptics also handed down two other modes – and this time, relativity has dropped out (PH 1.178–9):

> They also offer two other modes of suspension of judgement. Since everything apprehended is thought to be apprehended either by means of itself or by means of something else, they are thought to introduce puzzlement about everything by suggesting that nothing is apprehended either by means of itself or by means of something else.

That nothing is apprehended by means of itself is, they say, clear from the dispute which has occurred among natural scientists over, I suppose, all objects of perception and of thought – a dispute which is undecidable, since we cannot use either an object of perception or an object of thought as a standard because anything we may take has been disputed and so is unconvincing.

And for the following reason they do not concede either that anything can be apprehended by means of something else. If that by means of which something is apprehended will itself always need to be apprehended by means of something else, they throw you into the reciprocal or the infinite mode; and if you should want to assume that that by means of which another thing is apprehended is itself apprehended by means of itself, then this is countered by the fact that, for the above reasons, nothing is apprehended by means of itself.

The first of the Two Modes combines disagreement with what Agrippa called hypothesis – a statement accepted as true without proof. But in this version, the 'hypothesis' is claimed to be a self-evident truth; and that was exactly what the dogmatists of the time, Epicureans and Stoics, postulated to avoid regress or circle. The second mode combines regress and circle as ways of refuting any attempt of justifying a judgement. Of course, these modes also lead to the conclusion that nothing can be known or apprehended, but the initial premise – that whatever one comes to know must be either known 'by means of itself' that is, be self-evident, or based on something else – could hardly be rejected by the Sceptics' dogmatist opponents, unlike the relativity principle. It is a pity that Sextus has not preserved for us the name of the 'younger Sceptic' who came up with the Two Modes.

So far nothing has been said about Pyrrho as the founder of the Sceptic movement. We do not know why Aenesidemus chose to call himself a Pyrrhonist, but the reason was probably not that he saw Pyrrho as a more radical sceptic than his fellow Academics. Looking back at Timon's testimony, Pyrrho would seem to be what Sextus calls a dogmatist in the negative sense – someone who confidently asserts that nothing can be known, which would prompt the question how he knows that nothing can be known. The Academics and later Sceptics were more sophisticated: Arcesilaus denied that he knew even the last point that Socrates had – allegedly – left for himself, knowing that he knew nothing (Cicero, *Ac.* 1.45), and the same is attested for Aenesidemus (Photius, *Bibl.* 169b). As Sextus puts it, the Sceptics are also called Pyrrhonists because Pyrrho 'appears to them to have attached himself to Scepticism more systematically and conspicuously than anyone before him' (PH 1.7). Pyrrho served as a role model, not as a teacher. However, by appealing to Pyrrho as a kind of figurehead or founder of Scepticism, Aenesidemus had set himself up as a competitor to the Hellenistic schools of philosophy that advocated their doctrines as guides to the happy life. The Pyrrhonists would not call themselves a school in the sense of adherents of a doctrine, but they did say that Pyrrhonists 'follow an account which, to all appearances, shows us a life in conformity with traditional customs and the law and ways of living and our own feelings' (PH 1.17). While the Academics had simply taken the stance of critics of other philosophers' doctrines, the Pyrrhonists openly advocated their method as an alternative path to the best life.

This invited two obvious questions. First, how can a philosopher who claims to suspend judgement on everything fill long books with sentences that look like straightforward assertions? And second, how can a Sceptic act without belief? – the old inactivity argument.

The Pyrrhonists came up with a variety of responses to the first question, ranging from 'we only report our own affections' to happily accepting the point that a pronouncement like 'no more this than that' applies to itself and thereby refutes itself (PH 1.14). What better way could there be of saying nothing? Sextus generally uses the first answer – the Sceptic merely reports what appears to him without asserting that things are as they appear. Such reports, he says, do not constitute judgements or involve assent. So he carefully presents the aspiring Sceptic's path to tranquillity as a biographical story (PH 1.26):

> For Sceptics began to do philosophy in order to decide among appearances and to apprehend which are true and which false, so as to become tranquil; but they came upon equipollent dispute, and being unable to decide this they suspended judgement. And when they suspended judgement, tranquillity in matters of opinion followed fortuitously.

Finding herself again and again unable to decide – a situation abundantly illustrated by the Ten Modes – the Sceptic discovers that her worries fall away once she gives up trying to make a decision. The suggestion is, of course, that others who follow the Sceptical method may be equally lucky. In the next paragraph, Sextus presents a more specific explanation for the Sceptic's tranquility (PH 1.27):

> For those who hold the opinion that things are good or bad by nature are perpetually troubled. When they lack what they believe to be good, they take themselves to be persecuted by natural evils and they pursue what (so they think) is good. And when they have acquired these things, they experience more troubles; for they are elated beyond reason and measure, and in fear of change they do anything so as not to lose what they believe is good. But those who make no determination about what is good and bad by nature neither avoid not pursue anything with intensity; and hence they are tranquil.

In response to the inactivity argument, Sextus offers an account of the Sceptics' criterion or standard of action that is much closer to the initial reply of Arcesilaus than to Carneades' theory of convincing or unconvincing impressions (PH 1.22–3):

> We say, then, that the standard of the Sceptical way of living is what is apparent, implicitly meaning by this the appearances; for they depend on passive and unwilled feelings and are not objects of investigation. . . . Thus, attending to what is apparent, we live in accordance with everyday observances, without holding opinions – for we are not able to be utterly inactive. These everyday observances seem to be fourfold, and to consist in guidance by nature, necessitation by feelings, handing down of laws and customs, and teaching of kinds of expertise. By nature's guidance we are naturally capable of perceiving and thinking. By the necessitation of feelings, hunger conducts us to food and thirst to drink. By the handing down of customs and laws, we accept, from an everyday point of view, that piety is good and impiety bad. By teaching of kinds of expertise we are not inactive in those we accept.

It turns out, then, that the Sceptic may lead a perfectly normal life, including even the moral views of his community and the exercise of crafts (after all, Sextus himself was a doctor). For moral views can be inculcated by education and followed passively without reflection, and skills can be acquired in the same way. What distinguishes the Pyrrhonist from her fellow citizens is only her detachment from the truth or falsity of the appearances that come to her without any contribution of her own. Her actions may be seen as prompted by natural instincts, like eating when hungry, or as reflexes conditioned by education and technical training. In a later passage, emphasizing the difference between

Pyrrhonist Sceptics and Academics, Sextus rejects even the recourse to a weak form of assent suggested by Carneades because taking some appearances to be more convincing than others might lead, in the case of goods and evils, to the intensity of pursuit or avoidance that allegedly leaves ordinary people in perpetual trouble (see PH 1.230–1).

The Pyrrhonist ideal of tranquillity based on indifference to truth and falsity, embodied in the supreme equanimity of Pyrrho, does not seem to have found many adherents either in ancient or in modern times. It is not surprising that Sextus' works were read by early modern philosophers as being concerned with epistemology rather than peace of mind. The Pyrrhonists' refusal to observe even the modest distinction between convincing and unconvincing impressions or appearances made them look more radical in their scepticism than the Academics, whom Hume famously described as 'mitigated sceptics' (*Enquiry concerning Human Understanding*, pt. III, s.129; see Chapter 6, this volume). Both ancient versions of scepticism together supplied ample material for the epistemological debates from the sixteenth century onwards. What a modern reader might find missing is Descartes' notorious doubt about the existence of an external world. Perhaps one should remember, though, that this kind of doubt is inspired by the view that every judgement accepted as true must be either supported by proof, or else shown to be indubitable. It seems to me that this assumption might well be questionable.

Note

1 Ancient authors whose works are quoted in the text are cited with the following abbreviations:

Cicero, *Academica*, book 1: *Ac.*
Cicero, *Lucullus*, book 2: *Luc.*
Diogenes Laertius, *Lives of the philosophers*: DL
Plutarch, *Against Colotes*: adv. Col.
Photius, *Bibliotheca*: Bibl.
Sextus Empiricus (SE), *Outlines of Pyrrhonism*: PH (books 1–3)
Sextus Empiricus (SE), *Against the Professors*: M (books 7–11)
Translations from Sextus' *Outlines* (PH) are by Annas and Barnes (2000), with occasional modifications.

Further reading

The best ancient accounts of Academic and Pyrrhonist scepticism can be found in Cicero's *Academic Books* and in the first book of Sextus Empiricus' *Outlines of Pyrrhonism*. Both are available in excellent recent translations:

Cicero, *On Academic Scepticism*, translated with introduction and notes by C. Brittain (Indianapolis: Hackett, 2006).

Sextus Empiricus, *Outlines of Scepticism*, translated with introduction and notes by J. Annas and J. Barnes, 2nd edn (Cambridge: Cambridge University Press, 2000).

See also J. Annas and J. Barnes, *The Modes of Scepticism: Ancient Texts and Modern Interpretations* (Cambridge: Cambridge University Press, 1985): translations of the Modes in Sextus Empiricus and other ancient versions, with introduction and philosophical commentary.

Modern literature

There is recently *The Cambridge Companion to Ancient Scepticism*, (ed.) R. Bett (Cambridge: Cambridge University Press, 2010), with chapters on the history of ancient Scepticism, some of the main problems, and the influence of Scepticism in modern times. It also contains an extensive bibliography.

An older collection worth consulting is *The Skeptical Tradition*, (ed.) M. Burnyeat (Berkeley: University of California Press, 1983). A collection of papers about the vexed question of whether the Pyrrhonists really pretended to live without any beliefs is *The Original Sceptics: A Controversy*, (eds) M. Burnyeat and M. Frede (Indianapolis: Hackett, 1997).

CHAPTER 5

THE EPISTEMOLOGY OF DESCARTES

Desmond M. Clarke

There is no single theory of knowledge in Descartes' works that could be described correctly as his epistemology. His philosophical views changed over time and, as they did so, he offered reflections on different kinds of knowledge. Any attempt to summarize his epistemology must therefore acknowledge the historical context in which he wrote, and the influences in response to which he penned varying accounts of what constitutes knowledge in different disciplines. For example, Descartes' work includes comments on logic and mathematics (Gaukroger, 1989). However, the two accounts of knowledge to which he devoted most effort arose from reflections on (1) natural philosophy and (2) metaphysics. These are reviewed in Sections 1 and 2, while Section 3 compares the accounts given in each one of the distinction between the appearance and reality of things that are known.

One of Descartes' earliest efforts to sketch an account of knowledge, in addition to those just mentioned, is found in the incomplete *Rules*, which was abandoned by its author in 1628 and remained unpublished during his lifetime. This draft represented a philosopher's contribution, at the beginning of his career, to a long-established tradition of writing commentaries on Aristotle's *Organon*. The young Galileo had written similarly in a book that bore little relationship to the natural philosophy for which he later became famous (Wallace, 1992). There were many claims in Descartes' *Rules* that were familiar in the Aristotelian tradition, for example, that 'every science is certain and evident knowledge' and that there are only two ways to acquire such knowledge, viz. by 'intuition and deduction' (AT X 362, 368; Descartes, 2003a: 119, 123). Since Descartes identified mathematics as a paradigm of this kind of knowledge, it is not surprising that the projected method was abandoned when he attempted to apply this inappropriate ideal to questions in natural philosophy. Without the later published work, therefore, one could reasonably classify the Descartes of the 1620s as a critical or reforming Aristotelian. In stark contrast, the first specifically Cartesian account of knowledge was developed by reflecting on developments in natural philosophy.

1. Knowledge in natural philosophy

Descartes' philosophical interests assumed a distinctive new focus when he went to live in the United Provinces (approximately, the Netherlands today) in 1629. He began almost immediately to investigate natural phenomena, and continued those investigations for the rest of his life. When he was reported as claiming, about 1645, that his dissecting table was his library (Clarke, 2006: 304), the emphasis on experimental work reflected accurately the way in which Descartes had spent the final two decades of his life. He almost never read the writings of either ancient or contemporary philosophers, and focused instead throughout the period 1630–50 on developing a new natural philosophy that accommodated the results of his own empirical research and that of others. The results of these investigations were written up in a manuscript entitled *The World*, which was ready for publication but withdrawn suddenly when the author heard in 1633 about the condemnation of Galileo. Four years later, Descartes published his first book, the bulk of which comprised three essays on scientific topics: dioptrics, meteorology and geometry. Descartes later incorporated much of this natural philosophy into Parts II, III and IV of the *Principles of Philosophy* (1644), and he continued to revise a physiological treatise on animals until the end of his life (although it too remained unpublished at his death in 1650). This twenty-year engagement with genuine empirical work, which included what would today be called scientific or laboratory experiments, was the context in which Descartes abandoned the scholastic theory of knowledge that he had learned in college.

The publisher of the essays on natural philosophy invited Descartes to write a preface, in which he could outline the method(s) used to explain the rather disparate phenomena that he examined. This preface was completed, in the months immediately before publication in 1637, as the *Discourse on the Method for Guiding one's Reason and Searching for Truth in the Sciences*. One issue that the *Discourse* had to address was that the *Dioptrics* and *Meteorology* were not guided by Aristotle's ideal of demonstration. If genuine knowledge were acquired only by intuition and deduction, as the *Rules* had suggested, then Descartes should have concluded that his essays in natural philosophy provided readers with only 'knowledge that is merely probable' (AT X 362; Descartes, 2003a: 119) rather than genuine knowledge. This realization initiated a radical but not adequately acknowledged re-evaluation, on Descartes' part, of what was meant by 'knowledge'.

The options available to Descartes at this point in time were similar to those that Galileo had faced earlier in his controversy with Rome (McMullin, 2005). Aristotle had proposed the ideal of demonstration in the *Posterior Analytics*, and commentators repeated for almost two thousand years that knowledge-claims are either completely certain or uncertain, and that only the former provide genuine knowledge. Secondly, this tradition repeated the assumption that the certainty of knowledge-claims could derive only from first principles that are known by 'intuition', and that the derivation involved must be constructed with valid syllogisms. Descartes had already expressed reservations even in the *Rules* about the limited scope of scholastic logic; the latter did not include all possible forms of valid deduction, especially those found in mathematics. He now had to confront a much more intractable problem concerning the logic of confirmation, which arose as follows.

Descartes rejected the tradition of explanation in terms of 'substantial forms' that was associated with the scholastic tradition, primarily because scholastic forms merely renamed the phenomena to be explained in slightly camouflaged but circular re-descriptions. In the example made famous by Molière's caricature, sleeping powder was said to cause sleep because it has a sleep-inducing power. Even if 'sleep-inducing power' is translated into 'soporific form', no explanatory progress is made. The substantial forms of scholastic explanations thus identified the cause of any phenomenon as nothing more than a capacity for giving rise to the effects to be explained. Descartes had proposed, in *The World*, an alternative explanatory strategy: that all natural phenomena be explained by features of small particles of matter (such as their size, motion, configuration, etc.) and, if that enterprise were successful, all appeals to forms would become redundant. However, this approach to explanation – which was the method adopted in the *Dioptrics* and the *Meteors* – gave rise to a new problem, because it relied on properties that were hypothesized rather than known by experience.

For example, Cartesian explanations of optical phenomena assumed that we need not know the nature of light; it is sufficient to assume that light is composed of moving particles and that optical phenomena may be explained in terms of the motions of unobservable particles. In fact, one may extend the scope of the explanatory enterprise to include what happens in the eye and the brain when visual perceptions occur. The *Dioptrics* thus expanded from a scientific essay about the diffraction of light in lenses to an explanation of visual perception, and it thereby provided a model for the explanation of all sensory perceptions which were assumed to result from the impact of otherwise unobservable particles on our eyes, ears, etc. Such explanations presupposed an understanding of how parts of matter move and interact with each other. This issue was addressed by Descartes' three laws of nature, which he formulated initially in *The World*. There was no argument offered to show that everything in the natural world is capable of explanation on this rather slim foundation. The project, rather, was to attempt to explain as many natural phenomena as possible in terms of the motions of particles of matter, in accordance with the three laws of nature.

Having made many detailed assumptions about matter and its motions, and having hypothesized various interactions of particles that could result in the natural phenomena that we observe, Descartes acknowledged in the *Discourse* that it was possible to construct different hypotheses that are consistent with the laws of nature to explain the same natural phenomenon:

> I must also acknowledge that the power of nature is so extensive and so great, and these principles are so simple and general, that I hardly ever notice any particular effect about which I do not realize immediately that it can be deduced from these principles in a number of different ways, and my biggest difficulty is usually in identifying in which of these ways it depends on them. (AT VI 64–5; Descartes, 2003a: 46)

He conceded that he knew of no way to resolve this issue except by 'looking for some experiences such that their occurrence is not the same if the effect should be explained in one rather than another of these ways' (AT VI 65; Descartes, 2003a: 46) – in other words, to look for crucial experiments to isolate the most plausible explanations.

Even if crucial experiments appeared to support uniquely one rather than another hypothesis, readers of the *Discourse* had identified the fallacy of affirming the consequent as an insurmountable objection to any attempt to prove the truth of hypotheses. Hence, even if a given hypothesis, H, implies a phenomenon P, and if P is observed in nature, it does not follow that H is true. Many different hypotheses could equally well imply the same results, and there was no way to evade the logic of this objection. However, Descartes argued – as have philosophers of science since then – that the plausibility of hypotheses depends on a number of factors: for example, that a single hypothesis explains many disparate phenomena, that it implies novel results which, when investigated, turn out to be true, or that it is consistent with a small number of simple, fundamental laws, etc. He argued thus in response to Jean-Baptiste Morin (in 1638):

> You say that 'proving effects by a cause, and then proving this cause by the same effects is a vicious circle', which I accept. But I do not accept, for that reason, that it would be a vicious circle to explain effects by a cause and then to prove the cause by the effects, because there is a big difference between proving and explaining. . . . Finally, you say that 'there is nothing simpler than to adjust a particular cause to an effect'. But . . . it is not so easy to adjust one and the same cause to many different effects if it is not the real cause from which they result . . . if one then compares other people's hypotheses with mine, that is, all their real qualities, substantial forms, elements, and things like that . . . with the single hypothesis that all bodies are composed of some parts, which is something that can be seen with the naked eye in many cases . . . and if one compares what I have deduced from my assumptions concerning vision, salt, the winds, the clouds, snow, thunder, the rainbow, and similar things, with what others have deduced from their assumptions about the same phenomena, I hope that will be enough to convince those who are not too prejudiced that the effects that I explain have no other causes apart from those from which I deduced them. (AT II 197–200: Descartes, 2003a: 75, 76)

No amount of special pleading could ever turn this type of argument into an Aristotelian demonstration, and Descartes had to concede this, however reluctantly. Nonetheless, he also argued in reply to Mersenne that those who demanded a *demonstration* of explanations in natural philosophy were demanding the impossible:

> You ask whether I believe what I have written about refraction [in the *Dioptrics*] is a demonstration . . . to demand geometrical demonstrations from me, in something which depends on physics, is to expect me to do the impossible. If one wishes to apply the term 'demonstration' only to geometrical proofs, then one must say that Archimedes never demonstrated anything in mechanics, nor Witelo in optics, nor Ptolemy in astronomy. . . . Now what I claim to have demonstrated about refraction does not depend on the truth about the nature of light . . . but only on my assumption that it is an action or power which follows the same laws as local motion . . . those who simply say that they do not believe what I have written because I deduce it from certain assumptions that I have not proved . . . do not know what they are asking for, nor what they ought to ask for. (AT II 141–4; Descartes, 2003a: 73, 74)

It would be anachronistic to attribute to Descartes, or to any other author in the seventeenth century, a satisfactory formulation of the logic of confirmation. All the major contributors to natural philosophy from Galileo to Huygens struggled with the realization that the explanation of natural phenomena is necessarily hypothetical, and that such hypotheses could never be 'demonstrated' in the narrow sense defined by Aristotle. Therefore, unless the new natural philosophy were to be excluded from the scope of genuine knowledge, it was necessary to relax the definition of 'knowledge' to include plausible hypotheses.

Descartes himself constructed a very large number of hypothetical explanations – of magnetism, of blood circulation, of the formation of snowflakes, of the transmission of information from the external senses to the brain, etc. His work sponsored a new Cartesian natural philosophy that was substituted for its scholastic predecessor in many colleges in France and the Netherlands (Clarke, 1989). The enthusiasm of its promoters was matched by the severity of some of its critics; among the latter, it evoked caricatures in which natural phenomena were explained by wild guesses that were not remotely confirmed by empirical evidence. Newton's famous disclaimer, in the second edition of the *Mathematical Principles of Natural Philosophy*, can be read as such a critique, when he wrote: 'hypotheses, whether metaphysical or physical, or based on occult qualities, or mechanical, have no place in experimental philosophy' (Newton, 1999: 943). However, Newton failed to acknowledge that hypotheses are unavoidable in natural philosophy, even if they should be limited to those that are confirmed by empirical evidence.

Descartes, in contrast, never resiled from the concession in the *Discourse*, that one can construct explanations of natural phenomena only hypothetically. Even in his final published work, *The Passions of the Soul* (1649), he offered an analysis of human emotions as a '*physicien*', that is, as a natural philosopher. This meant that various passions, although understood as mental events in some sense, were triggered by and associated with specific physiological events in the human body, which provided the kind of natural philosophical explanation of emotions that was consistent with the core principles of Cartesianism. This was the culmination of the project that had originally been conceived in the *Treatise on Man*, in which the scope of natural philosophy was described in very extensive terms:

> I desire that you consider that all the functions that I have attributed to this machine [i.e. a machine similar to the human body], such as the digestion of food, the beating of the heart and the arteries, the nourishment and growth of the bodily parts, respiration, waking and sleeping; the reception of light, sounds, odours, smells, heat, and other such qualities by the external sense organs; the impression of the ideas of them in the organ of common sense and the imagination, the retention or imprint of these ideas in the memory; the internal movements of the appetites and the passions; and finally the external movements of all the bodily parts that so aptly follow both the actions of objects presented to the senses, and the passions and impressions that are encountered in memory; and in this they imitate as perfectly as is possible the movements of real men. I desire, I say, that you should consider that these functions follow in this machine simply from the disposition of the organs as wholly naturally as the movements of a clock or other automaton follow from the dispositions of its counterweights and wheels. (AT XI 201–2; Descartes, 1998: 169)

While implementing this extremely ambitious project over two decades, Descartes never acknowledged any sceptical objections to the reliability of the methods that he used or the plausibility of the conclusions that he drew. The opposite was the case. Although he invited readers to submit objections to his first book, he never conceded that any of his theories might be mistaken. Instead, he replied to critics with a conviction that one might associate with an uncritical dogmatist. This refusal to modify his views or to concede that he might be mistaken characterized all his subsequent correspondence with critics. If these correspondents shared an evaluation of Descartes, they could never have described him as sceptical; they thought that he claimed much more certainty for his views in natural philosophy than was warranted by the evidence or arguments he provided to support them.

2. Metaphysical knowledge

It is not clear why Descartes interrupted this twenty-year research project in natural philosophy to write about metaphysics. Following the condemnation of Galileo (1633), he had studiously avoided any engagement with theological issues. He also realized that it was easy to cross the threshold from philosophy into what the Christian churches regarded as their exclusive domain, i.e. orthodox interpretations of what was allegedly revealed by God in Scripture, as Galileo had learned to his detriment. Since Descartes understood metaphysics as any discussion of God and the soul that was based on reason, his initial diffidence about transgressing into theology by discussing those issues was understandable. Despite that, however, and for reasons that remain obscure, he mentioned in correspondence in 1640 that he was working on what he called 'An Essay on Metaphysics'. This draft essay eventually emerged, in 1641, under the editorial control of Mersenne in Paris, as the *Meditations on First Philosophy, in which God's existence and the immortality of the soul is demonstrated*. The title was corrected in the second edition that was published under Descartes' own direction, in Amsterdam, as *Meditations on First Philosophy, in which God's existence and the distinction of the soul from the body are demonstrated* (1642).

This was not the first occasion on which Descartes had published comments on God's existence and the soul. He had included a brief summary of his views in Part IV of the *Discourse* (1637), and during the period 1638–39 he considered publishing a Latin edition of that text together with replies to selected objections from readers. This prompted an acknowledgement that the discussion of God and the human soul in the *Discourse* was too brief; the reason offered, especially for his failure to mention scepticism in that context, was to avoid misleading those who could read a text that was written in French and was therefore accessible to a general readership: 'I was afraid that this introduction [i.e. the *Discourse*], which could have appeared as if it were designed to introduce the views of sceptics, would disturb weak minds, principally because I was writing in the vernacular . . .' (AT I 353–4). However, once he decided to discuss questions about God and the soul, but now more safely in Latin, he concluded that he had to address sceptical objections that challenged the very possibility of such knowledge.

One reason why scepticism seemed more destructive in metaphysics was that Descartes had assumed, in natural philosophy, that the concepts with which we work and the evidence on which we rely there are acquired, to a significant extent, from sensory experience. Metaphysics, however, involved addressing questions about realities that were traditionally assumed to lie outside the scope of the senses. One could not see or hear God, whereas one could 'see with the naked eye' that bodies are composed of small parts. For that reason, Descartes claimed that he could not avoid confronting some well-known sceptical objections if he wished to discuss, in the *Meditations*, God's existence and the distinction of the soul from the body.

The three sceptical objections that are mentioned in the First Meditation were inspired by the work of Sextus Empiricus (2000), which had acquired a new readership in France when it was translated from Greek into Latin in 1562. Even for those who did not read Latin, Pyrrhonism was familiar to readers of Montaigne's *Essays*. The three sceptical objections that Descartes reported – that our senses often deceive us; that the experiences we have while awake and while dreaming are so similar that they appear indistinguishable; and that the very intellectual faculties on which we rely to acquire knowledge may be fundamentally unreliable – were discussed in Montaigne's *Apology for Raymond Sebond*, the longest chapter in the *Essays* (Montaigne, 1993: 634–5, 669, 674). In addition to these sources, Descartes was familiar with the discussion of God's existence and the human soul in two books written by one of his correspondents, Jean Silhon: *Les Deux Vérités* (1626) and *De l'Immortalité de l'âme* (1634). Silhon had not only addressed sceptical objections to the possibility of knowing God and the soul; he also proposed a very similar response to that subsequently adopted by Descartes by arguing that, as long as one is thinking, one can be certain of at least one proposition, viz. that one is thinking (Ariew et al., 1998: 199).

The historical evidence thus confirms Descartes' claim, in reply to the Jesuit, Pierre Bourdin, that scepticism was a popular option for many authors at the time:

> We should not believe that the sect of sceptics has been extinct for a long time. It is very much alive today, and almost everyone who regards themselves as more intelligent than others takes refuge in scepticism, when they find nothing in the commonly accepted philosophy to satisfy them and cannot see any alternative which is more true. (AT VII 548–9)

When Bourdin accused Descartes of endorsing rather than merely reporting the sceptical arguments that he rehearsed in the First Meditation, he replied that no one thinks of Galen as publishing a method for getting ill simply because he discussed various illnesses and diagnosed their causes. Likewise, Descartes claimed, 'I did not propose any reasons for doubt with the intention of teaching them but, on the contrary, in order to refute them' (AT VII 573–4). The same clarification had been offered in the *Discourse*, where he claimed that he was not imitating 'the sceptics who doubt only for the sake of doubting . . . my whole plan was designed only to convince myself and to reject the shifting ground and sand' (AT VI 29; Descartes, 2003a: 22).

Thus one should read the *First Meditation* as rehearsing sceptical arguments that were prevalent at the time and, if successful, would have undermined the feasibility of Descartes' metaphysical agenda in that work. The most fundamental sceptical objection was presented in the guise of an evil genius which systematically misleads anyone who engages in metaphysical meditations. The objection could be expressed without reference to such mythical forces as follows: if our cognitive faculties were defective while appearing to be otherwise, how could one validate them without begging the question? This challenge, which is known as the problem of the Cartesian circle, can be mounted even if Descartes' other sceptical objections are adequately answered because, if it were successful, it would undermine his efforts to move beyond the claimed certainty of his awareness that he is thinking. Antoine Arnauld was the first to raise this objection, in the Fourth Objections to the *Meditations*, as follows:

> How can he [i.e. Descartes] avoid committing the fallacy of a vicious circle when he says that we are certain that what is perceived clearly and distinctly is true only because God exists? But we can be certain that God exists only because we

perceive it clearly and distinctly. Therefore, before we are certain that God exists, we have to be certain that whatever we perceive clearly and distinctly is true. (AT VII 214; Descartes 2003b: 90)

While Arnauld expressed the objection in the language of the *Meditations*, the fundamental objection is that one must rely on one's cognitive faculties in all attempts to reply to scepticism. However, we have no more reason, in the twenty-first century, to begin philosophy from the assumption of systemically defective cognitive faculties than we have to imagine the existence of a deceptive evil genius. Any defence of our capacity to acquire knowledge must assume that, when due caution is exercised, we succeed in reasoning validly (especially when we can model the validity of our reasoning in formal logics). Although that leaves the evil genius type of objection unanswered, such a remedy is consistent with the theory of knowledge that Descartes had developed independently to accommodate the uncertainty of knowledge that is acquired in natural philosophy.

As is well known, Descartes assumed the reliability of his cognitive faculties in order to address the two questions that he had listed in the subtitle of the *Meditations*, viz. the existence of God, and the distinction of the human soul from the body. In this context, he faced an epistemological problem that did not arise in his natural philosophy, i.e. how to acquire an idea of God. He proposed that, by meditating or reflecting on the activity of thinking, one could acquire an idea of a thinking subject, and that this idea could be used by analogy to conceive of God. He explained the method involved as follows: 'I would have you spend enough time on this meditation to acquire by degrees a very clear and, I would say, an intuitive notion of intellectual nature in general. This is the idea which, if considered without limitations, represents God, and if limited, is the idea of an angel or of a human soul' (AT I 353). He gave a similar reply to Hobbes, who denied having any idea of God. 'Who is there who does not perceive that there is something that they understand? Who therefore does not have the form or idea of understanding and, by extending this indefinitely, does not form the idea of God's understanding?' (AT VII 188).

This reflective approach to concept acquisition led Descartes to claim that the idea of God is innate in some sense. The use of the term 'innate' gave rise immediately to misunderstanding among readers of the *Meditations*, because it suggested that there are some fully formed ideas in each human mind even before one begins to think, and it provided the original source of the theory against which Locke later argued in Book One of the *Essay*. Descartes, however, was explicit in rejecting that misunderstanding of what he meant by 'innate'. He replied to Hobbes's objections: 'When we say that some idea is innate in us, we do not think that it is always being presented to us; in that sense, no idea would be innate. We mean only that we have within us a power to produce the idea in question' (AT VII 189; Descartes, 2003b: 89). Another critic, Henricus Regius, argued that the 'mind, in order to think, does not need any innate ideas, notions, or axioms that are distinct from the faculty of thinking' (Regius, 1648: 12). Descartes replied:

> By 'innate ideas' I have never understood anything else apart from what he himself [i.e. Regius] explicitly claims as true . . . namely: 'that we have in us a natural power by which we are capable of knowing God.' I have never either thought or written that the ideas in question are actual, or that they are species which are in some unknown way distinct from the faculty of thinking. (AT VIII-2, 366)

The *Meditations* can thus be seen as addressing epistemological problems (such as Pyrrhonism and concept formation) that arose only in the context of engaging with the two metaphysical issues that it discussed, namely, the distinction of the human soul from the body and the existence of God. While that explains why Descartes discussed scepticism, it does not resolve questions about the success or otherwise of his proposed solutions.

Despite the relative brevity of the *Meditations*, there is much disagreement among commentators about the conclusions for which its author argued or even about the structure of the arguments deployed by him. Most readers accept that Descartes attempted to move, deductively, along the following path:

1. I am aware of my own thinking activity.
2. This awareness provides me with a clear and distinct idea of a thinking thing.
3. I can modify the idea of a finite thinking thing to generate an idea of an infinite thinking thing.
4. The latter provides an admittedly inadequate idea of God, but one that is sufficient for proving God's existence.

5. I can prove God's existence validly by using the arguments rehearsed in the Third and Fifth Meditations.
6. Therefore God exists.
7. God is not a deceiver.
8. It would be equivalent to deceit on God's part if (a) He equipped human creatures with cognitive faculties that are systematically misleading and (b) He failed to provide them with any way of recognizing and/or avoiding being misled.
9. Therefore, since God can be known to exist and not be a deceiver, we can conclude validly that our cognitive faculties are not systematically misleading.

Having addressed the most fundamental sceptical objection thus, Descartes dismisses almost casually the other two objections, about mistaken judgements based on sensory information and the possibility that we may be merely dreaming about the realities that we seem to experience. 'For from the fact that God is not a deceiver it follows that, in such cases, I am completely free from error' (AT VII 90; Descartes, 2003b: 70). He claims that the 'hyperbolic doubts of recent days should be rejected as ridiculous' (AT VII 89; Descartes, 2003b: 70), because he can check the reliability of sensory experiences by comparing what he learned from different senses and by being very careful about the judgements that he makes. Secondly, he can also dispose of the dreaming argument 'because dreams are never joined by memory with all the other activities of life, as happens with those that occur while we are awake' (AT VII 89; Descartes, 2003b: 70).

While this summary rejection of sceptical doubts as 'ridiculous' coincides with Descartes' original assessment of their insignificance for doing natural philosophy, the arguments that are assumed to support that conclusion fail to address the most fundamental sceptical objection raised. There are at least two reasons for this, in addition to the unavoidable circularity to which Arnauld drew attention: (a) the kind of certainty that Descartes assumed was required for metaphysical knowledge; and (b) the weakness of the Cartesian arguments for God's existence.

There are clear indications, in Descartes' early Aristotelian writings, that genuine knowledge requires one's beliefs to be absolutely certain. Rule Two of the *Rules* recommends that 'we reject all knowledge that is merely probable, and we decide to believe only what is known perfectly

and cannot be doubted' (AT X 362; Descartes, 2003a: 119). This dichot-
omy between what is probable and what is certain is reflected in the
choice, in Rule Three, of intuition and deduction as the only means
by which to gain knowledge 'without any fear of error' (AT X 368;
Descartes, 2003a: 123). However, by the time Descartes completed the
Principles in 1644, he acknowledged a distinction between two kinds
of certainty, moral and metaphysical, and conceded that many of his
claims in natural philosophy realized only the former (AT VIII-1, 327–9).
Moral certainty was defined as the certainty that is sufficient for making the kinds of decision that are required for daily living. In contrast,
'metaphysical or absolute' certainty is such that – according to an addition in the French edition of the *Principles* – 'we think that something
could not possibly be otherwise than we judge it to be' (AT IX-2, 324).
Descartes seems to have assumed that discussion of metaphysical questions required metaphysical certainty, and that this presupposes the
kind of metaphysical foundation that he offered in the *Meditations* and
in Part I of the *Principles*. This assumption may have been influenced
by another contemporary commonplace about the certainty of revelation, namely, that what is taught by the Scriptures is indubitable. One
of Descartes' most vociferous critics contrasted the degree of certainty
that is appropriate and feasible for different kinds of belief: 'Just as
it would be a mistake to demand of medicine a degree of certainty
that is comparable to the dogmas of theology, so likewise one could
not excuse those who would demand, for all the dogmas of physics,
that their demonstrations achieve the exactitude that is found only in
mathematics' (Schoock, 1643: 123). Despite endorsing the uncertainty
of natural philosophy, Descartes was attempting to emulate the alleged
certainty of religious belief in his philosophical apologetics.

The second reason why Descartes' response to the possible unreliability of our cognitive faculties failed is that the proofs of God's existence
provided in the *Meditations* are much less convincing than the allegedly
doubtful claims for which Descartes wished to provide a 'metaphysical' foundation. Descartes had claimed in the Fifth Meditation that 'the
certainty and truth of all knowledge depends only on the knowledge
of the true God in such a way that, before I knew him, I was incapable
of knowing anything else perfectly' (AT VII 71; Descartes, 2003b: 57).
He repeated this in Part I of the *Principles*, where he considered it 'reasonable to doubt such conclusions [e.g. those found in mathematical

proofs] and believe that it [the human mind] cannot have knowledge which is certain before it discovers the author of its origin' (AT VIII-1 10; Descartes, 2003b: 116). However, the Cartesian proofs of God's existence are much less convincing than any of the mathematical proofs or other claims in natural philosophy that they are intended to protect from sceptical objections. Even contemporary sympathetic readers of the *Meditations* found the proofs of God's existence unconvincing, and some – such as the notorious critic, Gisbertus Voetius – suspected that Descartes' real objective was to support atheism by presenting such manifestly weak arguments for God's existence that they would have the opposite effect to what was apparently intended.

Descartes' attempt to provide a secure foundation for the reliability of our cognitive faculties thus fails for many reasons. It uses those same faculties in the construction of a defensive foundation (as Arnauld objected), and it requires of metaphysical knowledge-claims an unnecessary and unattainable degree of indubitability that is absolute. Rather than embark on a search for an absolutely secure foundation, he might have deployed the dismissive comments with which he replied to an objection by Mersenne:

> Once we think that something is perceived correctly by us, we are spontaneously convinced that it is true. If this conviction is so strong that we could never have any reason to doubt what we are convinced of in this way, then there is nothing further to inquire about; we have everything that we could reasonably hope for. Why should we be concerned if someone happens to pretend that the very thing, about the truth of which we are so firmly convinced, appears false to God or to an angel and therefore that it is false, absolutely speaking? Why should we care about such an absolute falsehood, for we do not believe in it at all and have not the slightest evidence to support it? (AT VII 144–5; Descartes, 2003b: 81)

3. Appearance and reality

The two epistemological theories that are outlined above result from Descartes' reflections on two different kinds of knowledge, namely, knowledge in natural philosophy and metaphysical knowledge. They differ in the degree to which uncertainty is tolerated in the former but not the latter, and in the concerns about radical scepticism that emerge in the latter but are completely absent from the former. They also differ in how they address the distinction between objects of knowledge and our perceptions of them.

In the early 1630s Descartes endorsed a distinction that was first made explicitly by Galileo (Drake, 1957: 274–7), to the effect that our sensations may not have the same properties as the realities of which they are sensations. Descartes invoked the same example as Galileo had used, about the sensation of tickling and the reality of what is involved in being tickled, to illustrate the principle that he expressed in the first sentence of *The World*:

> Since my plan here is to discuss light, the first thing that I want to bring to your attention is that there may be a difference between our sensation [*sentiment*] of light, i.e. the idea which is formed in our imagination by means of our eyes, and whatever it is in the objects that produces that sensation in us, i.e. what is called 'light' in a flame or in the sun. (AT XI 3; Descartes, 2003a: 85)

This distinction coincided with one that was also developed by Boyle and that subsequently provided the basis for Locke's distinction between 'primary' and 'secondary' qualities. Descartes' version of the distinction implied that one may not assume that our sensations (which Descartes included in the extension of the term 'idea') are 'completely similar' [*entièrement semblable*] to the realities of which they are sensations. It is therefore always illegitimate to examine the kinds of experiences we have, and to conclude that the objects that stimulate those experiences have exactly similar properties. This is now so familiar in scientific explanations that the novelty of its original discovery may not be appreciated. We are no longer even surprised by a scientific theory that, for example, the experience of a characteristic colour is explained by the wavelength of the light that impinges on our eyes, and that there is nothing 'blue' about light that causes a sensation of blue in us.

As already indicated above, Descartes used this argument to release him from the apparent expectation, within scholasticism, that one must explain our experiences by corresponding forms in the stimuli that cause them. He proposed instead to limit his explanation of such stimuli to the size, motion, etc. of small parts of matter, and to accept the uncertainty that results from the hypothetical character of such inferences from sensations to their possible causes.

The sceptical objections that were discussed in metaphysics, however, seemed to prevent Descartes from adopting a similar latitude. Once he had considered that the external physical world may not exist and had conceded that he must prove its existence before recovering any of the knowledge that had been classified as doubtful in the First Meditation, Descartes felt constrained to argue that the external world must correspond [in some sense] to his perceptions of it; indeed, he had nothing else available on which to reconstruct that world, at that point in the argument, apart from his own ideas. Thus, in natural philosophy he speculated (from without to within) about how hypothetical physical bodies could cause our sensations, while in metaphysics his argument began with ideas and moved outward towards the kind of reality that must cause them. The contrast between the two approaches is evident in the first section of Part II of the *Principles*. Having rehearsed the sceptical arguments of the *Meditations* in Part I of the *Principles*, Descartes began Part II by arguing that an external physical world must exist. The argument assumed that God is not a deceiver, and then concluded that there is matter in the universe:

> We have a clear understanding of this matter as something that is quite different from God and from ourselves or our mind; and we *appear* to see clearly that the idea of it comes to us from things located outside ourselves, which it wholly resembles [*quibus omnino similis est*]. . . . The unavoidable conclusion, then, is that there exists something extended in length, breadth, and depth, and possessing all the properties which we clearly perceive to belong to an extended thing. And it is this extended thing that we call 'body' or 'matter' (AT VIII-1, 41; CSM I 223, emphasis added)

The phrase in Latin above was translated into French by exactly the same phrase [*entièrement semblable*] that Descartes had used eleven years earlier to deny the validity of this same inference, and it might seem on first reading as if Descartes contradicts in metaphysics what he had asserted as a first principle in natural philosophy.[1] Granted, he does not claim in this text that the external stimuli that cause our sensations have exactly the same qualities as those sensations, but merely that they appear to have them. To avoid inconsistency, Descartes should be understood along the following lines.

The arguments deployed in the *Meditations* and in the *Principles* (Part I) do not show that the objects that trigger our sensations are 'exactly similar' to our sensations of them. He described this assumption on many occasions as naïve, and he compared it with the prejudices of childhood (AT VIII-1, 35; Descartes, 2003b: 140–1; Descartes to More, 5 February 1649: AT V 271). Accordingly, the meditator in the *Meditations* could not reasonably accuse God of being deceitful if the external realities that trigger our ideas are *not* exactly similar to them. He was entitled to conclude only that there is 'some kind of matter, which is extended in length, breadth and depth, and has various differently shaped and variously moving parts which give rise to our various sensations of colours, smells, pain and so on' (AT VIII-1, 40; CSM I 223). Descartes has thus reintroduced the hypothesis about matter on which *The World* was constructed as if it were deduced from our perceptions or ideas.

However, his conclusion is not that matter must have properties that are 'exactly similar' to our perceptions of them, but merely that there must be some reality (matter) that has properties that cause us to have the sensations that we experience. This leaves him free to speculate, in the subsequent paragraphs of the *Principles*, about the properties that we may hypothesize in matter in order to construct a viable natural philosophy. The principle that he had adopted in *The World* thus retained its validity: 'although everyone is commonly convinced that the ideas we have in our thought are completely similar to the objects from which they originate, I see no argument that guarantees that this is so' (AT XI 3; Descartes, 2003a: 85). Accordingly, the *Principles* reminds readers that 'sensations, emotions and appetites . . . may also be perceived clearly if we are very careful not to make any judgments about them apart from what is included precisely in our perception and of which we are inwardly aware' (AT VIII-1, 32; Descartes, 2003b: 138). In other words, such judgements are secure only on condition that they do not assume naively that the stimuli that trigger sensations also resemble them.

Rather than hold God guilty of deception, therefore, we should hold ourselves responsible for naïve and unwarranted inferences if we assume that the realities that cause us to have perceptual experiences – whatever they turn out to be – have exactly similar properties to those that we experience. This conclusion may appear inconsistent with another of Descartes' repeated claims, about the 'truth' of so-called 'clear and distinct' ideas. The latter might suggest that we are able to inspect our ideas and, based on some kind of phenomenological inspection, decide whether there are mind-independent realities that correspond exactly to them. Here again the distinction between two kinds of knowledge is relevant. In his natural philosophy, Descartes relied on sensory information to confirm hypotheses about the realities that apparently stimulate our senses. Likewise, he claims in the *Principles* that 'we have sensory awareness of, or rather as a result of sensory stimulation we have a clear and distinction perception of, some kind of matter' (AT VIII-1, 40; CSM I 223). However, the physical theories about matter that are introduced by Descartes in the subsequent pages are not warranted by an inspection of the clarity and distinctness of his ideas, but by their success in explaining various natural phenomena.

4. Conclusion

By following the historical sequence of Descartes' engagement with epistemological issues, various changes of emphasis and focus can be accommodated within a coherent account of different kinds of knowledge. In the *Rules* he briefly attempted to work within the Aristotelian ideal of demonstration that was almost commonplace at that time. However, he subsequently developed different analyses of knowledge that focused on two philosophical enterprises that had little in common. One was the newly emerging natural philosophy, to which he contributed significantly, and the other was a traditional apologetic enterprise – inspired by various church councils – that invited Catholic scholars to provide philosophical arguments to support their religious faith (AT VII 3; Descartes, 2003b: 9). These two kinds of 'knowledge' were as disparate as the descriptions of them that Descartes offered, and it is a fundamental mistake to read the *Meditations* as if they offered a single Cartesian theory of knowledge that fits the full range of disciplines, including mathematics, on which he offered philosophical reflections. This mistake probably results from a completely contingent factor about the interests of modern readers and the relative accessibility or otherwise of various Cartesian texts. Descartes' natural philosophy has been superseded by modern scientific theories, and there are relatively few readers today of the scientific essays for which the *Discourse on Method* was written as a preface. In contrast, the *Meditations* are still read in translation even by undergraduate students of philosophy, despite the scholastic Latin in which it was written. Since Descartes' reflections on the epistemology of natural philosophy are found in his scientific essays and correspondence, while his concerns about the significance of Pyrrhonism for metaphysics are found in the *Meditations*, it is understandable though regrettable that the *Meditations* are often seen as the exclusive source of a Cartesian epistemology that is concerned primarily with scepticism.

Note

1   This was brought to my attention by Delphine Kolesnik.

Further reading

There are many general collections of articles on Descartes' philosophy, such as: Janet Broughton and John Carriero (eds), *A Companion to Descartes* (Malden, MA: Blackwell, 2008), and John Cottingham (ed.), *The Cambridge Companion to Descartes* (Cambridge: Cambridge University Press, 1992). The natural philosophy of Descartes is discussed in Stephen Gaukroger, John Schuster and John Sutton (eds), *Descartes' Natural Philosophy* (London: Routledge, 2000); Daniel Garber, *Descartes' Metaphysical Physics* (Chicago: University of Chicago Press, 1992); William R. Shea, *The Magic of Numbers and Motion* (Canton, MA: Science History Publications, 1991); Desmond M. Clarke, *Descartes' Philosophy of Science* (Manchester: Manchester University Press, 1982). The standard foundationalist interpretation of the *Meditations* is found in Bernard Williams, *Descartes: The Project of Pure Inquiry* (Harmondsworth: Penguin, 1978), and in Margaret Wilson, *Descartes* (London: Routledge, 1978), while Steven Nadler, *Arnauld and the Cartesian Philosophy of Ideas* (Manchester: Manchester University Press, 1989), reviews contrasting interpretations of what Descartes meant by an idea. The Dutch context in which Descartes wrote all his work is summarized in Theo Verbeek, *Descartes and the Dutch* (Carbondale: Southern Illinois University Press, 1992). Descartes' attempt to provide a scientific explanation of some mental phenomena is examined in Desmond M. Clarke, *Descartes's Theory of Mind* (Oxford: Clarendon Press, 2003).

References

Ariew, R., Cottingham, J. and Sorell, J. (eds) (1998), *Descartes' MEDITATIONS: Background Source Materials*. Cambridge: Cambridge University Press.

Clarke, D. M. (1989), *Occult Powers and Hypotheses: Cartesian Natural Philosophy under Louis xiv*. Oxford: Clarendon Press.

—(2006), *Descartes: A Biography*. Cambridge: Cambridge University Press.

Cottingham, J., Stoothoff, R. and Murdoch, D. (eds and trans.) (1985), *The Philosophical Writings of Descartes*, 2 vols. Cambridge: Cambridge University Press (identified as CSM, with volume and page number).

Descartes, R. (1964–76), *Oeuvres de Descartes*, (eds) C. Adam and P. Tannery. Paris: Vrin/CNRS (identified as AT, with volume and page number).

—(1998), *The World and Other Writings*, ed. and trans. S. Gaukroger. Cambridge: Cambridge University Press.

—(2003a), *Discourse on Method and Related Writings*, trans. D. M. Clarke. London: Penguin.

—(2003b), *Meditations and Other Metaphysical Writings*, (trans.) D. M. Clarke. London: Penguin.

Drake, S. (ed. and trans.) (1957), *Discoveries and Opinions of Galileo*. New York: Doubleday.

Gaukroger, S. (1989), *Cartesian Logic: An Essay on Descartes' Conception of Inference*. Oxford: Clarendon Press.

McMullin, E. (ed.) (2005), *The Church and Galileo*. Notre Dame, IN: University of Notre Dame Press.

Montaigne, M. de (1993), *The Complete Essays*, trans. M. A. Screech. London: Penguin.

Newton, I. (1999), *The Principia. Mathematical Principles of Natural Philosophy*, (trans.) I. B. Cohen and A. Whitman. Berkeley: University of California Press [first published in 1713].

Regius, H. (1648), *Brevis Explicatio Mentis Humanae, sive Animae Rationalis*. Utrecht: T. Ackersdicius.

Schoock, M. (1643), *Admiranda Methodus Novae Philosophiae Renati Des Cartes*. Utrecht: J. van Waesberge.

Sextus Empiricus (2000), *Outlines of Scepticism*, trans. J. Annas and J. Barnes. Cambridge: Cambridge University Press.

Wallace, W. A. (1992), *Galileo's Logical Treatises*. Dordrecht: Kluwer.

CHAPTER 6

LOCKE, BERKELEY, HUME: EPISTEMOLOGY
P. J. E. Kail

1. Introduction

John Locke (1632–1704), George Berkeley (1685–1753) and David Hume (1711–1776) are the three figureheads of the first significant wave of 'British Empiricism'. Each wrote copiously on a vast range of subjects but produced masterpieces that are reference points of empiricism. The impact of Locke's *An Essay concerning Human Understanding* (1st edition 1690) on the eighteenth century and beyond is difficult to overestimate. Berkeley's *A Treatise concerning the Principles of Human Knowledge* (1710) and *Three Dialogues between Hylas and Philonous* (1713) exploit Locke's empiricist principles to deny the existence of matter and to build a world of experiences sustained by God and perceived by human spirits. Hume's *A Treatise of Human Nature* (1739–40) is a heady mixture of empiricism, scepticism and naturalism. Its ambition and complexity was so formidable that Hume recast its epistemological part in the more accessible *An Enquiry concerning Human Understanding* (1748). This emphasis on the primacy of experience is not new, since forms of empiricism are prominent in ancient philosophy. However, the rigour with which it is pursued in the context of the scientific revolution is something unprecedented.

'Empiricism' is derived from the Greek for experience, and if episte-mology is the study of knowledge and justification, then knowledge and justification for empiricists is related – somehow – to experience. Here I try to give a flavour of how these thinkers understood this thesis. I shall frame matters by discussing Locke's views on knowledge, probability and the external world and self, and then consider aspects of Berkeley's and Hume's responses to these views. We shall see that Locke's views encourage scepticism, and this is a tendency to which Berkeley and Hume react very differently. Some caveats need to be borne in mind, however. Obviously this chapter is concerned with epistemological matters, but it would be mistaken to see Locke, Berkeley and Hume as solely, or even primarily, concerned with epistemology. Locke and Hume are as much naturalistic psychologists as they are epistemologists, and their influence in other areas like political and moral philosophy, and philosophy of religion, is just as important as their epistemology. Berkeley inherits some epistemological views from Locke, and is heavily critical of others, but is not concerned with the ins and outs of epistemology so much as developing a metaphysical system. Furthermore, grouping the three philosophers under a single label can mislead in at least two respects. First, the extent to which they agree is vastly outweighed by many, sometimes fundamental, differences. Second, it can encourage a blunt opposition between these 'empiricists' and the 'rationalists' Descartes, Malebranche, Spinoza and Leibniz where the British disagree entirely with the Continentals. There *is* one important difference between the two groups of thinkers, as we shall see, but we should not forget that empiricists agree with rationalists on many important issues. Finally, given the complexities of the views discussed here, I can barely scratch the surface of the epistemologies of Locke, Berkeley and Hume and some surfaces (like for example Hume's moral epistemology) remain unscratched.

2. Ideas and knowledge

Empiricism comes in different forms. One is *genetic*, holding that all our ideas or concepts are derived from sensory experience. *Justificatory* empiricism holds that the justification of any claim must rest in experience. A third form of empiricism holds that the content of thoughts or mental representations is entirely composed of elements of experience. Only the second form is a strictly epistemological doctrine, though the other two forms of empiricism bear on it to a greater or less extent.

All three thinkers agree on the genetic doctrine and connect it with the issue of representation. Locke spends Book I of the *Essay* arguing against innate principles. His target here is wider than the thesis that there are innate *ideas* or concepts and includes the claim that we have innate knowledge of general principles (logical truths for example) and of moral or practical principles. The narrower concern about the origins of concepts, however, bears on the representation issue. Ideas are concepts, and ideas are derived from experience. What our ideas can represent is constrained by what we can sense. This marks the key contrast between the empiricists and the rationalists, the latter group maintaining we have *non-sensory* or *intellectual* representations. These representations enable us to understand the fundamental structure of the world. For Descartes and Leibniz our possession of these non-sensory representations is explained by an appeal to innateness, and so rejecting innateness is part and parcel of the rejection of the intellect. There are no non-sensory representations and no way of understanding the world outside of experience. 'In all that Great extent', writes Locke 'wherein the mind wanders . . . it stirs not one jot beyond those *Ideas*, which *Sense* or *Reflection*, have offered for its Contemplation' (E 2.1.24).[1] In other words, ideas originate in experience (including experience of the operations of our own minds), and their reach is constrained by that fact. Berkeley, in his notebooks, writes 'Pure Intellect I understand not' (PC 810), and for Hume 'we can never think of any thing which we have not seen without us, or felt in our own minds' (T Abstract 6).

The claim that representation is limited by experience is connected to a view of the meanings of terms and the sentences in which terms figure. What we mean must be relatable to experience. Terms that cannot be so related lack a meaning. It is a matter of controversy quite how severe this restriction is for each of these philosophers. John Toland used Locke's theory, soon after the publication of the *Essay*, to argue that the Christian mysteries are meaningless, but it is unclear whether Locke would endorse this claim. Berkeley certainly did not endorse the claim that talk about such mysteries is meaningless, and offers a subtle discussion, particularly in his *Alciphron* (1732) of the different senses of 'meaning' and its relation to ideas. And, as we shall see in Section 4, Hume exploits the claim that ideas are derived from experience to argue that we have no idea of power, but the force of this claim is a matter of debate.

For the purposes of this chapter, however, we shall consider primarily the role of ideas in epistemology. Though ideas function as concepts or representations, they are also objects or mental particulars (images) about which judgements are made. The objects of *knowledge* for these empiricists are these mental particulars and the relations in which they stand. This makes knowledge very narrow in its scope. In one sense, probability, understood as an epistemic position that is inferior to knowledge, becomes more important than knowledge for the empiricists just because knowledge is so limited. But in another sense the restricted view of knowledge is centrally important because of its profound effect on the empiricists' views of our epistemic situation, as we shall see. Locke offers a complex taxonomy of knowledge centred on the thesis that knowledge is 'nothing but the perception of the connexion and agreement, or disagreement and repugnancy of any of our Ideas' (E 4.1.2). 'This agreement comes in different sorts, identity or diversity, relations, co-existence or necessary connexion and real existence' (E 4.1.3). These comprise the knowable facts, and there are two ways in which they are knowable, intuition and demonstration. In intuition the agreement or disagreement of ideas is 'immediately evident' to the mind. Locke tells us that in 'this, the mind is at no pains of proving or examining, but perceives the Truth, as the Eye doth light, only by being directed toward it' (E 4.2.1). Intuition is assent compelling (it 'forces itself immediately') and epistemically first-rate (we 'cannot conceive of . . . a greater certainty'). In demonstration, the paradigmatic example of which is knowledge of mathematical proof, one moves from some intuited facts to intuitive knowledge of what is not presently evident by a series of steps, each of which involves intuitive knowledge of relations that one can 'see'. This is a lower 'degree' of knowledge, since the steps involved in such a demonstration leave room for mistakes (E 4.2.3–7).

Locke's examples of the kinds of agreement or disagreement mentioned above are blue is not yellow (identity and diversity), two triangles upon equal basis, between two parallels are equal (relation), iron is susceptible to magnetical impressions (co-existence) and God exists (real existence) (E 4.1.7). A plausible account of the first two categories of relation is that they comprise conceptual or analytic relations among ideas that we can attend to and discover through intuition and demonstration. Of real existence, one can have intuitive knowledge of one's own existence (E 4.9.3), and this figures as a premise for a demonstrative argument for the existence of God (E 4.10). Nevertheless almost all knowledge concerns the conceptual connections of ideas, including relations of co-existence.

I shall explain why co-existence concerns concepts rather than objects below, but note that, with one exception, anything falling short of intuition or demonstration 'with what assurance soever embraced, is but Faith or Opinion, but not Knowledge' (E 4.2.14). This is a very severe restriction, even for Locke's time, as he acknowledges (E 4.4.1). His reason for this is as follows. Knowledge is 'real' only when there is 'a conformity between our *Ideas* and the reality of Things' (E 4.4.3). But since we cannot directly compare ideas with external things ('when the mind perceives nothing but its own *Ideas*') our knowledge is almost entirely restricted to relations among ideas. The exception is 'sensitive knowledge' which purportedly allows for knowledge of a world external to the mind. Leaving this aside for the moment (see Section 4), there are perhaps a number of further assumptions underlying Locke's view of knowledge that account for its restricted nature. One is an extreme form of epistemic internalism as a condition of knowledge, whereby one cannot be in a state of knowledge unless one has direct and infallible awareness of what renders one's state of knowledge (see, for example, Alston (1989) for a discussion of epistemic internalism). This internalism is likely driven by Locke's view that knowledge is an intellect achievement, acquired through one's own personal endeavours, and not a state that one happens to be in. One must achieve knowledge through reflecting on what is available to one's mind.

The ideas that comprise the present content of one's consciousness are so intimately related to us that it is impossible for us to go wrong, and, what's more, ideas cannot themselves deceive. Hence they are the objects of knowledge. As Hume puts it, everything that 'enters the mind, being in *reality* a perception 'tis impossible any thing shoul'd to *feeling* appear different. This were to suppose, that even where we are most intimately conscious, we might be mistaken' (T 1.4.2.7).

A second reason for this restricted view of knowledge is as follows. Locke works with an assumption about the ontological structure of the world that yields a view of knowledge his general empiricism cannot meet. I said that we come to know the relations of co-existence, but these comprise the 'nominal essences' of things, complex ideas of substances that are descriptions of the collections of sensible qualities we use to classify things into kinds. But such knowledge is knowledge only of the relations of *ideas* that figure in our classificatory conventions, and not knowledge of the ontological relations that figure in the constitution of the real essences of substances. Our knowledge of the real essences of things is restricted by the fact that our ideas are derived solely from experience, meaning that the internal structure, and the crucial relations of ontological dependence, is hidden from us (E 4.3.9–17). A grasp of those relations of dependence *would* show to us the intelligible structure of that world. So there is an ideal of knowledge as a grasp of ontological relations, but an ideal that we cannot meet. The reasons for this restriction are sometimes contingent (e.g. that we lack sufficiently powerful microscopes) but sometimes involve claims about our failure to find certain relations even conceivable (E 4.3.13). What we are left with is knowledge only of conceptual relations. When relations are not 'supposed of an external archetype', knowledge is 'real' because its objects comprise solely ideas and their relations (E 4.5.5). This is true for mathematics and for morality. Moral and mathematical facts consist in analytic relations among ideas (e.g. that there are discoverable relations between the ideas of property and injustice) he holds that we are capable of demonstrative knowledge and certainty (E. 4.4.7).

Even if we leave aside large questions about this restrictive view of knowledge, it is unclear how successful the account is on its own terms. Among the many worries is our apparent knowledge of modal truths and universal propositions. How do we know, for example, that that the sum of the angles on *all* triangles is 180°, given a model of knowledge as the perception of relations among particulars? Locke's answer is that we gain knowledge of the particular case and extend it to all resembling shapes. But how do we distinguish between features that are accidental to the particular we considered and those that are essential to that particular? How can we tell in advance that the area of the particular triangle doesn't affect the sum of its angles? An appeal to intuition seems unsatisfactory.

Berkeley had little interest in the taxonomy of knowledge, but he did hold that we have intuitive knowledge of our ideas. Ideas are 'immediately perceivable' and constitute the 'objects of knowledge' (PHK 2). He also writes in a way that suggests that can have intuitive knowledge of necessity and possibility (PHK 3) and is critical of Locke's view of universal knowledge (PHK Introduction, 15 & 16). Hume shows more traces of engagement with Locke on the topic of knowledge. He thinks we can have intuitive knowledge of certain relations among the ideas, resemblance, contrariety and degrees in quality (T 1.3.1.2). He also holds that we can have demonstrative knowledge of proportions in quantity or number (T 1.3.1.3). However, he picks up on Locke's admission that demonstration has a lower degree of knowledge, because we are liable to make mistakes in chains of intuition, to produce a 'scepticism with regard to reason' (T 1.4.1). One's capacity to make mistakes in first-order judgements encourages second-order judgements to secure the first-order ones, but this leads to a regress that leaves a 'total extinction of belief and evidence' (T 1.4.1.6). Hume thinks not that we ought to conclude that the sceptic is right, but instead we should acknowledge that reasoning is best thought of as a natural causal process rather than a voluntary and independent faculty of comparison. We shall return to this in the next section.

3. Probability

Where knowledge fails we have probability. Probability is not a formal notion, the mathematical representation of the rules for ideal reasoning, but a psychological state of lower epistemic standing inasmuch as it does not carry with it infallibility. Probability falls short of knowledge because whereas in knowledge 'each step has its visible and certain connexion', in probability that 'which make me believe, is something extraneous to the thing I believe; something not evidently joined on both sides to, and so not manifestly shewing the Agreement, or Disagreement of those *Ideas*, that are under consideration' (E 4.15.3). For example, Locke holds that if we see a man walk on ice we have knowledge since we observe the fact of a man walking on ice (we see a connection between the two ideas). However, if that fact is reported to me, my judgement has the status of probability since the connection between the two is not evident to me.

Without probability, 'the greatest part of Men must be . . . very Scepticks' (E 4.16.2). Probable judgement concerns either possible objects of experience and testimony or those that are not the possible objects of human experience and testimony (E 4.16.5). The latter includes spirits like angels, deeply but contingently unobservable bodies and the in-principle hidden inner structures of material objects (E 4.16.5 – see above). Probable judgement is made on the basis of analogical reasoning, and here, as in many other places, Locke shows his engagement with Isaac Newton and his methodology. The third of Newton's 'Rules of Reasoning' expresses the idea that unobservable entities and processes are to be modelled on what is observable, and Locke here extends its application.

Locke's discussion of probability also concerns testimony, and here he is often thought to show another very restrictive view of epistemology. He appears to evince what is known as 'epistemic individualism'. Epistemic individualism in this context holds roughly that the testimony of A that p at best justifies the belief that A believes that p, and never justifies the belief that p. Notoriously Locke writes that 'we may as rationally hope to see with other Mens Eyes, as to know by other Mens Understandings. So much as we ourselves consider and comprehend of Truth and Reason, so much we possess real and true Knowledge. The floating of other Mens Opinions in our brains makes us not one jot the more knowing, though they happen to be true' (E 1.4.23). But however much this passage might suggest epistemic individualism, other passages suggest a different view. Thus, for example, one can acquire a justified belief from a mathematician, the 'Man, on whose Testimony he receives it, not being want to affirm any thing contrary to, or besides his Knowledge . . .' (E 4.15.1). The key point is that that justification can only come from a testifier who *knows* that p rather than one only having probable opinion.

Locke also discusses grades of probability in terms of the nature of the relevant testimony and its relation to the subject's own experience. At one end of the scale is the universal testimony of others (its universality giving it credence) regarding something that concurs with the subject's constant experience. At the other end of the scale are those that 'contradict common experience and the reports of History and Witness clash with the ordinary course of Nature' (E 4.16.9) and fall outside the subject's own experience. This last example concerns miracle reports, a subject never far from discussions of testimony in the period, and for Locke miracles function to give credence to revelations. This is an aspect of his general strategy of subordinating revelation to reason. Any claim to revelation must be tested against reason, and his strategy here rests on distinguishing between having a divinely revealed experience that p

and the experience that p is divinely revealed. The former must either show itself to be knowledge, and so falls under the ordinary canons of epistemology or if not, it is mere belief and cannot have authority. If however the claim is to know that the experience is divinely revealed, it must be tested against something independent of that experience.

Hume famously wrote on the connection between probability and reported miracles, and I shall discuss this below. But the topic of probability more generally is one of the most central aspects of his philosophy, and he follows Leibniz's criticism of Locke and others for 'being too concise when they treat of probabilities, and those other measures of evidence on which life and action entirely depend' (T Abstract 4). Hume's approach however is not merely to fill in detail but instead to produce what was a radical account of the probable reason itself. Hume argues for a view of reason as a natural faculty, intelligible in terms of certain natural or associative relations between perceptions. Probable reason turns out to be 'nothing but a species of instinct or mechanical power' (E 9.6), and a faculty that is no different in kind from the inferential faculties of non-human animals. The approach he takes is naturalistic in the sense he seeks to explain the psychology of such inferences and the results are naturalistic inasmuch as he concludes the processes underlying human reasoning are no different in kind from the causal processes underlying the natural world.

For Hume probable inference is inference based on the relation of cause and effect. We cannot penetrate into the essences of objects to perceive the powers upon which effects depend (see below). Our knowledge of what causes what depends on our past observations of causes being regularly followed by their effects. I discover, for example, that three cups of coffee in the morning is regularly followed by my failure to sleep at night, and so I conclude that three cups of coffee is the cause of sleeplessness. In light of this discovery, I can reason on its basis that the next time I have three cups of coffee in the morning I shan't sleep. The inference I draw is a form of reasoning – based on the relation of cause and effect – and, what's more, it seems based on a *good reason* or *justification* for what I believe. If I said that my reason for thinking that I won't fall asleep is because rabbits eat lettuce, you would conclude that I have no reason at all, since there is no connection between these two claims. Since, however, we agree that too much coffee is the *cause* of sleeplessness, you view me as having a good reason.

Hume seeks to understand how we draw such inferences, and to understand 'those other measures of evidence on which life and action entirely depend' (T Abstract 4). He argues that we do not draw such inferences *because* we possess a good reason to do so, or to put his negative claim in a different way, he argues that reason does not *determine* us to draw such inferences. On the basis of such statements, many have thought that Hume's entire discussion had the sole aim of showing that all such inferences have no positive epistemic standing. That is, Hume's main aim was to put forward the 'problem of induction'. We may put the problem thus: we normally think that what we have observed in the past provides us with good reason for beliefs about what we have yet observed. Such reasons however appear to rest on a general assumption, namely that the future will resemble the past. But what reason do I have to think that the future will resemble the past? I cannot know a *priori* that it will, and so it seems that my only other option is to argue since the future *has* resembled the past it will continue to do so. But this begs the question, namely, what reason do I have to assume that the future will resemble the past?

Before we take up this issue in connection with Hume, it is worth noting that Berkeley, though he didn't consider this question, has a ready answer to it. The laws of nature for him are underwritten by the will of God, which of course underwrites our general assumption that the future will resemble the past. Berkeley, as we shall see, rejects the existence of objects other than ideas and sees the world as consisting in patterns of experience underwritten by God. The relation between experiences however is not a causal one. Instead it is the relation of sign and signified. Fire does not cause pain, but instead our idea of a fire, caused in us by God, is a sign for, or warning of, impending pain. So the regularities in experience are not causal but providential, and understanding them is a matter of interpreting their meaning. So our confidence that the future will resemble the past is secure.

Hume has no such views and so the sceptical question remains. As I said, Hume is often read as a sceptic who holds that such inferences are not epistemically good ones, but inferences we cannot help making anyway. There is no denying the importance of this reading for the history of philosophy, nor, indeed, the fact that some passages of his writings seem to support it. On the other hand it does not sit at all well with much of what Hume says and does. For one thing his naturalistic approach to human nature is based on generalizations drawn from experience. But if he did hold that we have no reason to believe such claims, then he must conclude that we have no reason to believe his system. Second, he often applies terms of epistemic approval to probable inference (for example such inferences can be 'just and conclusive' (T 1.3.13.3). Third, he contrasts conclusions drawn from cause and effect from other inferences in a way that suggests the latter are second-class or 'merely the offspring of the imagination' (T 1.3.9.4).

In the light of these, and other considerations, commentators now tend to view claims such as the inference's not being 'determin'd by reason' or that there is no argument for the inference not as negative evaluations of those inferences but as claims about the *causal mechanism* of such inferences. What cannot be operative in the drawing of such inferences is some *argument* in its favour (there can be no such argument) but it does not follow from that alone that probable inferences – inferring effects from causes – are not epistemically praiseworthy. His positive claim is that such inferences are the operations of the mechanisms of association or 'custom' that his predecessors had previously distinguished sharply from reason and identified with the mechanism underlying animal minds. This naturalistic claim regarding the mechanism of reason can be seen as naturalistic in an epistemological sense, roughly the idea that the justification of a belief can be understood in terms of the natural processes that produce that belief. Hume says reason is 'a kind of cause, of which truth is the natural effect' (T 1.4.1.1) and it is possible to see this as a nascent form of reliabilism. That is to say, a belief is justified by its being a product of a causal mechanism that reliably produces true belief (see Chapter 10 of this volume for discussion). Hume of course does not explicitly use concepts such as reliability but nevertheless the way he views such inferences suggests he assumes that such inferences are reliable (though that we cannot know that there are so).

Hume talks of probable inference as a potential source of *proof.* He does not mean by this that the evidence entails the relevant conclusion, but instead the evidence leaves the conclusion 'entirely free from doubt and uncertainty'. It is 'ridiculous' to say ''tis only probable that the sunrise tomorrow' (T 1.3.11.2), criticizing philosophers, Locke included, who reserve the term 'proof' to knowledge in the strict sense. There are epistemic and psychological faces to the notion of proof, the former in terms of frequency, the latter in terms of psychological conviction or the 'force and vivacity' characteristic of Hume's theory of belief. The more frequently we experience A causing B, the more stable our patterns of inference and the conviction that accompanies it. Probability, and its degrees, is determined by the frequency of observed relation between A and B and impacts on psychological conviction proportionately. This helps us to understand Hume's scepticism with regard to reason mentioned at the end of the previous section. Knowledge, recall, is a matter of comparison and discovery of relations, but in demonstration there is the possibility that we have made a mistake in the chain of reasoning. A probable judgement is then applied, but has the effect of diminishing the psychological assurance. This continues until all conviction reaches zero. Hume does not recommend his conclusion, but uses it to confirm his hypothesis that 'all our reasonings concerning causes and effects are nothing but the effects of custom and that belief is more properly an act of the sensitive, than the cogitative part of our natures' (T 1.4.1.8).

Hume's most celebrated application of his theory of probable reason is his discussion 'Of miracles'. What he is driving at here, and how successful he is, is hotly debated, but one way to take it is as follows. Hume argues that, *pace* Locke, it is never rational to believe a reported miracle. A miracle is a violation of a law of nature. Laws of nature are those causal regularities for which we have proofs ('proof' in the sense mentioned above). A testimonial proof of any event should be such that doubt is impossible, and there are various aspects of this including the quality and quantity of the testifiers. So conceivably there could be a 'proof against proof' (EHU 10.11). Which of these proofs are we to prefer? I should accept the testimony if 'the falsehood of his testimony would be more miraculous, than the event which he relates; then, and not till then, can he pretend to command my belief or opinion' (EHU 10.13). But it is always more probable that such testimony, however sincere, is false than that the event itself occurred, so in deciding between the two proofs it is more rational to believe in the falsehood of the testimony than in the event reported.

4. World and mind, existence and nature

Locke's dictum 'the Mind knows not Things immediately, but only by the intervention of the *Ideas* it has of them' (E 4.4.3) raises the spectre of scepticism, or rather a number of different scepticisms. The first question it raises is whether we can know that there are the physical objects that ideas supposedly represent. Locke, aware of the challenge of Descartes' *Meditations*, did not wish to hold that we have no knowledge of the external world, nor did he want to take what Hume described as the 'very unexpected circuit' (EHU 12.13) of appealing to God to guarantee that an external world exists. So in addition to the categories of knowledge discussed above, Locke claimed that we have 'sensitive knowledge' of the *particular existence of finite beings* without us' (E 4.2.14). Locke is very brief in his discussion, and it is not hard to get the impression that he doesn't really address the problem. The most sympathetic reading of sensitive knowledge holds that ideas are *signs* of their causes, and so we are entitled to know *that* there is something outside our experience, even if we cannot know *what*. So our perceptual relation to physical objects is indirect. We indirectly perceive external objects by directly perceiving ideas of sensory states that are caused by physical objects.

Though we do not have knowledge of what the causes of our ideas are, Locke offers a hypothesis regarding them and our perceptual relation to them. The ordinary pre-theoretical view that we perceive objects directly (that is, without first perceiving a mental of object or idea) is assumed by him to be false. Instead, objects cause ideas in observers, who become indirectly aware of those objects by being directly aware of those ideas. Locke also has a view of what those objects are like, guided by a speculative-cum-scientific hypothesis about the behaviour of physical objects called 'corpuscularism'. This is a probable 'hypothesis' (E 4.3.16), based on an analogy with the behaviour of observable objects, and is the furthest we can go in explaining the behaviour of physical objects. Roughly speaking, physical objects are constituted by particles or corpuscles that have 'primary qualities', those properties which we think any physical object must have. These comprise figure, number, solidity, extension and motion or rest. Differences in physical objects involve differences in the 'arrangement' of these qualities, and in explaining their interaction we need only appeal to these qualities and the powers with which their different arrangements equip them. Our *ideas* of objects are also caused by particular arrangements of primary qualities. Locke holds that our ideas of primary qualities represent those qualities by *resembling* them. Others – our ideas of secondary qualities – are caused by arrangements of primary qualities, but their ideas do not resemble those causes. So my visual experience is extended and this extension resembles the extension of the book before my eyes. My experience of its colour, however, is akin to the pain I feel when I stub my toe. The cause of the pain is nothing 'like' the pain itself. The difference between pain and colour experience is that we mistakenly suppose that the cause of our colour experiences is 'like' that experience, but instead such causes are simply the particular arrangements of corpuscles that have the power to produce the idea.

We have then knowledge that our ideas have external causes, and a probable hypothesis regarding what those causes might be. Furthermore, we are ignorant to a great extent of the essences and natures of the external bodies. Our ideas of bodies as arrangements of primary and secondary qualities, and the powers they have to affect other bodies, really constitute a convention employed in classification and not a grasp of the true nature of material substance. It is not hard to see how these implications of thesis 'the Mind knows not Things immediately, but only by the intervention of the *Ideas* it has of them' leaves the door ajar to scepticism. Berkeley saw the 'way of ideas' as providing a way of shutting it. As his notebooks attest (see e.g. PC 563), he was singularly unimpressed with Locke's brief account of sensitive knowledge. His response to the incipient scepticism rests on the identification of ordinary objects – tables and chairs, etc. – with what is immediately perceivable. What, however, is immediately perceivable are sensations or ideas. That closes the gap between ideas and the world by the simple expedient of identifying the constituents of the world with ideas.

Berkeley did not see this as some revision of what we ordinarily understand by 'external object', but instead its correct interpretation. But how can he think that? Do we not think that objects – unlike ideas – continue to exist unperceived? What his answer is to this question is a matter of controversy, but one way to understand it is as follows. Berkeley denies that objects exist independently of *all* minds. The 'absolute existence of unthinking without any relation to their being perceived . . . [is] perfectly unintelligible' (PHK §3). However, it does not follow that objects cannot exist outside *particular* minds. Instead their continuity is maintained by an omniscient God in the following way. Any given object is a collection of actual and possible ideas and that collection continues to exist unperceived by us in virtue of the fact that God has a standing volition to produce ideas in observers under the relevant circumstances.

The gap between ideas and objects is not the only source of scepticism that Berkeley saw as endemic to Lockean philosophy. Since our ideas are essentially sensory, Locke holds that we cannot penetrate into the natures or essences of external bodies. He saw this as expression of modesty, rather than of scepticism. God has 'fitted our Senses, Faculties, and Organs, to the conveniences Life, and the Business we have to do here. . . . But it appears not, that God intended, we should have a perfect, clear, and adequate Knowledge of [substances]; that perhaps is not the Comprehension of any finite being' (E 3.23.6). Berkeley however saw scepticism. In the preface to the *Three Dialogues between Hylas and Philonous*, Berkeley writes that modern philosophy encourages '*scepticism* and *paradox*. It is not enough, that we see and feel, that we taste and smell a thing. Its true nature, its absolute external entity, is still concealed'. This source of scepticism is removed by Berkeley's philosophy. There is no 'hidden nature' to objects that eludes the reach of sense experience. The complexity of worldly objects is the result of the rules governing the composition of ideas by which God operates to render the world orderly and intelligible and so fit place for humanity to inhabit.

Hume, however, pushes open wide the sceptical door left ajar by Locke and others. One aspect of this, which we will discuss later, concerns our grasp of the nature of the world external to our minds. But what of the prior question of whether we can have knowledge *that* there are objects other than perceptions? In the *Treatise*, Hume approaches the issue of our belief in external objects by asking what causes it, declaring at the opening of his account that he will not call into question the existence of external objects. 'We may well ask', he writes, '*What causes induce us to believe in the existence of body*? but 'tis in vain to ask, *Whether there be body or not*? That is a point, which we must take from granted in all our reasonings' (T 1.4.2.1). He agrees with one aspect of Locke's theory, namely that it is false that we perceive physical objects directly. However, he thinks we ordinarily believe that we do, and tries to explain why we do by appeal to the imagination. However, whereas Locke thought his view that we perceive objects indirectly is supported by a probable hypothesis, Hume uses his account of probable reason to argue that such a belief cannot be caused by probable reason and cannot be justified by it. As we saw, probable reason for Hume is based on an inference from observed effects to observed causes. But we cannot directly experience an external object, and so observe such a causal relation between it and our idea. The belief cannot be the product of probable reasoning. Instead the philosophical belief is caused by the same imaginative propensity behind the mistaken view that we perceive objects directly. So having reviewed the cause of our belief in body, Hume tells us that he is no longer confident in that belief, despite saying earlier that 'we ought to have an implicit faith in our senses . . . I feel myself *at present* of a quite contrary sentiment, and I am inclin'd to repose no faith at all in my senses' (T 1.4.2.56). In becoming aware of the causal origins of the belief, our confidence in it is shaken, though when we leave the study we forget our worries. It seems that we cannot really justify the belief but we can't help believing.

Whether this is Hume's settled view on the matter is a difficult question to answer, and commentators are divided on whether he thinks we can justify to ourselves the natural assumption of a world of objects external to our minds or whether he holds that such a belief is merely psychologically inescapable. Be that as it may, there is another aspect of Hume's scepticism that might be considered as an extension of Locke's empiricism. Recall that Berkeley found Locke's claim that the real essences of bodies lie hidden from us to be a form of scepticism. Hume agrees with Locke, writing that his own intention 'never was to penetrate into the nature of bodies' because 'such an enterprise is beyond the reach of human understanding' (T 1.2.5.26). Locke also supposed that such bodies had active forces or powers by which they operate, that idea of which, albeit a very imperfect one, is drawn from the experience of our wills. Hume, by contrast, thinks that we have *no* idea of power derived from causally related objects or from the operation of our wills. Our idea of power is in fact derived from a subjective reaction, a 'feeling of determination', derived from repeated experience of regularities, which is in turn projected back onto them. We cannot talk meaningfully of power in the objects since we lack an idea of it, and so 'when we say we desire to know the ultimate and operative principle, as something, which resides in the external object, we either contradict ourselves, or talk without a meaning' (T 1.4.7.5). Some commentators take this to imply that Hume holds that there is nothing more to causation than regular succession. So what makes it true, roughly speaking, that event *a* causes event *b* is that every event of type A is regularly followed by events of type B. For others, Hume holds that causation involves hidden powers and is arguing that they are completely unintelligible to us. All we can *understand* of causation is regular succession, and that the 'ultimate springs and principles are totally shut up from human thought and enquiry' (EHU 4.12). Again, this is an issue over which commentators are deeply divided. But whether Hume reduces causation to regularities, or holds that we cannot understand powers that lie beyond experience, all agree that his arguments involve the empiricism about representation mentioned at the beginning of Section 2. Hume's general approach involves what is known by commentators as his 'Copy Principle'. This is his 'first principle' of his 'science of human nature' (T 1.1.1.12), and holds that all our simple ideas are derived from simple impressions, which they exactly represent. What our ideas represent is to be determined by the impression of which they are a copy, and where there is no impression, we have no idea. The genetic claim is therefore related to a claim about representation.

But what about the idea we have of our own minds? For Hume, the true idea of the human mind is not that of a substance or 'owner' of perceptions, but simply that of a collection or bundle of perceptions. We cannot have an impression of some invariable 'owner of perceptions', and so we have no idea of it. The bundle mind, however, plays tricks on itself. The bundle of perceptions that constitutes the mind produces a 'fiction', a false belief that there is some substance that connects these perceptions. Famously, Hume thinks that his account is faulty. In the *Appendix* he wrote to the *Treatise*, he tells us that he has found himself in a 'labyrinth' and that he doesn't know how to 'correct' his 'former opinions, nor how to render them consistent' (T Appendix 9). It is difficult to know where Hume thinks he has gone wrong since it can hardly be said that he stated his worries clearly. Berkeley had, before Hume, flirted with the idea that the self is nothing but a collection of ideas. He realized that we can have no idea of the self and never abandoned this claim. Nevertheless, he did not want to reduce the self, ontologically speaking, to a collection of perceptions and held that we have a 'notion' of the self as an active centre of ideas. Locke, consistent with his claim that we do not have knowledge of the real essence of material substance, argued that we are equally ignorant of the real essence of the mind. To illustrate our ignorance, Locke suggests that, for all we know, thinking might not require a mental substance, but instead that God might 'superadd' thinking to material substance (E 4.3.6). Ironically, although used to illustrate the extent of ignorance of our minds, the suggestion kick-started materialist conceptions of the mind of which Locke would not approve.

5. Summary

Locke placed experience at the centre of his epistemology for a number of reasons. One has to do with his Newtonian views that experience is central to science as opposed to the *a priori* methods of the rationalists, who thought that nature of the world could be known through pure intellect. Another, which he records in the *Essay*'s 'epistle to the reader', is that we can settle where we can and where we cannot have knowledge, putting an end to potentially dangerous disputes. If we know that such disputes fall outside what we can know, we must agree to disagree. Experience is limited, and hence so are we, but Locke saw this as sensible modesty. But, as we have noted, the modesty is extreme. Knowledge is very limited indeed, and our relation to the world outside of experience is a tenuous one by Locke's principles. For Berkeley and Hume Locke's modesty is really scepticism. Berkeley saw Locke's epistemology as rendering the existence of the world doubtful and its nature hidden from us. His solution was to identify the natural world with experiences organized by God. Hume on the other hand took Locke's scepticism to show something about the nature of human cognition, namely that our natural propensities are more central to life than reason is. The high demands for knowledge set by Locke also lead Hume to see probability as central to human endeavour and knowledge as marginal. His interest in probability and how it is embodied in human cognition issued in a new and radical account of human reason where it becomes another natural propensity.

Note

1 The standard edition of Locke's *Essay concerning Human Understanding* (E) is (ed.) Peter Nidditch (Oxford: Clarendon Press, 1975). In referring to the Essay, I follow the convention of book, chapter and section number.

Further reading

There are a number of reliable editions of Berkeley's *Principles of Human Knowledge* (PHK) and the *Three Dialogues Between Hylas and Philonous*. The Oxford Student Editions, edited by Jonathan Dancy (both Oxford: Oxford University Press, 1998) have very good introductions. The *Alciphron* and his *Philosophical Commentaries* (PC) can be found in *The Works of George Berkeley, Bishop of Cloyne*, (eds) A. A. Luce and T. E. Jessop (London: Nelson, 1948–1957), in nine volumes. Recommended student editions of Hume's works are *A Treatise of Human Nature* (T), (eds) D. F. Norton and M. J. Norton (Oxford: Oxford University Press, 2000), and *An Enquiry concerning Human Understanding* (EHU), (ed.) T. L. Beauchamp (Oxford: Oxford University Press, 1999). Reference to the *Treatise* is by book, section, and paragraph number and to the *Enquiry* by section and paragraph number.

The secondary literature is vast. Recommended introductions to Locke include E. J. Lowe, *Locke on Human Understanding* (London: Routledge, 1995), and N. Jolley, *Locke: His Philosophical Thought* (Oxford: Oxford University Press, 1999). An accessible, but more advanced, collection of essays some of which bear on Locke's epistemology is V. Chappell (ed.), *The Cambridge Companion to Locke* (Cambridge: Cambridge University Press, 1994). On the particular topic of internalism, see W. P. Alston, 'Internalism and externalism in epistemology', ch. 8 in his *Epistemic Justification: Essays in the Theory of Knowledge* (Ithaca: Cornell University Press, 1989).

Tom Stoneham's *Berkeley's World: An Examination of the Three Dialogues* (Oxford: Oxford University Press, 2002) and Alasdair Richmond's *Berkeley's Principles of Human Knowledge: A Reader's Guide* (London: Continuum, 2009) are both very good. Two very different, but equally interesting, introductions to Hume are Harold Noonan's *Hume on Knowledge* (London: Routledge, 1999) and John Wright's *Hume's A Treatise of Human Nature* (Cambridge: Cambridge University Press, 2010). A good collection of more advanced articles is Elizabeth Radcliffe (ed.), *A Companion to Hume* (Oxford: Blackwell, 2008).

References

Alston W. P. (1989), 'Internalism and externalism in epistemology', ch. 8, in *Epistemic Justification: Essays in the Theory of Knowledge*. Ithaca: Cornell University Press.

Berkeley (1948–1957), *Philosophical Commentaries* (PC), in *The Works of George Berkeley, Bishop of Cloyne*, nine volumes, (eds) A. A. Luce and T. E. Jessop. London: Nelson.

Berkeley (1998), *Principles of Human Knowledge* (PHK), The Oxford Student Editions, (ed.) Jonathan Dancy. Oxford: Oxford University Press.

—(1998), *Three Dialogues Between Hylas and Philonous*. The Oxford Student Editions, (ed.) Jonathan Dancy. Oxford: Oxford University Press.

Hume (1999), *An Enquiry concerning Human Understanding* (EHU), (ed.) T. L. Beauchamp. Oxford: Oxford University Press.

—(2000), *A Treatise of Human Nature* (T), (eds) D. F. Norton and M. J. Norton. Oxford: Oxford University Press.

Locke (1975), *Essay concerning Human Understanding* (E), (ed.) Peter Nidditch. Oxford: Clarendon Press.

CHAPTER 7

KANT AND KANTIAN EPISTEMOLOGY

Melissa McBay Merritt and Markos Valaris

1. Introduction

What can I know? Kant, like many of his early modern predecessors, took this question about the extent and bounds of our knowledge to be the most fundamental one for philosophy. Our aim in this chapter is to give an introduction to Kant's attempt to answer this question in the *Critique of Pure Reason*, as well as a survey of Kant's influence on later work in epistemology in the analytic tradition.[1]

In the first part of this chapter we will sketch the main elements of Kant's epistemology. In order to understand the motivation for Kant's project, it is crucial to note that for Kant – as for many of his predecessors in the early modern period – the urgency of epistemological questions was felt primarily with regard to metaphysics. So, for example, Locke warns that we take things backwards if 'we let loose our Thoughts into the vast Ocean of *Being*' before making an assessment of our own cognitive powers.[2] As Locke and others noted, nothing distinguishes the history of metaphysics so much as seemingly endless debate on fundamental issues; and the natural (and perhaps healthy) response to this failure to make decisive progress is scepticism. The real problem was not the intrinsic undesirability of scepticism, but rather the nourishment that scepticism was thought to provide to atheism – at least when metaphysics concerns itself with issues of immediate consequence for human conduct, such as freedom of the will.[3] In a similar spirit, Kant develops his account of empirical and *a priori* knowledge in the *Critique of Pure Reason* not for its own sake, but in order to guide metaphysics onto the 'secure path' of a science.[4] In our discussion we will focus almost exclusively on Kant's epistemology. Nevertheless, it will be important to keep Kant's metaphysical motivations in mind.

Although Kant thought he had 'exhausted all possible answers' to the fundamental epistemological question in the *Critique of Pure Reason* (A 805/B 833), the history of epistemology does not end with him. In fact, Kant's own views have played a major part in the more recent history of epistemology, and continue to be influential to this day. In the second part of this chapter we will discuss the work of the two philosophers who did the most to keep Kant's influence alive in twentieth century analytic philosophy: Wilfrid Sellars and P. F. Strawson.

2. Kant

As we already saw, the result of Kant's epistemological inquiry was meant to be a new conception of metaphysics. Metaphysics had been pursued in the rationalist tradition under the assumption that we can have knowledge of objects that cannot be met with in sensible experience. Making claims about such supersensible objects could accordingly depend only on the resources of the intellect.[5] So, for example, it was thought that we could determine the existence of God simply through analysis of the concept of an absolutely perfect being.[6] But with such claims we overreach our cognitive capacities, Kant maintains; this is why metaphysics has failed. We can correct our course if we heed an important insight from the empiricist tradition, namely that we can have knowledge only of *sensible* objects. Indeed, even mathematics does not yield knowledge of special non-sensible mathematical objects; rather, mathematics provides knowledge only if its results are applicable, at least in principle, to sensible appearances (B 147) – an insight Kant finds exemplified in the spectacular success of the physical sciences from Galileo to Newton.

Kant's endorsement of the empiricist position that we can have knowledge only of sensible objects might seem to rule out the possibility of metaphysics altogether. But it rules out only a metaphysics of the supersensible.[7] If metaphysics in general is inquiry into the essential nature of things, there remains a place for a metaphysics of the sensible world, or nature. Such metaphysics would not consist in knowledge of contingent facts about particular objects; if it is to be a metaphysics at all, it must be concerned with what is necessarily the case with sensible objects in general. Its results would be articulated, most basically, as a battery of principles that hold of necessity of all sensible objects. In the *Critique of Pure Reason*, Kant tries to provide the epistemological foundation of this reconceived metaphysics.

Strict empiricism, however, has no room for the project Kant pursues. We can explain this point with regard to Hume, whom Kant credits with being the first wholly consistent proponent of empiricism in the early modern tradition (B 127). Hume divides all human reasoning into two categories, depending on its subject matter: we reason either about *'Relations of Ideas'*, he says, or about *'Matters of Fact'*.[8] We can only have knowledge of necessary truths when we reason about relations of ideas. When we do this, we merely make explicit the inferential connections among our representations. As Kant and later philosophers would put it, we arrive at this knowledge simply by analysing the content of our concepts: for this reason, such judgements are called 'analytic'. Examples might be *all triangles have three sides*, or as Kant suggests, *all bodies are extended*, or take up space (A 7/B 11).[9] Analytic judgements merely concern the content of our concepts, which may or may not pertain to real things in the world.[10] By contrast, Hume maintains, all claims about real things in the world concern matters that (for all we can know) could perfectly well be otherwise. Our grounds for such claims can consist only of evidence drawn from past experience. Claims about matters of fact, according to Hume, can only be *a posteriori*.

So Hume gives us two options. We can have knowledge that holds of necessity, but it can concern only the content of our concepts; and since I can perfectly well analyse the content of the concept *gnome*, or *phlogiston*, simply by taking note of my inferential commitments, it follows that analytic judgement entitles us to no claims about the reality of things. Alternatively, we can make claims that concern the reality of things, but such claims are only contingent.

However, Kant rejects Hume's division of human reasoning: it is possible, he maintains from the outset, to have knowledge that both holds of necessity and yet concerns matters of fact. As an example,

Kant points to the success of the experimental method in physics. Even though the physicist must rely upon experience in order to determine what the particular laws of nature are; still she has some more fundamental appreciation of nature itself as a law-governed whole. The particular question posed through a well-designed experiment registers only within the framework of more fundamental knowledge regarding the general *lawfulness* of nature. Such knowledge Kant deems both *synthetic*, because it concerns real objects,[11] and also *a priori*, because we have it independently of experience. The metaphysics of sensible nature would be based on an account of our capacity for synthetic *a priori* knowledge; and this account would need to be exhaustive if it is to articulate the basic framework of the laws of nature. In the section of the *Critique* called 'Analytic of Principles', Kant spells it out as a set of fundamental principles, such as that every alteration takes place in accordance with the law of cause and effect.

The example of the sciences provides only initial support for the viability of Kant's project in the *Critique*. Pointing to this example, Kant takes as given from the outset that we have synthetic *a priori* knowledge. His task is to explain how we could have such knowledge. Hence the guiding question of the *Critique* is '*How* is synthetic *a priori* judging possible?'[12]

Kant sets out with an initial hypothesis to show how this question could be answered. He likens it to the revolutionary 'first thoughts of Copernicus', since it calls for a revolution in the way in which we conceive of the relation between subject and object in knowledge. If we assume that 'all of our knowledge must conform to objects', we leave ourselves no way to account for the possibility of synthetic *a priori* knowledge, which would require that we are able to have some kind of knowledge of sensible objects 'prior to their being given' in sensible experience (B xvi). So Kant inverts the standard assumption, and proposes that 'objects must conform to our knowledge' (B xvi). The Copernican hypothesis does not require that we give up on the idea that the world is there anyway, whether or not we ever come to cognitive terms with it. However, the hypothesis entails that what it is to be an object is to be an object of possible knowledge. Thus objects necessarily conform to the principles that determine what can be known by us. The metaphysical implications of this claim are controversial, and we cannot consider them here. For present purposes, the crucial point is this: given the Copernican hypothesis, answering the question how synthetic *a priori* knowledge is possible comes down to giving an account of the principles that constitute our cognitive capacity.[13]

Knowledge of sensible objects requires – on any account – a *receptive* capacity, or 'sensibility': it must be the case that sensory representations can arise in us through affection by external objects. However, if *a priori* knowledge of sensible objects is to be possible, Kant argues, we must distinguish between two aspects of sensible representations. When I look at this piece of paper, I have a *sensation* of its white colour. Sensation is the aspect of the representation that corresponds to the stimulation of a distinct sensory modality – in this case, vision. However, my representation involves something more than sheer whiteness. This whiteness must have some extension and stand in spatial relations to all other extended things. So Kant argues in the *Critique*'s 'Transcendental Aesthetic' that I must have a representation of space in order to have a representation of some particular expanse of whiteness. Kant makes a similar point about time, and concludes that any sensible appearance that we can have is necessarily determinate in space and time. The representations of space and time are themselves prior to our representation of spatio-temporal particulars. Space and time are therefore *a priori* representations of human sensibility.

However, we must do more than simply enjoy sensible appearances in order to have knowledge of objects. Knowledge also requires a capacity for thought. Hence Kant maintains that knowledge requires the involved cooperation of two *distinct* capacities, sensibility and understanding.[14] Sensibility and understanding are both necessarily involved in knowledge, and yet – as Kant maintains against both empiricist and rationalist traditions – they 'cannot exchange their functions' (A 51–2/B 75–6). Sensible representations, which Kant calls 'intuitions', are singular (i.e. they represent some individual thing); whereas intellectual representations, which Kant calls 'concepts', are general (i.e. they represent some kind of thing). Sensible representations are not confused versions of intellectual representations, as the rationalists maintain; and intellectual representations are not reducible to sensible representations, as the empiricists maintain.[15] If we follow the rationalists on this point, we will be inclined to suppose that pure intellectual representations on their own entitle us to make claims about the reality of things, encouraging us to make cognitive claims about supersensible objects. And if we follow the empiricists, then we will be unable to account for concepts such as *substance* and *cause*, which clearly seem to be central to the way in which we make sense of the world, but yet (as we will see in a moment) do not seem to arise from experience. Thus, the Copernican hypothesis not only requires that we identify *a priori* conditions of the *sensible* representation of objects; it also requires that we identify *a priori* conditions of *thought* about objects. Accordingly, Kant specifies a set of twelve fundamental concepts, or necessary rules of thought about objects, and calls them the 'categories'.[16]

Included among the twelve categories are concepts that were long conceived as fundamental concepts of metaphysics, such as substance and cause. Let us consider how, for example, the concept of substance was handled by Kant's predecessors, so that we may better understand what is at stake for Kant. In a famous passage of Descartes' *Meditations on First Philosophy*, the Meditator takes a piece of wax, notes a bunch of its sensible properties, and then places the wax next to a flame. Every one of the previously noted sensible properties disappears: the wax no longer has the same smell, the same hardness, the same colour, and so forth – 'yet the wax remains' (Descartes, 1996: 20). The Meditator does not suppose that the stuff he held in his hands has simply gone away. But everything that he was able to represent about the wax through mere sensible perception has changed; only what he represented about the wax through the resources of the intellect alone remained constant. The perception of the wax depends upon the concept of substance, which Descartes claims must be 'innate', or in the mind prior to any sense perception. Locke, in reply, recognizes the centrality of the concept of substance to our thought about objects, and agrees that we cannot obviously derive the representation of substance from sensible experience:[17] we cannot see or otherwise perceive what it is that persists through all of the wax's changes. But neither Locke nor any of his successors in the empiricist tradition can accept the Cartesian account of the origin of this concept. The history of early modern empiricism can be tracked, at least in large part, in terms of the evolution of their struggle about what to say about fundamental concepts such as substance and cause.

For Kant, however, the real philosophical problem does not have to do with how we acquire these concepts – whether they are implanted in us by a benevolent creator, or whether they are instead acquired through experience.[18] The real philosophical problem concerns our *entitlement* to employ these concepts as we do (A 84/B 116ff.). When we experiment with the wax, we do not simply enjoy a random succession of sensations of a particular smell, colour, hardness and so forth. These representations are unified in a certain way, as successive states of a persisting substance. However, there is nothing in these sensible representations themselves that dictates how they must be combined so that we have an experience of an enduring material object. This is the role that the categories are meant to play. They purport to be necessary rules for combining sensible representations so that we may have knowledge of objects; and their source, Kant explains, is the understanding alone. Kant aims to address the legitimacy of this claim in the pivotal chapter of the *Critique*, the 'Transcendental deduction of the categories'.

Kant's argument in the 'Deduction' is too complex to do much justice to here. But we can sketch out its general strategy. Knowledge requires the involved cooperation of two *distinct* capacities (sensibility and understanding). We still need a principled account of how, precisely, sensibility and understanding necessarily cooperate in the production of knowledge. Kant's strategy is to show that the manner in which objects are 'given' to us in space and time must always already accord with the conditions of thought about objects, or the categories.

Kant makes his case, in large part, by arguing for a new conception of our cognitive capacity. Our capacity to know, he suggests, is most fundamentally a capacity for reflection. This capacity for reflection involves not just being able to ascribe particular judgements to oneself, but also the ability to be aware of the source of those judgements in oneself, and the readiness to adjust them in order to meet demands of intra-subjective and inter-subjective coherence.[19] Here again he aims to correct what he takes to be a crucial mistake of the empiricist tradition. Although most empiricists are prepared to recognize that we have a capacity to be aware of our own cognitive activity, the automatic processes of comparing, connecting and separating sensible representations are thought to be sufficient for knowledge. Reflection in the Kantian sense is a mere afterthought, required only in order to account for a mode of knowledge that is more refined than that which animals are capable of. By contrast, in Kant's view, this capacity for reflection is a fundamental requirement of knowledge, and no knowledge is possible without it.

Most notably, Kant's 'Deduction' leaves us with a new conception of experience as empirical knowledge. Setting out with the undeniable success of early modern physics firmly in mind, Kant in effect asks: What must experience be like if it is to contribute to scientific knowledge of material nature? Experience cannot be something that we merely suffer as a result of sensible affection, if it can so much as answer the question that is posed through a well-designed experiment. Experience, Kant argues, must be made possible by a tacit, and anticipatory, grasp of how sensible appearances are necessarily unified in any objective representation. Anyone who has come into the use of his cognitive faculties has this tacit understanding. Kant makes it explicit as a set of fundamental principles, called the 'principles of pure understanding', which include the principle of causality and the principle of the permanence of substance. As we saw earlier, Kant thinks of the categories as rules that determine how appearances in general must be combined if knowledge of objects is to be possible. The principles of pure understanding are derived from the categories, as rules that determine how *specifically human* (i.e. spatio-temporally structured) sensory appearances must be combined if knowledge of objects is to be possible. Thus, they are set out in the aftermath of the 'Deduction', once Kant has validated the general claim of the categories. With this, Kant has answered his question about how synthetic *a priori* knowledge is possible, and has provided the basis for the metaphysics of sensible nature that has been at issue.

3. Kant's influence

Kant's work has exerted a profound influence in nearly every field of philosophy, and on schools of thought far too diverse to survey in this chapter. In what follows we will focus only on Kant's influence on epistemology in the analytic tradition.

The history of analytic philosophy's engagement with Kant goes through several distinct phases. Much early analytic philosophy, starting with Frege and ending roughly with the waning influence of Logical Positivism, was articulated in relation to – although usually in opposition to – Kantian views.[20] Early analytic philosophers engaged with Kant mostly in a negative way: by and large, their goal was to rid philosophy of what they thought of as pernicious Kantian influences. Largely as a result of these efforts, by the middle decades of the twentieth century Kant no longer seemed relevant to most analytic philosophers working in epistemology, metaphysics or philosophy of mind.

Two important exceptions were Wilfrid Sellars and P. F. Strawson, whose work helped return Kant to the forefront of philosophical discussion. These two philosophers were influential not merely by writing detailed expositions of Kant's views, but primarily by giving Kantian themes a central place in their own original views.[21] As a result, Sellars and Strawson became points of reference not only for later Kant scholars, but also for later generations of philosophers drawing from Kant in their own work. This is why the rest of this section will be devoted to their work.

3.1 Wilfrid Sellars

Although Kant's main goal in the *Critique of Pure Reason* was to give an account of synthetic *a priori* knowledge, it is his views on experience and empirical knowledge that are most influential today, at least in the analytic tradition. In large part, this influence filters through the work of Wilfrid Sellars, and especially through his celebrated essay 'Empiricism and the philosophy of mind' (Sellars, 1963a; hereafter EPM, and references will be by section number). Although direct exegesis is not on the agenda of EPM, the essay is famous for developing two distinctively Kantian thoughts: first, that the content of experience is (at least in part) *conceptual*, and, second, that the epistemic authority of experience depends on a capacity for *reflection*.

At the core of EPM lie Sellars' arguments against the view he calls 'traditional empiricism', and particularly its commitment to what he calls 'the Myth of the Given'.[22] Like Kant, Sellars believes that empiricism contains an important insight. Empiricists are right to insist that sensory experience plays an essential *epistemic* (rather than merely causal) role in our knowledge about the world. It is not enough, for example, to say that we are prompted by its looking to us as if the sky is blue to believe that the sky is blue. Experience justifies us in forming this belief, or makes it rational for us to form this belief. Sellars' argument against traditional empiricism is that it cannot give a coherent account of how experience plays this role.

Traditional empiricism offers a seemingly straightforward account of the epistemic role of experience. According to traditional empiricism, experiential episodes are cases of *basic knowledge*, in the following sense: they are cases of knowledge that presuppose no other knowledge. Since experiential episodes are cases of *knowledge*, they are the sort of thing that can function as a reason for belief. And since they are cases of *basic* knowledge, we can, without fear of circularity, use them as reasons for beliefs about the world. For example, on such a view it might be that my having an experience as of a blue sky entails that I know that the sky looks blue.[23] I might then use this knowledge as a reason for believing that the sky is blue.

According to Sellars, however, this account of the epistemic role of experience is fatally flawed. At its heart is the idea that experiential episodes are instances of knowledge that presupposes no other knowledge. But this is a myth, in Sellars' view – the 'Myth of the Given' (EPM 32).[24]

In order to better appreciate Sellars' arguments against the Myth of the Given it might help to begin by looking at the broader epistemological view he is working towards. In a famous passage, Sellars asserts the following (EPM 36):

> In characterising an episode or a state as that of *knowing*, we are not giving an empirical description of that episode or state; we are placing it in the logical space of reasons, of justifying and being able to justify what one says.

Sellars is not going to deny that experiential episodes can be cases of knowledge. In a Kantian spirit, he accepts this as an insight of empiricism. What he will deny is that experiential episodes constitute an autonomous level of basic knowledge, in the way that traditional empiricism requires. This is also a Kantian thought: as we saw, Kant argues that experience requires the application of concepts in accordance with synthetic *a priori* principles; thus, experience always presupposes other knowledge. Moreover, this passage sets the stage for Sellars' rejection of the Myth of the Given. Knowledge, according to Sellars, depends on our ability to *justify* what we claim to know – that is, at a minimum, on our ability to *reflectively recognize* our beliefs and the reasons for our beliefs. As we will see later, this is inconsistent with the Myth of the Given.

One of Sellars' most characteristic claims in EPM is that, in order for experience to play its distinctive epistemic role, it must 'contain propositional claims' (EPM 16). Experiential episodes, according to the view developed in EPM, must have propositional content. For example, in having an experience as of a blue sky one draws upon the same conceptual resources that one would draw upon in consciously entertaining the proposition that the sky is blue. In Sellars' metaphorical terms, we might put this by saying that the experience 'contains the claim' that the sky is blue – the experience *claims that* the sky is blue. If that were not so, according to Sellars, it would be unclear how we could rely on the experience in order to *justify* our belief.[25] In Kantian terms, we can put the point by saying that experience must draw upon the capacities of the understanding, not just sensibility: 'intuitions without concepts are blind' (A 52/B 75).

Sellars' argument so far suffices to rule out some forms of traditional empiricism, which are discussed early on in EPM (1–7). According to those views, having an experience is simply a matter of standing in a primitive, unanalysable relation to a particular thing – having a sensation, or sensing a sense-datum. But, according to Sellars, experience conceived along these lines cannot be used to justify anything, because it lacks conceptual content – it does not contain any claims.

However, not all forms of traditional empiricism deny that experiential episodes have propositional content. Thus not all forms of traditional empiricism fall to this argument.[26] For this reason, Sellars develops a more general argument (EPM 35–8), which relies directly on a requirement for reflection.

As we have seen, experiential episodes must have *epistemic authority*: they must have the sort of status that makes it legitimate for us to take them as reasons for beliefs about the world. Putting the point in Sellars' metaphorical terms, it is not the case that being the subject of just any mental episode that contains the claim that the sky is blue gives me a reason for believing that the sky is blue; for example, *imagining that* the sky is blue gives me no such reason. I only have such a reason if the relevant episode has the right sort of authority – i.e., only if it is legitimate for me to trust what it claims.

So what would the authority of experiential episodes consist in? According to Sellars, a correct answer to this question must start from considerations of *reliability*. For example, looking at this page, you are undergoing an experience that contains the claim 'this is white'. In order for this experience to have the right sort of authority, it must be the product of reliable perceptual capacities. In Sellars' terms, it must be 'the manifestation of a tendency to produce [such claims] if and only if a [white] object is looked at in standard conditions' (EPM 35).[27] But, Sellars insists, reliability is not sufficient for authority. Epistemic authority needs to be *reflectively recognized*.[28] (In this respect, epistemic authority resembles political authority: the post of, say, Prime Minister has authority only to the extent that it is recognized as having authority.) For example, an experiential episode that contains the claim 'this is white' cannot have the relevant sort of authority unless its subject knows that episodes of this sort are, in general, reliable indicators of the presence of white objects in standard conditions. Otherwise, she would not be able to reflectively recognize the authority of that episode.

The implications of this for traditional empiricism are straightforward, and devastating (EPM 36). As we saw earlier, traditional empiricism's reliance on the Myth of the Given requires that experiential episodes count as cases of knowledge of a kind that presuppose no other knowledge. Given Sellars' view of epistemic authority, however, there can be no such thing as knowledge that presupposes no other knowledge. In particular, experiential episodes can count as knowledge only if the subject *knows that* episodes of the relevant sort are, in general, authoritative. Contrary to traditional empiricism, therefore, experiential episodes cannot count as cases of basic knowledge. Traditional empiricism fails, because it is incompatible with giving our capacity for reflection the central place in our epistemic lives that it deserves.

3.2 *P. F. Strawson*

Strawson's *The Bounds of Sense* (1966; hereafter BoS) came at a time when Kant's work was no longer considered relevant by most analytic philosophers, and its goal was to show that this attitude was mistaken. Strawson's project was to extract what he considered to be the timeless philosophical insights of the *Critique of Pure Reason* from its idiosyncratic metaphysical framework, thus making them more accessible to his contemporaries. Although the faithfulness of Strawson's reconstruction to the original has been repeatedly questioned, his work played a major role in analytic philosophy's renewed interest in Kant.

According to Strawson, Kant's core project in the *Critique of Pure Reason* is one of conceptual analysis. In particular, its aim is an analysis of the concept of *experience* (BoS 15):

> It is possible to describe types of experience very different from the experience we actually have. But not any purported and grammatically permissible description of a possible kind of experience would be a truly intelligible description. No philosopher has made a more strenuous attempt than Kant on . . . the investigation of the set of ideas which forms the limiting framework of all our thought about the world and experience of the world.

According to Strawson, Kant's aim is to discover those features of our experience which are essential to it, in the sense that any phenomenon that lacked those features would no longer be recognizable as experience. Such features cannot be discovered empirically, for example through an investigation of the physiology of experience. They cannot be discovered in this way, because we can imagine creatures whose physiology is wildly different from ours, but which are still capable of experience. The essential features of experience are, rather, to be discovered by an analysis of the *concept* of experience itself.

Why should this project seem important, however? Why should it matter that there are limits to how much variation our concept of experience allows for? Strawson's answer is that these limits correspond to a set of commitments about the nature of the world and the extent of our knowledge of it, which we have no choice but to accept.[29]

This thought motivates the strategy of so-called *transcendental argument*.[30] A transcendental argument typically is formulated in response to a sceptical challenge. For example, a traditional sceptic about the external world might argue that our subjective experience cannot justify us in believing that there is a world independent of our subjective conscious states, because our subjective experience might be just the same even if there were no such world. More precisely, according to this sceptic we cannot trust our subjective experience as a guide to the external world unless we have some prior reason to believe that there really is such a world, and that we gain glimpses of it in experience. But, the sceptic continues, what prior reason do we have for that belief?

Transcendental arguments of the type Strawson outlines do not aim to *answer* the sceptic's question. Rather, they seek to show that the question is in some sense illegitimate. They seek to turn the tables on the sceptic, by bringing to light commitments the sceptic has already taken on by using the concept of experience. In particular, according to Strawson, Kant purports to show that using this concept entails commitment at least to the existence of an objective spatio-temporal world, independent of our conscious states, which is partially revealed to us in experience. If this is correct, then there would seem to be something seriously wrong with the sceptic's suggestion that our experience might be just the same, even though there were no external world: the existence of the external world is, on this view, entailed by the claim that we have experience at all.

Philosophical opinion remains divided over the prospects of transcendental arguments in general, and of particular transcendental arguments in the literature. We will not enter into such disputes here; interested readers should consult the 'Further reading' section. It is, rather, time to turn to the conceptual claim Strawson attributes to Kant – namely, the claim that our concept of experience is the concept of a type of episode or state that partially reveals the layout of an objective world, independent of our conscious states.

On the face of it, this claim is startling. It does not seem hard to conceive of creatures whose stream of consciousness is like a dream, a series of sensations lacking any internal connection to each other or to any independent reality. Certainly, many philosophers – sceptics and non-sceptics alike – have not shied away from describing our *actual* experience in such terms. So how does Kant, according to Strawson, argue for his view? We only have space here to discuss this argument in barest outline, beginning with Strawson's own summary (BoS 87):

> We shall find that its fundamental premise is that experience contains a diversity of elements (intuitions) which, in the case of each subject of experience, must somehow be united in a single consciousness capable of . . . conceptualizing the elements so united. We shall find that its general conclusion is that this unity requires another kind of unity . . . on the part of the multifarious elements of experience, namely just such a unity as is also required for experience to have the character of experience of a unified objective world.

The fundamental premise of Kant's argument, as Strawson reads it, is a claim about the intellectual capacities that are necessary for experience. We rely on experience to construct a more or less coherent world-picture.

Thus, it must be possible for us to unite a series of experiences in a 'single consciousness'; for example it must be possible for me to hold together in consciousness the way things looked a second ago and the way things look right now, so as to compare the two and potentially make sense of any differences that come to my attention. The capacity to do this, as Strawson points out, essentially involves a capacity for *reflection*: a capacity to *ascribe* these experiences to myself. Strawson's fundamental premise, therefore, is that experience is inconceivable without a capacity for reflection. His conclusion, then, follows from a further argument – the details of which we cannot consider here – that ascribing experiences to oneself requires thinking of each of them as a partial and perspectival glimpse of an objective world, i.e., of a world whose existence and character is independent of our subjective states.

4. Conclusion

In closing this chapter, we should take note of some Kantian features that Sellars and Strawson share, and which have become characteristic of a loose neo-Kantian strand in analytic philosophy. In fact, given Kant's highly abstract and idiosyncratic handling of these ideas, it may well be that they can be more readily grasped when encountered in the more concrete settings given to them by his followers.

Both Sellars and Strawson follow Kant in placing special emphasis on *experience* as a source of knowledge about the world. They both also follow Kant in denying that experience is a cognitively *simple*, or *presuppositionless*, form of contact with the world. If experience is to fulfil its epistemic role, then it must involve fairly complex capacities on the part of the experiencing subject. Of course, it is not controversial that experience requires complex capacities at either the physiological level or the level of sub-personal information-processing. But this is not what Sellars and Strawson argue. Following Kant, they argue that experience requires capacities at the conceptual level, and in particular a capacity for *reflection*. In Kantian terms, experience requires the involvement not just of *sensibility*, but also of the *understanding*.

But we should also note a divergence from Kant, which Sellars, Strawson and their contemporary followers share. Kant conceived of his project as an investigation into the foundations of the metaphysics of sensible nature and of physical science. According to Kant, physical science is about the world of our experience. From this, as we saw, he inferred that an investigation into our faculty of knowledge would also reveal the fundamental principles on which physical science is based (the principles of pure understanding). Contemporary philosophers do not follow Kant on this. This is because they would not accept his premise, at least not without serious qualifications. As twentieth century scientific developments made clear, the world as revealed by physical science need not bear any resemblance to our experience of it. Aligning our common sense picture of the world with physical science is a difficult challenge for recent and contemporary philosophers in a way that it was not for their counterparts before the twentieth century.[31]

Notes

1   References to the *Critique of Pure Reason* follow the pagination of the first (A) and second (B) editions; quotations are from the Norman Kemp Smith translation (Kant, 2007), modified on occasion. References to Kant's other works follow volume and page of the German Academy of Sciences edition (Kant, 1902–).

2   John Locke, *An Essay concerning Human Understanding* I.1.4–7. Citations follow book, chapter and section of the text, and the pagination in the Nidditch edition (Locke, 1975).

3   Locke alludes to these difficulties as the impetus for his *Essay*; see its 'Epistle to the Reader' (Locke, 1975: 7). For an illustration of how fundamental problems of metaphysics might engender endless debate, consider his remarks about whether mind and body could causally interact (*Essay* IV.iii.6; Locke, 1975: 542).

4   This is the overarching theme of the *Critique*'s second-edition 'Preface'; see also A 3/B 6–7, and B 22–4. However, the problem of sorting out what we can legitimately say about some morally significant topics in metaphysics (such as freedom of the will, the existence of God, and the immortality of the soul) gets a full treatment only in the *Critique of Practical Reason* (see Kant, 1902–), where Kant draws out the implications of his distinction between theoretical and practical knowledge. Our topic in this chapter is Kant's epistemology with regard to the *theoretical* employment of reason (i.e. in regard to our reasoning about what is the case in the domain of nature); we will bracket the fact that, for Kant, there must also be an epistemology for the *practical* employment of reason (i.e. in regard to our reasoning about what to do). Likewise, the metaphysics at issue

in this chapter is only the metaphysics of material nature; Kant pursues a meta-physics of morals in other work. For the distinction between theoretical and practical knowledge, see B ix–x, A 633/B 661, and *Critique of Practical Reason* (5: 56).

5 Supersensible objects were deemed *intelligibilia* or *noumena* – objects of the intellect alone – in contrast to sensible objects, called *sensibilia* or *phenomena*.

6 For examples of this general strategy, see Descartes' 'Meditation V', in *Meditations on First Philosophy* (Descartes, 1996), or what was pursued under the heading of 'natural theology' in the German metaphysics with which Kant was most familiar – e.g., in the selections from Christian Wolff and Alexander Baumgarten in Watkins (2009).

7 Kant's epistemology excludes the possibility of our having theoretical knowledge of supersensible objects, or noumena. In 'Phenomena and Noumena' (A 235–60/B 294–315), Kant points to this result as the guiding principle of his ensu-ing adjudication of the errors of traditional metaphysics in the 'Transcendental Dialectic'. Although the epistemological import of Kant's distinction between phenomena and noumena are relatively clear, its metaphysical implications are much less so. We will not go into this topic here.

8 *Enquiry concerning Human Understanding*, §IV.1 (Hume, 2000: 24).

9 The examples are somewhat controversial. Hume takes mathematics to consist entirely of analytic truths, and offers as his examples the identity thought in the Pythagorean theorem and '*That three times five is equal to the half of thirty*' (*Enquiry concerning Human Understanding* §IV.1: Hume, 2000: 24); he does not display much interest in other types of putatively analytic truths under the heading of 'relations of ideas'. Kant wholly disagrees with Hume's assessment of mathematics; this should be evident already from Kant's endorsement of the view, already noted above, that mathematics is (as it were) the language of nature. Kant takes the bulk of our mathematical knowledge to be 'synthetic', making an exception only for propositions like 'the whole is equal to itself' or 'the whole is greater than its part' (B 14–17).

10 'Propositions of this kind, are discoverable by the mere operation of thought, without dependence on what is any where existent in the universe' (*Enquiry concerning Human Understanding*, §IV.1; Hume, 2000: 24).

11 Exactly how the distinction between analytic and synthetic judgement is to be drawn is a vexed question in Kant interpretation. For our purposes we do not need to enter into these debates, except to note that it is generally agreed that while analytic judgements concern the content of our concepts, synthetic judge-ments concern real objects.

12 In the course of the Preface and Introduction to the *Critique*, Kant shows that the initial problem about metaphysics can be transposed into this more general question about the possibility of synthetic *a priori* knowledge.

13 In this sense, the *Critique* simply makes explicit principles which we tacitly employ in our ordinary cognitive dealings with the world. It may then seem,

Kant says, that the *Critique* was not worth the effort if it only teaches us 'what, in the merely empirical employment of understanding, we should in any case have practiced without any such subtle inquiry' (A 237/B 296). But this positive account of our cognitive capacity can then be used to adjudicate the errors of traditional metaphysics in the latter half of the *Critique*. Later, Kant argues that Hume's attempt at a similar project failed because empiricism lacks the resources to provide an account of our 'necessary ignorance' on certain matters. Such an account of our cognitive *incapacity* can only rest on an exhaustive account of our cognitive *capacity*, which can only be completely specified through a battery of principles that necessarily determine anything that can figure as a sensible object for us at all. Since empiricism cannot accommodate synthetic *a priori* principles, Kant maintains, it lacks the resources to provide the exhaustive account on which the denial of 'dogmatic metaphysics' must rest (see A 738–69/B 766–97).

14 There are further complications in Kant's conception of the intellect, which need not concern us here. In short, Kant distinguishes between three aspects of the 'higher cognitive faculty' or intellect, of which understanding is only one (A 130/B 169).

15 'In a word, Leibniz *intellectualised* appearances, just as Locke . . . *sensualised* all concepts of the understanding' (A 271/B 327).

16 Kant also refers to them as 'pure concepts of the understanding'. This name indicates that they do not contain any empirical representations in them at all (see the account of the term 'pure' at B 2–3), and that they are constitutive of the understanding (see Kant's gloss on pure intellectual concepts at *Jäsche Logic* 9: 94).

17 See especially *Essay* I.iv.18 (Locke, 1975: 29).

18 The genesis of these concepts is not what interests Kant in the *Critique*. However, he denies that the categories are innate; he hints at this at A 86/B 118, and is explicit about it in 'On a discovery' (8: 221–3). For interpretation of this point, see Waxman (1991) and Longuenesse (1998).

19 Kant expresses the general point about reflection as a principle regarding the 'synthetic unity of apperception' in §§16–17 of the Transcendental Deduction. Although Kant explicitly identifies the terms 'pure apperception' and 'reflection' (*Überlegung, Reflexion*) in *Anthropology from a Pragmatic Point of View* (Kant 1902–, 7: 134n.), the implications of this have only begun to be examined in recent commentary. See Henrich (1989), Smit (1999), Merritt (2009).

20 So, for example, Frege argued at length against Kant's view that arithmetic is synthetic, while the logical positivists struggled with the apparently empirical refutation (by Einstein's theory of relativity) of Euclidean geometry's claim to describe physical space. We will not consider this early history here. It has been extensively documented elsewhere (see 'Further reading' section).

21 Strawson's *Individuals* (1959) is an original work in metaphysics, heavily influenced by his reading of Kant. In this chapter we will concentrate, however, on *The*

Bounds of Sense (Strawson, 1966), which is more exegetical in nature. Sellars' most detailed direct discussion of Kant is in *Science and Metaphysics* (Sellars, 1968). In this chapter, however, we will focus on his 1956 essay 'Empiricism and the philosophy of mind' (reprinted as Sellars, 1963a).

22 Sellars does not make it entirely clear which philosophers he thinks fall under this label, but it seems fair to say that Locke, Hume, and several of the Logical Positivists would all fit the bill, and all are at least obliquely invoked in EPM.

23 As Sellars notes, different versions of traditional empiricism embody different conceptions of basic knowledge, not all of which are expressible by 'looks' statements. Sellars devotes §§10–30 of EPM to discussing 'looks' statements.

24 Sellars thinks that empiricists are not the only ones to have been taken in by the Myth of the Given (EPM §0). For present purposes, however, we will only focus on the empiricist version of the Myth.

25 Although this view is controversial, it is not part of our aim here to evaluate it. There is also controversy as to how Sellars argues for it. According to some, Sellars relies on a general principle according to which an episode or state can only give reason for a belief if its content could function as a *premise* in an argument in support of that belief. It is, however, doubtful whether Sellars subscribes to this principle. For one thing, he identifies the idea that experience provides premises as an instance of the Myth of the Given (see e.g. EPM 32). For another, in later work Sellars suggests that the conceptual content of experiential episodes is *not* propositional in form. On this later view, experiential episodes have sub-propositional content; for example, facing a cube in broad daylight I might have an experience with the content 'this cube' (Sellars, 1968: 5). Since only propositions can function as premises, this suggests that Sellars did not think that the epistemic role of experience rests on its ability to provide premises.

26 Sellars suggests a way to turn these considerations into a general argument against all forms of traditional empiricism (EPM 14–19), but he does not seem to place much weight on it. We will set it aside for present purposes.

27 The notion of reliability has enjoyed plenty of time in the epistemological spotlight since the time of Sellars' essay. Reliabilism – the attempt to give an account of knowledge or justification in terms of reliability – remains an influential project today. Sellars anticipates reliabilism, but he does not endorse it; indeed, he also anticipates some of the most influential arguments against it. For a discussion of reliabilism, see Chapter 10 of the present volume.

28 This, as we saw earlier, is a Kantian thought too: Kant emphasized that our capacity for knowledge depends on our capacity to be aware of our judgements and their subjective sources, and to defend and adjust them in response to demands of coherence.

29 These commitments are what, in Strawson's picture, correspond to Kant's principles of the pure understanding. Making them explicit is the task of the project

Strawson in *Individuals* (1959) calls 'descriptive metaphysics'. Note that, whereas for Kant the principles of the pure understanding are synthetic *a priori*, what in Strawson's system corresponds to them would be *analytic* – they are discoverable by analysis of the concept of experience.

30 This title was coined by Barry Stroud (1982) to refer to the style of argument Strawson attributes to Kant. It has been questioned whether Kant really relies on this type of argument in the *Critique of Pure Reason*, and even whether responding to scepticism (the purpose for which transcendental arguments are typically used) was especially high in Kant's agenda (see Engstrom, 1994). For present purposes we will not go into this debate.

31 For a classic statement of the problem, see Sellars (1963b).

Further reading

There are many editions of Kant's work to choose from. The standard scholarly edition is the multi-volume German Academy of Sciences edition currently published by Walter de Gruyter (Kant 1902–). Any good edition of Kant's work in English will include the German Academy pagination in the margins of the text, since the standard way of citing Kant's texts is by volume and page of the Academy edition (with the exception of the *Critique of Pure Reason*, which is cited according to the pagination in the first and second editions of 1781 and 1787 respectively). Translations vary, and it is good practice to consult several, if possible. A good place to start is with the English translations in the ongoing Cambridge Edition of the Works of Immanuel Kant, edited by Paul Guyer and Allen W. Wood.

For a more summary statement of some of the core ideas of the *Critique of Pure Reason*, see Kant's 1783 *Prolegomena to Any Future Metaphysics*; and for the metaphysics of nature that is promised by the epistemological project of the *Critique*, see his 1786 *Metaphysical Foundations of Natural Science*. (These are in Kant, 1902–.)

The secondary literature on Kant's *Critique* is vast. A classic work with a strong focus on epistemology is Allison (2004). For a recent collective commentary, see Guyer (2010). For Frege's engagement with Kant on arithmetic, see his *The Foundations of Arithmetic* (1950). The history of the logical positivists' relation with Kant is extensively discussed by Michael Friedman, in the essays collected in Friedman (1999).

Sellars presented his reading of Kant as his 1966 John Locke Lectures at the University of Oxford. They were subsequently published as *Science and Metaphysics* (Sellars, 1968). For commentaries on EPM, see Brandom (1997) and deVries and Triplett (2000).

For the debate on transcendental arguments see Stroud (1982), as well as the essays in Stern (1999). Transcendental arguments of a similar style, though not necessarily with a focus on experience, have been used by various philosophers, both earlier and later than Kant. For recent examples, see Davidson (1984) and Putnam

(1981). Strawson restates his position on the topic in *Skepticism and Naturalism* (1985).

John McDowell's *Mind and World* (1994) is probably the most famous contemporary work in analytic philosophy that explicitly draws on both Kant and Sellars. McDowell's views on Kant and Sellars are further elaborated in several essays (McDowell, 2009).

References

Allison, H. E. (2004), *Kant's Transcendental Idealism: An Interpretation and Defense*, 2nd edn. New Haven: Yale University Press.

Brandom, R. (1997), 'Study guide', in Sellars (1997), pp. 119–81.

Davidson, D. (1984), 'On the very idea of a conceptual scheme', in his *Inquiries into Truth and Interpretation*. New York: Oxford University Press, pp. 184–98.

Descartes, R. (1996 [1641]), *Meditations on First Philosophy with Selections from the Objections and Replies*, revised edn, (ed.) J. Cottingham. Cambridge: Cambridge University Press.

deVries, W. A. and Triplett, T. (2000), *Knowledge, Mind, and the Given: Reading Wilfrid Sellars's 'Empiricism and the Philosophy of Mind'*. Indianapolis: Hackett.

Engstrom, S. (1994), 'The transcendental deduction and skepticism', *Journal of the History of Philosophy*, 32, 359–90.

Frege, G. (1950 [1884]), *The Foundations of Arithmetic: A Logico-Mathematical Enquiry into the Concept of Number*, (ed. and trans.) J. L. Austin. Oxford: Basil Blackwell.

Friedman, M. (1999), *Reconsidering Logical Positivism*. Cambridge: Cambridge University Press.

Guyer, P. (ed.) (2010), *The Cambridge Companion to Kant's Critique of Pure Reason*. Cambridge: Cambridge University Press.

Henrich, D. (1989), 'Kant's notion of a deduction and the methodological background of the first Critique', in E. Förster (ed.), *Kant's Transcendental Deductions: The Three Critiques and the Opus Postumum*. Stanford: Stanford University Press, pp. 29–46.

Hume, D. (2000 [1748]), *An Enquiry concerning Human Understanding*, (ed.) T. L. Beauchamp. New York: Oxford University Press.

Kant, I. (1902–), *Gesammelte Schriften*, (eds) German Academy of Sciences. Berlin: Walter de Gruyter (and predecessors).

—(2007 [1781/1787]), *Critique of Pure Reason*, 2nd edn, trans. N. K. Smith. Basingstoke: Palgrave Macmillan.

Locke, J. (1975 [1690]), *An Essay concerning Human Understanding*, (ed.) P. H. Nidditch. Oxford: Clarendon Press.

Longuenesse, B. (1998), *Kant and the Capacity to Judge: Sensibility and Discursivity in the Transcendental Analytic of the Critique of Pure Reason*, (trans.) C. T. Wolfe. Princeton: Princeton University Press.

McDowell, J. (1994), *Mind and World*. Cambridge, MA: Harvard University Press.

—(2009), *Having the World in View: Essays on Kant, Hegel and Sellars*. Cambridge, MA: Harvard University Press.

Merritt, M. (2009), 'Reflection, enlightenment, and the significance of spontaneity in Kant', *British Journal for the History of Philosophy*, 17, 981–1010.

Putnam, H. (1981), *Reason, Truth and History*. Cambridge: Cambridge Univesity Press.

Sellars, W. F. (1963a), 'Empiricism and the philosophy of mind', in his *Science, Perception and Reality*. London: Routledge & Kegan Paul, pp. 127–96. (Reprinted as Sellars, 1997.)

—(1963b), 'Philosophy and the scientific image of man', in *Science, Perception and Reality*. London: Routledge & Kegan Paul, pp. 1–40.

—(1968), *Science and Metaphysics: Variations on Kantian Themes*. London: Routledge and Kegan Paul.

—(1997), *Empiricism and the Philosophy of Mind*, including 'Study Guide' by R. Brandom. Cambridge, MA: Harvard University Press.

Smit, H. (1999), 'The role of reflection in Kant's Critique of Pure Reason', *Pacific Philosophical Quarterly*, 80, 203–23.

Stern, R. (ed.) (1999), *Transcendental Arguments: Problems and Prospects*. Oxford: Clarendon Press.

Strawson, P. F. (1959), *Individuals: An Essay in Descriptive Metaphysics*. London: Methuen.

—(1966), *The Bounds of Sense: An Essay on Kant's Critique of Pure Reason*. London: Methuen.

—(1985), *Skepticism and Naturalism: Some Varieties*. New York: Columbia University Press.

Stroud, B. (1982), 'Transcendental arguments', in R. C. S. Walker (ed.), *Kant on Pure Reason*. Oxford: Oxford University Press, pp. 117–31.

Watkins, E. (ed. and trans.) (2009), *Kant's Critique of Pure Reason: Background Source Materials*. Cambridge: Cambridge University Press.

Waxman, W. (1991), *Kant's Model of the Mind: A New Interpretation of Transcendental Idealism*. New York: Oxford University Press.

CHAPTER 8

AMERICAN PRAGMATISM: FALLIBILISM AND COGNITIVE PROGRESS

Christopher Hookway

According to Hilary Putnam, one central goal of pragmatism is the reconciliation of anti-scepticism and fallibilism (Putnam, 1994: 152). Anti-scepticism is not just the claim that the familiar sceptical challenges of Pyrrhonism and the Cartesian philosophy can be defeated. It normally takes the stronger form of holding that these challenges do not even need to be addressed philosophically. If we find ourselves taking sceptical challenges seriously, we have already gone wrong. Fallibilism involves the recognition that our methods of forming our opinions are not proof from error. Even our best scientific theories may need to be revised as our knowledge develops. Since Cartesian approaches to philosophy construct reasons for doubt from the fact that we often make mistakes and that even our most confident opinions cannot be secure from error, it can seem that a commitment to fallibilism provides the material that are needed for the development of arguments for scepticism.

If Putnam is right, then we should expect pragmatist philosophers to provide explanations of why philosophers do not need to worry about scepticism. They should also provide frameworks for an epistemology which can account for our confidence in our cognitive achievements while recognizing the fallibility of the methods of inquiry that we employ. This chapter will explore how these themes are developed in the work of some of the most important classical pragmatists. In doing this, we shall be concerned with their responses to the Cartesian tradition in philosophy.

The pragmatist tradition originated in the United States in the 1870s, in the meetings of a Metaphysical Club in Cambridge Massachusetts (Menand, 2001). Members of this club included the philosophers Charles Sanders Peirce and William James, as well as a number of lawyers and other intellectual figures. The third 'classic pragmatist' was John Dewey, and contributions to pragmatism were made by a number of other thinkers, including C. I. Lewis, the idealist Josiah Royce, and (outside the United States) F. P. Ramsey.[1] The differences between these thinkers can sometimes appear as striking as their similarities. James, Dewey, Lewis and other pragmatists tend to recognize Peirce as the original pragmatist, although it was James who did most to introduce pragmatist ideas to wider philosophical debate. Although most pragmatists have made contributions to epistemology, we shall concentrate on the classic pragmatists, beginning by examining Peirce's response to pragmatism, his rejection of foundationalism, and his emphasis on the importance of *inquiry* as a central concept in responding to epistemological issues. The second half of the chapter will introduce a number of different ideas which have been used by pragmatists in their attempts to defend fallibilism while giving no weight to sceptical arguments.

1. Peirce and the spirit of Cartesianism

Discussions of epistemological issues are found in the earliest published writings of all the classical pragmatists. The three papers by Peirce that were published in 1868 and 1869 in the *Journal of Speculative Philosophy* are often interpreted as a 'critique of Cartesianism' (Bernstein, 2010: 32ff.) or as an attack on 'the modern epistemological framework' (Cooke, 2006: 7). Peirce's writings on the logic of inquiry provide an argued rejection of the Cartesian approach to knowledge, and they defend an approach to epistemology which was distinctive and original.

The second of these papers, 'Some consequences of four incapacities' (EP1: 28–55), starts by describing the 'spirit of Cartesianism', listing four epistemological theses, all of which Peirce rejected. The first is that 'philosophy must begin with universal doubt' (EP1: 28): we are justified in believing propositions only if it is not possible to doubt them. The second is the individualist claim that 'the ultimate test of certainty is to be found in the individual consciousness' (EP1: 28). In each case, Peirce emphasizes that each of these theses was an innovation, marking a break with scholastic thought and, probably, with common-sense and the successful sciences. The third mark of Cartesianism is that '[t]he multiform argumentation of the middle ages is replaced by a single thread of inference depending often upon inconspicuous premises' (EP1: 28). It is a consequence of this that, if any one of the premises upon which a belief depends is rejected, then this provides a reason for doubting the proposition believed. This may provide support for the first thesis: it does not take much for us to have reasons for doubt which will need to be defeated.

The fourth thesis (EP1: 28) will concern us less than the first three. Peirce holds that Cartesianism must find many important facts 'absolutely inexplicable', unless they can be grounded in God's contribution to making them so. Perhaps he is thinking about Descartes' strategy of making our confidence in clear and distinct ideas depend upon the benevolence of God. All of the pragmatists will reject all of these theses. We shall examine the first three of them in turn, focusing on the arguments employed by different pragmatists, and tracing the consequences for epistemology of agreeing with the pragmatist stance.

2. Scepticism and the method of doubt

The method of doubt requires us to try to suspend judgement in all things: we are justified in our beliefs only if we have conclusive reason for believing them. So the lack of conclusive reasons for some belief itself constitutes a reason for doubting it. In early writings, Peirce showed no sympathy for the method of doubt. 'We cannot begin with complete doubt' (EP1: 28). We have no alternative to beginning with the 'prejudices' that we possess when we begin doing philosophy (EP1: 28–9). These prejudices 'are things which it does not occur to us *can* be questioned' (EP1: 29). Cartesian doubt 'will be a mere self-deception, and not real doubt'. Philosophers who doubt propositions on the basis of the Cartesian challenges will experience 'pretend doubt' rather than 'real doubt'.

As it stands, this is not compelling: the mere fact that we are psychologically incapable of believing a proposition does not establish that there is not sufficient reason for doing so; it does not establish that we already possess knowledge. However, we may read Peirce as identifying some views about our current practice of forming and defending beliefs that conflict with some underlying assumptions of Descartes' arguments. First, he recognizes that we sometimes do rationally come to doubt what we had previously believed, but, when this occurs, we have positive reason to do so. We do not simply rely on the principle that we abandon any belief for which we lack conclusive reason. Once again, this begs the question: whether lack of reason for belief constitutes a reason for doubt is precisely what is at issue.

However, Peirce supplements his rejection of the method of doubt by identifying other features of the methods employed in the 'successful sciences' (EP1: 29) which depart from Cartesian procedures. The latter, we noted his saying, 'teaches that the ultimate test of certainty is to be found in the individual consciousness' (EP1: 28). He first rejects the individualist component of this 'most pernicious' view (EP1: 29). We can identify four elements in the pragmatist rejection of these views. We can only seek truth in philosophy for 'the *community* of philosophers' (EP1: 29). If 'disciplined and candid minds' refuse to share our views, that gives us reason for doubt. But, once we have stable agreement, 'the question of certainty becomes an idle one'. And he also calls on philosophers to 'imitate the successful sciences in its methods' (EP1: 29):

> [We should] proceed only from tangible premises which can be subjected to careful scrutiny, and to trust to the multitude and variety of its arguments than to the conclusiveness of any one. Its reasoning should not form a chain which is no stronger than its weakest link, but a cable whose fibres may be ever so slender, provided they are sufficiently numerous and intimately connected.

So long as we are careful in our reasoning, we can trust fallible methods of belief formation, probably in the hope that any errors will eventually surface and be corrected; but we can do this responsibly only as members of a community of inquirers. We don't *need* to employ the Cartesian method.

As we have seen, this combination of anti-scepticism and fallibilism is characteristic of pragmatist thought. Both James and Dewey share this outlook with Peirce. His writings from the 1860s and 1870 also develop two other pragmatist epistemological strategies which echo throughout the work of the other classical pragmatists. One of these involves identifying, and criticizing, philosophical views which lead us to find Cartesian approaches to epistemology. The other is found in some of Peirce's most influential papers, 'The fixation of belief' and 'How to make our ideas clear', the first two of a series of papers on 'The logic of science' in 1877 and 1878.[2]

3. Peirce's critique of foundations and intuitions

Peirce presents his anti-sceptical, fallibilist outlook as a consequence of four conclusions which were defended in 'Questions concerning certain faculties claimed for man', the first of the *Journal of Speculative Philosophy* papers (EP1: 11–27). Peirce identified four cognitive capacities whose possession was required by Cartesian strategies and then argued that we do not possess any of these four capacities.

We can begin (as Peirce does, in the second of those papers) by describing the four capacities in question (EP1: 28–30):

1. Philosophers such as Locke and Hume (see Chapter 6 of this book) relied upon introspection in order to show that the contents of our minds include impressions and ideas. Peirce denied that we had any powers of introspection: our knowledge of the 'internal world' arises from an inference to the most plausible explanation of external facts about our behaviour.
2. Foundationalist epistemologists hold that our knowledge is grounded in what Peirce calls 'intuitions'. An intuition is a belief, or perhaps some other kind of cognition that is 'not determined by a previous cognition of the same object, and therefore so determined by something out of the consciousness' (EP1: 11). This may correspond to epistemological conceptions of 'the given'. There are no absolute first premises, nor are there any other states (such as the possession of a simple sense datum) which are determined solely by the 'transcendental object'. Descartes' method of doubt appears to be a tool for identifying intuitions. Since the question of whether we have intuitions cannot be settled by introspection, it must be settled by hypothetical reasoning: psychological phenomena show that many beliefs or experiences

which *appear* to be intuitions result from tacit or explicit reasoning. We have no power of intuition: every cognition is determined logically by previous ones. All our beliefs and experiences are influenced by the background beliefs which provide a context for our thinking.

3. For early modern philosophers such as Hume and Locke (again see Chapter 6), thought is a matter of 'ideas', primarily simple ideas which bear their contents on their sleeves. Peirce argues that, if we are to study the world of internal thought on the basis of external facts, we will conclude that all thought is in signs, grounded in external facts (see Bernstein, 2010: 32ff).

4. For scepticism to be taken seriously, we have to recognize that how things *really are* need not be as they appear to us. We may inhabit a world of things in themselves whose properties and relations may not be knowable to us. This requires us to *understand* the possibility of there being things which are 'absolutely incognizable' (EP1: 30).

So far, we have identified some negative theses: pragmatist approaches to epistemology take seriously the fact that we tend not to take scepticism seriously. And we have seen that Peirce rejects a number of views which may be necessary for adopting Cartesian foundationalist strategies in epistemology. His critique of intuitions has much in common with Sellars' rejection of the *given* (see Chapter 7). Most of the pragmatists share the practice of rejecting scepticism by criticizing philosophical views which make foundationalism and scepticism attractive.

Peirce then gives an early version of his account of *reality* (EP1: 52):

> The real, then, is that which, sooner or later, information and reasoning would finally result in, and which is therefore independent of the vagaries of me and you. Thus, the very origin of the conception of reality shows that this conception essentially involves the notion of a COMMUNITY, without definite limits, and capable of an indefinite increase of knowledge.

It is an important element in this way of thinking about reality that we are fallible: whatever we believe now may not be what we will believe if we continue investigating the matter. Any of our beliefs could turn out to be mistaken in its account of the realities. But it is compatible with this that reality is *knowable* in principle.

So far we have examined some negative theses defended in Peirce's writings from the late 1860s. These have been influential in the development of pragmatism. Even more influential were the first two papers (mentioned above in Section 2) in a series published in the *Popular Science Monthly*, under the title *Illustrations of the Logic of Science*: again, 'The fixation of belief' and 'How to make our ideas clear' (EP1: 109–41).

4. Inquiry and the method of science

'The fixation of belief' is a study of the 'guiding principles' we should employ in regulating our beliefs. For the most part, our logical principles are manifested in habits of reasoning, and logical theory attempts to explain which habits of reasoning are good ones. Peirce argues that the most important and fundamental logical principles are those that can be derived from the facts we take for granted when we ask the question which standards of reasoning we should adopt.

Most contemporary epistemologists study these issues by asking what is required for being justified in believing a proposition or by explaining when we possess knowledge. Pragmatist epistemologists have generally formulated their problems rather differently. There are facts that are already taken for granted when we ask the 'logical question' of what guiding principles we should expect. These include the fact that there are such states as belief and doubt, 'that a passage from one to the other is possible . . . and that this transition is subject to some rules which all minds are alike bound by' (EP1: 113). Moreover, belief is a stable, settled state which guides our desires and shapes our actions (EP1: 114). But doubt 'is an uneasy and dissatisfied state from which we struggle to free ourselves and pass into the state of belief' (EP1: 114). The term 'inquiry' is used for this struggle. So Peirce employs the framework of belief, doubt and inquiry in order to identify the fundamental guiding principles.

Peirce then argues that the only method of inquiry which is compatible with the presuppositions of the logical question is what he calls 'the method of science'. He relies on the assumption that the aim of inquiry is, simply, settled belief. We might suppose that our goal is *true* belief, but, since it is a tautology that whenever we believe a proposition we believe it to be true, this additional requirement has no pragmatic significance (EP1: 115). The method of science yields stable belief, at least in the long run. Other methods that Peirce considers fail to yield settled belief; their use inevitably leads to doubt of our opinions. For example, the method of tenacity involves adopting any proposition one pleases and then sticking to it through thick and thin. This method fails because it cannot guarantee that we will not encounter people who have other opinions, and disagreement naturally gives rise to doubt. The fundamental hypothesis of the method of science is this (EP1: 120):

> There are real things, whose characters are entirely independent of our opin-
> ions about them; those realities affect our senses according to regular laws,
> and, though our sensations are as different as our relations to the objects, yet,
> by taking advantage of the laws of perception, we can ascertain by reasoning
> how things really are, and any man, if he have sufficient experience and reason
> enough about it, will be led to the one true conclusion.

Most of the pragmatists sought to use the method of science in inquiries in all areas of inquiry, although there may be differences in how they understood the method of science.

Exactly what is involved in the method of science? And why should we trust in its outcomes? Peirce described the method of science as involving three phases which, in his earlier work, he identified with three kinds of arguments: abduction, deduction and induction. As we have seen, inquiry begins with a problem, most often a doubt. The doubt may arise from the fact that our current stock of beliefs leads to perceptual surprise, to unexpected results, or it may arise because we seek explanations of observed regularities. The first phase, abduction, is concerned with identifying hypotheses or solutions to problems which are worth taking seriously; it is the process of forming an explanatory hypothesis. Peirce discusses the sorts of considerations that should guide us in this: we should take guidance from the sorts of theories that have proved helpful in related areas of inquiry (EP1: 189); the 'economy of research' (EP2: 109) considers how we should, for example, first assess hypotheses that can be easily tested, and we should hope that we possess a capacity for guessing right (EP2: 107–14; see Cooke, 2006: 39ff.; Hookway, 1985: 222f.).

Having identified a hypothesis we wish to test, we can use deductive reasoning to make predictions about the experiential results we would expect our observations or experiments to have if the hypothesis was true. Inductive reasoning then evaluates the hypothesis by examining whether our predictions about the results of our experiments are confirmed. Peirce has a distinctive account of why it is rational to trust inductive reasoning. He does not hold that inductive reasoning can be trusted to yield conclusions that are true or even probable. Rather, induction is to be trusted because it is self-correcting. This is clear in what Peirce calls 'quantitative induction' (EP2: 103). Conclusions reached by inductive reasoning are fallible; but if they are mistaken, further inductive reasoning will, eventually, reveal the error and arrive at a more accurate conclusion. This is clearest in 'quantitative induction': although my first estimate of how many of the beans in a sack are white may be mistaken, further sampling will lead eventually to a more reliable assessment. Qualitative induction resembles this kind of quantitative induction: we test hypotheses by sampling the predictions that can be made on the basis of the hypothesis. This provides reason for trusting induction, while endorsing the fallibilist claim that any belief we now hold on the basis of induction may turn out to be mistaken.

Even if most everyday inductions are reliable, the conclusions we reach at the cutting edge of scientific research are probably more likely to be refuted than to stand the test of time. This leads Peirce to argue, like Popper (1972), that we should not *believe* our current scientific opinions. Scientific acceptance may consist in the recognition that some proposition is assertable at the current stage of inquiry, while involving no confidence that it will continue to be so as our knowledge and understanding develops.

5. William James: contextualism and conservatism

5.1 Conservatism

James's discussions of the rationality of belief introduce ideas which have become important for epistemology. The first is a doctrine that has already been mentioned in connection with Peirce's rejection of scepticism. Sometimes we can defend our beliefs by offering reasons for holding them. But more often we trust our settled beliefs without being able to explain why we now have reason for holding them or why we acquired them in the first place. As we saw, the argument of Descartes'

'Meditation I' holds that if we lack positive justification for a belief, then this itself constitutes a reason for doubting it. Epistemic conservatives reject this Cartesian assumption. Beliefs are justified unless we have positive reason for doubting them:

> If someone already believes some proposition, then they are prima facie rational in continuing to believe it.

We need reasons for our beliefs when we first acquire them or when someone has suggested that there is reason to doubt them. Why are we justified in ignoring the sorts of hypothetical reasons for doubt which are proposed by proponents of scepticism? Epistemic conservatism holds that beliefs are justified unless there is a positive reason for doubting them. This opens up a range of interesting issues about just what constitutes a reason for doubting a stably held belief. Why are we justified in ignoring the sorts of hypothetical reasons for doubt which are proposed by proponents of scepticism?

James accepts a principle of doxastic inertia in his 1906/7 lectures on *Pragmatism*, especially in lecture II in which he explains 'What pragmatism means' and introduces his pragmatist account of truth. Acknowledging the influence of Schiller and Dewey, he considers how we arrive at new opinions, concluding that the process by which this occurs is always the same (1907: 34–5):

> The individual has a stock of old opinions already, but he meets a new experience that puts them to a strain. Somebody contradicts them; or in a reflective moment he discovers that they contradict each other; or he hears of facts with which they are incompatible; or desires arise in him which they cease to satisfy. The result is an inward trouble to which his mind till then had been a stranger, and from which he seeks to escape by modifying his previous mass of opinions. He saves as much of it as he can, for in this matter of belief we are all extreme conservatives. So he tries to change first this opinion, and then that . . . until at last some new idea comes up which he can graft upon the ancient stock with a minimum disturbance of the latter.

Similar views are defended by a contemporary pragmatist, Isaac Levi, who defends a principle of doxastic inertia: 'there is no need to justify current beliefs, only changes in belief' (Levi, 1998: 78).

This form of conservatism is often defended by philosophers sympathetic to the common-sense tradition (see EP2: 346–54 on Peirce's 'critical common-sensism'). It is also found in Wittgenstein's *On Certainty* (1969) (see Chapter 9) and it is sometimes assumed by epistemologists defending externalist views of justification and knowledge (see Chapter 10). It is also found in the writings of pragmatist philosophers such as Isaac Levi and Peirce (Hookway, 2008). Peirce calls upon philosophers 'not [to] pretend to doubt in philosophy what we do not doubt in our hearts' (1868, EP1: 29). Later, in 1906, he wrote that 'what one does not doubt cannot be rendered more satisfactory than it already is' (Peirce, 1935: paragraph 498).

As already mentioned, James's commitment to the principle of doxastic inertia is evident from his lectures in *Pragmatism*. The conservatism is manifest when we preserve 'the older stock of truths with a minimum of modification, stretching them just enough to make them admit the novelty, but conceiving that in ways as familiar as the case leaves possible' (James, 1907: 35).

The insistence on this form of conservatism, this preservation of the 'older stock of belief', is very important for James. He suggests that taking this seriously was indispensable if we are to recognize what is wrong with many of the criticisms made of pragmatism. Indeed, he says that loyalty to the older truths 'is the first principle in revising and forming our beliefs rationally' (1907: 35). Pragmatism's critics are disturbed by the suggestion that there is no independent or objective *constraint* upon what we believe: perhaps, they suggest, we can reasonably accept anything which it suits our needs to believe. Rationalists and some other realists and empiricists offer different candidate explanations of why and how our opinions are constrained by reason, or by the facts, or by experience. Loyalty to the older facts provides another kind of constraint. They reflect what we know (fallibly) about reality and our determination to be loyal to these older facts and thus indicate that we want to revise our beliefs in a way that preserves what we take ourselves to know. We trust our beliefs until given reason to doubt them, not whenever we think it would suit us to change them.

5.2 Contextualism

Epistemic contextualism, the view that how much justification is required for us to be warranted in our beliefs depends upon context, has been much discussed in recent years (e.g. DeRose, 1992). What is the evidence that William James would have favoured this position?

The place to begin is 'The will to believe', James's response to W. K. Clifford's account of 'The ethics of belief'. James is responding to one of the fundamental principles of Clifford's paper. According to Clifford (1886: 346):

> It is wrong always, everywhere, and for any one, to believe anything upon insufficient evidence.

For Clifford, this rule is an ethical principle: Belief 'is desecrated when given to unproved and unquestioned statements, for the solace and private pleasure of the believer' (1886: 343). Such belief is 'sinful'. As is well known, Clifford used this principle to mandate agnosticism about religious matters.

James's paper argues that, in appropriate circumstances, it can be rational or appropriate to form or retain beliefs when you possess relatively little, or even no, relevant evidence. His argument rests upon identifying the particular circumstances in which belief can be formed on 'passional grounds'. In identifying these circumstances, he is specifying the sort of context in which belief may be legitimate when we have no or little relevant evidence.

James specifies the contextual requirements for such belief to be legitimate (1897: 2–4, 11). One requirement is that the correctness of the belief in question cannot be settled intellectually. Others concern the practical urgency of settling whether to endorse the proposition in question, and the lack of alternative courses of action which do not depend upon this belief. This urgency can depend upon the risks involved in suspending judgement in the proposition in question or in arriving at a belief which is in fact false.

A contextualist response to Clifford's position can take two different forms. One is to observe that the term 'sufficient evidence' is very vague. We may suppose that, in different contexts, different amounts of evidence will count as sufficient: someone may argue that the amount of evidence that would be sufficient for a casual belief where the risk of error has little weight would be insufficient when engaging in, for example, medical research. In that case, we could continue to endorse the principle as it was formulated by Clifford, but deny that it has the consequences which Clifford expects it to have. Alternatively, James could hold that Clifford's principle is applicable in some circumstances but not in others. As we shall see, James's response is of the second of these kinds.

In section VII of 'The will to believe', James writes (1897: 17):

> There are two ways of looking at our duty in the matter of opinion, – ways entirely different, and yet ways about whose difference the theory of knowledge seems hitherto have shown very little concern. *We must know the truth*; and *we must avoid error.*

These 'two separable laws' (1897: 17), 'Believe truth!' and 'Shun error!', can be in tension, and 'by choosing between them we may end by coloring differently our whole intellectual life' (1897: 18).[3] James's view is that in some contexts we should give prominence to one of these laws, and in other contexts we should rely upon the other. We want to obtain truth and we want to avoid falsehood, and we weigh these desiderata differently in different contexts.

In science, he tells us, 'and even in human affairs in general, the need of acting is seldom so urgent that a false belief to act on is better than no belief at all' (1897: 20). In science, we value the avoidance of error more than obtaining truth: we can wait to reach the truth. But '*Moral questions* immediately present themselves as questions whose solution cannot wait for sensible proof' (1897: 22). And the 'Law courts, indeed, have to decide on the best evidence attainable for the moment, because a judge's duty is to make law as well as to ascertain it' (1897: 20). James presents the issue by saying that there are two laws, and we can only follow one of them on any specific occasion, so we need an account of *which* we should follow. A more plausible kind of pragmatism would hold that we have, not two laws but rather two values which carry different weights in different circumstances, making use of Bayesian ideas and decision theory. Although James's way of describing the issue may have to be rejected, it is evidently a precursor of these more sophisticated views.

We have seen that one distinctive feature of pragmatist epistemology is that it is primarily concerned with the normative standards we should adopt for the conduct of inquiry. Inquiry is a problem-solving activity. Peirce describes it as the struggle to replace *doubt* by settled belief. This perspective is in line with the fallibilism which is defended by most pragmatists, and it marks a difference from familiar epistemological projects that focus on knowledge, certainty and justified belief. The idea that logic is 'the theory of inquiry' was central to the philosophy of John Dewey (1938), and it was developed in ways that differ from Peirce's.

6. Dewey on inquiry

John Dewey's work in this area is most manifest in a book such as *Logic: The Theory of Inquiry* (1938). His account of inquiry is significantly different from Peirce's. The latter sees inquiry as beginning with doubt, usually about whether to believe some proposition, and concludes in settled belief. Dewey, by contrast, holds that 'Inquiry is the controlled or directed transformation of an indeterminate situation into one which is so determinate in its constituent distinctions and relations as to convert the elements of the original situation into a unified whole' (Dewey, 1998, vol. 2: 171). We start with a problem, not knowing our way around; and inquiry comes to an end when we no longer find our situation problematic. Dewey insists that it is the whole situation which is problematic and which needs to be transformed by successful inquiry. It is not concerned simply with changing our mental states, our beliefs and our questions. Inquiry is concerned with the external *situation* and it aims to transform the situation, making it whole again. And where Peirce is primarily interested in the possibility of *scientific knowledge* and is impressed by the fact that current scientific views are provisional, likely to be revised in the course of our attempt to understand how things are, Dewey is primarily interested in how we can use intelligence to solve social and political problems, and with inquiry into how such problems can be solved. Indeed Dewey complains that many philosophers treat scientific knowledge as the paradigm case of serious inquiry: early modern philosophers such as Hume construct an account of knowledge of facts, based upon experience, and then conclude that 'knowledge' of values is second rate, failing to meet the standards used in the most advanced science. By contrast, according to Dewey, 'the conception that scientific judgments are to be assimilated to moral is closer to common sense than is the theory that validity is to be denied of moral judgments because they do not square with a preconceived theory of the nature of the world to which scientific judgments must refer' ('Practical character of reality' in Dewey, 1908: 132).

7. The pragmatist maxim

So far, we have identified some distinctive epistemological views defended by philosophers who are known to be pragmatists. We have identified a number of views, associated with Peirce, James and Dewey, that fit Putnam's observation that pragmatists typically embrace fallibilism while rejecting scepticism. We can now examine the philosophical views which are most distinctive of pragmatism and see how they contribute to these epistemological views. It is important here that the classical pragmatists all held views that were broadly empiricist. Peirce described his views as a kind of 'prope-positivism', and James described his position as 'radical empiricism'. However their position has a distinctive character: they all have a conception of experience which is much richer than would be accepted by traditional empiricists such as Hume (see Chapter 6). They recognize that we directly (although fallibly) perceive external objects, and our experience presents things as interacting causally with other things and as instantiating laws. Peirce models experience on experiment: in experiencing our surroundings, we are agents, eliciting experiences by interfering with our surroundings in order to see what happens; and in doing so we exploit our background knowledge and conceptual repertoire. Like John McDowell (1994), Peirce holds that our experience is shaped by concepts, describing our perceptual judgements as 'the extremest case of Abductive Judgment' (EP2: 229).

Pierce identified pragmatism with a logical maxim for clarifying ideas and theories and William James connected this with his pragmatism which he referred to as 'Peirce's Principle'. The content of a concept is elucidated by examining the effects of its objects, concentrating upon those which might, in principle, make a difference to what is rational for us to do. 'Our conceptions of these effects', he says 'is the whole of our conception of the object' (EP1: 132). All the information that can be relevant to the use of a concept in conversation of inquiry can be elicited in this way. There is nothing to the content of a concept apart from statements of how it affects what is rational for us to do, and since our activities, including inquiries, are regulated by experience, this means that we clarify our understanding of a proposition by identifying how we should expect its truth to make a difference to the experiential results we would expect our action to have in the context that we occupy.

These views have important implications for epistemology. Pragmatist clarifications are valuable in two different ways. First, if we can't find any 'practical consequences' that a concept or proposition can have in any circumstances, then we can conclude that the concept or proposition in question lacks content. This enables Peirce to undermine the Kantian concept of a 'thing in itself'. A priori 'ontological metaphysics' is dismissed as of no value for the same reason. The same holds of the concepts of truth and reality which were employed by Descartes in employing the method of doubt, as is the idea of real things whose only impact upon knowers is the production of what Peirce calls 'intuitions'. Generally we know about external things because they interact with us in law-like ways and give rise to patterns of experience which are best explained as effects of these things.

What does pragmatism have to say about truth and reality? Can we make sense of the importance these concepts have in identifying our aims in inquiry? Or must we recognize that these goals do not have the importance we take them to have? James was happy to recognize that we seek truth and that truth consists in an agreement with reality. But he gives this a pragmatist formulation. He holds that *'ideas . . . become true just in so far as they help us to get into satisfactory relation with other parts of our experience'* (1907: 34). A true proposition is one that it is *'good in the way of belief, and good, too, for definite, assignable reasons'* (1907: 42). Having said that, he allows that what we take to be true at one time may turn out not to be true as more experience comes in. Whether that is enough to explain what our aim in inquiry is remains unclear. Peirce uses his pragmatist maxim to come up with a more sophisticated account of truth, one that recognizes the mind-independence of reality without leaving reality too remote from our beliefs and experiences for us to use it as a goal. In 'How to make our ideas clear', he explains how he 'would explain reality': 'The opinion which is fated to be ultimately agreed to by all who investigate, in what we mean by the truth, and the object represented in this opinion is the real' (EP1: 139). The reality of something depends upon its being knowable, in principle, if only we can inquire well enough and are sufficiently fortunate in obtaining relevant evidence in the medium term. But it is not determined by what any individual or group of people actually believes. So we *can* obtain knowledge of the truth, so long as we come to believe what anyone would be fated to believe who understood the proposition in question. But we can also recognize that any of our beliefs could, in principle, turn out to be mistaken.

This does mean that we can never be absolutely certain that we have reached a belief that any inquirer would eventually converge on if they inquired for long enough. Often we can be sure that we have reached such a belief, especially in connection with everyday beliefs concerning ordinary matters. In other circumstances we can reasonably *hope* that we will accept a proposition only when it is true, while aware that if we are mistaken, we could, in principle, learn that this is the case. But whether we have succeeded is not a decidable matter. Richard Rorty (2000), following Donald Davidson, concludes, from the fact that fallibilism means that we cannot recognize whether we have succeeded, that truth cannot be our aim. At best, our cognitive goal must be to arrive at beliefs that meet prevalent standards of justification, or to arrive at beliefs that will obtain the acceptance of those that we admire and respect. Dewey similarly seems to adopt cognitive goals other than truth. Our aim is always to solve the problem that prompts us to inquire; we are content when we unify the elements of the indeterminate situation; but we do. And we are not surprised when new problems arise. Our inquiries arise within particular contexts and our responses are evaluated within that context too. Inquiry ends when we reach a state of 'warranted assertability', but this need not involve any assurance of truth.

Notes

1 We lack space to discuss the work of all these thinkers or that of more recent philosophers whose views have a pragmatist character. De Waal (2005) provides a very useful guide to the pragmatist tradition, and Talisse and Aikin (2008: ch. 2) complement the discussion of this chapter.
2 For further discussion on scepticism and pragmatism, see Olsson (2005), Cooke (2006), and Hookway (2008).
3 In the first of the 1906/7 lectures, James explores 'The present dilemma of philosophy' (1907: 9ff.), arguing that one's philosophical outlook (whether one is an empiricist or a rationalist, whether one is a determinist or a believer in free will, and so on) is a product of temperament or character. Empiricists tend to be 'tough-minded' while those who believe in free will are 'tender-minded'. This supports his general claim that our beliefs can be formed on the basis of 'passional considerations', our epistemic standards being expressed in passional responses.

Further reading

Since there is an extensive literature on and by pragmatist philosophers on epistemological matters, we can only mention a small sample of the literature here. A good place to start is the helpful chapter on Pragmatist Epistemology in *Pragmatism: A Guide for the Perplexed* by Robert Talisse and Scott Aikin (London: Continuum, 2008), a book which also provides a general account of background to pragmatist philosophy. *Peirce's Pragmatic Theory of Inquiry: Fallibilism and Indeterminacy* (London: Continuum, 2006) by Elizabeth F. Cooke, provides a detailed analysis of Peirce's epistemological views. John Dewey's *The Quest for Certainty* is one of his more readable works, complementing his *Logic: The Theory of Inquiry*. James Tiles's *Dewey* (London: Routledge, 1988) is a helpful guide to this. Graham Bird's account of James's philosophy can provide helpful guidance too: *William James* (London: Routledge & Kegan Paul, 1986). A work that links classical pragmatism with more contemporary discussions is C. I. Lewis' *Mind and the World Order: Outline of a Theory of Knowledge* (New York: Dover, 1929) which offers a pragmatist twist on Kantian epistemology, and defends a pragmatist account of the *a priori*.

A large number of philosophers illustrate contemporary uses of pragmatist ideas. *New Pragmatists* (Oxford: Clarendon Press, 2007), edited by Cheryl Misak, contains some excellent examples of this, as does Susan Haack's systematic defence of a Peircean approach to epistemology: *Evidence and Inquiry: Towards Reconstruction in Epistemology* (Oxford: Blackwell, 1993). Alan Malachowski's *The New Pragmatism* (Durham: Acumen, 2010) provides a useful account of some recent developments in pragmatism, especially those involving Richard Rorty and Hilary Putnam. Other contemporary philosophers who have been influenced by pragmatism include Robert Brandom and Huw Price.

References

Bernstein, R. J. (2010), *The Pragmatic Turn*. Cambridge: Polity Press.

Brandom, R. B. (ed.) (2000), *Rorty and His Critics*. Malden, MA: Blackwell.

Clifford, W. K. (1886 [1879]), 'The Ethics of belief', in his *Lectures and Essays*, 2nd edn, (eds) L. Stephen and F. Pollock. London: Macmillan and Co., pp. 339–63.

Cooke, E. F. (2006), *Peirce's Pragmatic Theory of Inquiry: Fallibilism and Indeterminacy*. London: Continuum.

De Waal, C. (2005), *On Pragmatism*. Belmont CA: Wadsworth.

DeRose, K. (1992), 'Contextualism and knowledge attributions', *Philosophy and Phenomenological Research*, 52, 913–29.

Dewey, J. (1908), 'Does reality possess practical character?', in *The Middle Works of John Dewey, 1899–1924*, vol. 4: 1907–1909. Carbondale, IL: Southern Illinois University Press, pp. 125–42.

—(1938), *Logic: The Theory of Inquiry*. New York: Henry Holt and Company. Also published as (2008), *The Later Works of John Dewey, 1925–1953*, vol. 12, (ed.) J. A. Boydston. Carbondale, IL: Southern Illinois University Press.

—(1998), *The Essential Dewey*, 2 vols, (eds) L. A. Hickman and T. M. Alexander. Bloomington: Indiana University Press.

Hookway, C. (1985), *Peirce*. London: Routledge & Kegan Paul.

—(2008), 'Peirce and skepticism', in J. Greco (ed.), *The Oxford Handbook of Skepticism*. Oxford: Oxford University Press, pp. 310–29.

James, W. (1897), *The Will to Believe and Other Essays in Popular Philosophy* (reprinted version). New York: Dover Publications.

—(1975 [1907]), *Pragmatism: A New Name for Some Old Ways of Thinking*. Cambridge, MA: Harvard University Press.

Levi, I. (1998), 'Pragmatism and change of view', in C. J. Misak (ed.), *Pragmatism. Canadian Journal of Philosophy*, Supp. Vol. 24, 177–201.

McDowell, J. (1994), *Mind and World*. Cambridge, MA: Harvard University Press.

Menand, L. (2001), *The Metaphysical Club: A Story of Ideas in America*. New York: Farrar, Straus, and Giroux.

Olsson, E. J. (2005), *Against Coherence: Truth, Probability, and Justification*. Oxford: Clarendon Press.

Peirce, C. S. (1935), *Collected Papers vol 6: Scientific Metaphysics,* (eds) C. Hartshorne and P. Weiss. Cambridge, MA: Harvard University Press.

—(1998), *The Essential Peirce*, two volumes, (ed.) The Peirce Edition Project. Bloomington and Indianapolis, IN: Indiana University Press. (References take the form 'EPn: m' giving volume n and page m.)

Popper, K. R. (1972), *Objective Knowledge: An Evolutionary Approach*. Oxford: Clarendon Press.

Putnam, H. (1994), *Words and Life*, (ed.) J. Conant. Cambridge, MA: Harvard University Press.

Rorty, R. (2000), 'Universality and truth', in Brandom (2000), pp. 1–30.

Talisse, R. B. and Aikin, S. F. (2008), *Pragmatism: A Guide for the Perplexed*. London: Continuum.

Wittgenstein, L. (1969), *On Certainty*, (eds) G. E. M. Anscombe and G. H. von Wright. Oxford: Basil Blackwell.

CHAPTER 9

WITTGENSTEIN ON KNOWLEDGE
Paul Snowdon

Ludwig Wittgenstein was born in Austria in 1889 and died in England in 1951. His intellectual roots were European, but a large part of his philosophical life was spent in Cambridge. He published the gnomic and compressed *Tractatus Logico-Philosophicus* in 1922. It presents a conception of the essence of language and of the world. But a number of years after that he renounced his earlier views and developed a new approach both to philosophy and to language. The most important presentation of his new views is in the posthumously published *Philosophical Investigations*. His intellectual life is, in consequence, normally divided into an early and a later period. He is acknowledged to be one of the giants of early-twentieth-century philosophy, along perhaps with Gottlob Frege and Bertrand Russell (the latter's presence in Cambridge was what took Wittgenstein there originally). He is someone whose system of thought has struck many people as correct, both during his lifetime and since, and it has continued to attract the attention even of philosophers who are not inclined to believe it, because of its originality and brilliance. The present essay aims to introduce, and scrutinize, some of the ideas about epistemology that he can be interpreted as proposing in his later period.

In his earlier philosophical period Wittgenstein, in fact, seems not to have been engaged by issues in epistemology at all. He was, rather, fascinated by language and the world, and their relations. Once he changed his views epistemology became a significant interest for him. However, there is a sense in which knowledge never became something of *primary* focus for him until towards the end of his life. Wittgenstein became obsessed with the writings of G. E. Moore and made the notes that were collected in *On Certainty*. Rather, the primary focus of Wittgenstein in the second part of his life was things such as language, meaning, rules, private experience, thought, action, seeing, mathematics and so on. (It is hard to give a *general* characterization of the topics that he primarily focussed on.) His aim was basically to remove what he saw as the errors that traditional bad philosophy generates in thinkers, without replacing these errors with new and supposedly correct theories. This can be summed up by saying that he is fundamentally a negative thinker.[1] In most of his later philosophical writings he does not *directly* target misconceptions about knowledge (or related epistemological notions). We might suspect that this reflects the fact that Wittgenstein himself did not really feel the pull of scepticism. Instead in the course of his engagement with these *other* primary topics he introduces and relies on some ideas which can be called 'epistemological'. I want to first describe some of these general ideas (and what became of them) before analysing in more detail the results of his concentrated engagement with epistemology in *On Certainty*.

1. Epistemology in the later philosophy

We are accustomed to philosophers analysing knowledge. Wittgenstein does not do that. He tends to be sceptical about our ability to define terms. Nor, it seems to me, does Wittgenstein in any concentrated way try to combat scepticism, which is the second standard task for epistemologists. At least, he does not do this before *On Certainty*. What Wittgenstein does is to assume that scepticism is incredible, hence to take it as a constraint that any account of the phenomena with which he is dealing must be consistent with that assumption. His commitment to the idea that the revisions which the sceptic is proposing are wrong can be related to his general negative approach to philosophy. What he thinks of as good philosophy leaves, as he puts it, everything as it is, apart from the errors that bad (i.e. traditional) philosophy produces. These are eliminated or exorcised. Clearly, this general conception requires Wittgenstein to be happy with the positive knowledge ascriptions we standardly make. It can also be said that if philosophy does not add to human knowledge then it will not provide unobvious analyses of anything, including of knowledge itself. It stands out though that it makes it difficult to draw consequences from the assumption that our positive knowledge ascriptions are correct if there is no theory of knowledge to draw on. The suspicion deserves voicing that, despite offering no explicit positive account of knowledge, Wittgenstein relied at times on an implicit picture of it which shaped some of the proposals he made.

I have represented Wittgenstein's anti-scepticism as a consequence of his negative conception of philosophy. But at a certain level in his later thought there is a positive element. Wittgenstein exorcises bad philosophy by persuading us not to adopt it. This method involves us in following certain arguments and so agreeing with their conclusions. There must be a positive level. In his positive thinking about language in general it can be said that the two most important concepts are those of use as determinative of meaning and the idea of the use of expressions as being like games we play according to rules. The use we make of expressions, in the language games we play, determines their meaning. So when Wittgenstein focuses on epistemological language he tries to say how it is used and what the rules of our epistemological talk are.

To convey some of Wittgenstein's central ideas about knowledge I want to start by saying something about his employment of the term 'criterion', a term that Wittgenstein frequently employs, and one that became central to a tradition of thought about knowledge which drew its inspiration from him. I also want to single out some claims he made about some specific sorts of knowledge.

2. Wittgenstein's general views

2.1 Criteria
In *The Blue Book* Wittgenstein introduces, in thinking about knowledge, the distinction between criteria and symptoms. These remarks give every appearance of being Wittgenstein's explication of the term

'criterion'. Thereafter the notion of criteria is, as we shall see, often employed by him in developing arguments and stating theses. It is, perhaps, the term that is most investigated when discussing Wittgenstein's approach to knowledge, and which has been taken up in a tradition of thinking about epistemology that would regard its inspiration as Wittgensteinian. Wittgenstein's account proceeds in three stages. In the first stage he starts by making some remarks about knowledge of other minds. It is worth noting that it is most often in relation to knowledge of other minds that Wittgenstein talks about knowledge and criteria. Knowledge of minds, one's own or more usually of others, seems to have been the case that fascinated him.

Wittgenstein starts *The Blue Book* by saying this (1958: 24):

> When we learnt the use of the phrase 'so-and-so has toothache' we were pointed out certain kinds of behaviour of those who were said to have toothache. As an instance of these kinds of behaviour let us take holding your cheek. Suppose that by observation I found that in certain cases whenever these first criteria told me a person had toothache, a red patch appeared on the person's cheek.

Now, Wittgenstein then points out that if I claim that someone has a toothache on the basis of seeing the red patch and I am asked how I know that red patches mean that someone has a toothache I can cite the coincidence between the red patch and holding the cheek. But he also says that if I am asked why holding the cheek means the subject has toothache we shall be at a loss and that we have hit the point where it is right to talk about conventions.

In the second stage Wittgenstein introduces the terminology of criteria and symptoms. The core idea of criteria is twofold. The criterion for a certain feature is something that if it is determined to obtain means conclusively that the feature is present. That is an epistemological aspect. But further giving the criterion counts as defining what the condition is. That is, so to speak, a conceptual feature. The contrasting notion is that of the symptoms for a feature; these are conditions that observation leads one to regard as a sign of the presence of the feature.

Finally, Wittgenstein claims that with actual cases of natural language, since our languages are not 'precise calculi' we cannot say what tests that we employ are the criteria for our terms and what merely the criteria. After that Wittgenstein moves onto other matters.

Where, then, do these remarks leave us as regards understanding the term 'criterion'? I want to make three points. First, when Wittgenstein points out that with most terms in natural language we could not say what the criteria are he seems to imply that the notion of criterion has no actual determinate application. This must leave us wondering how the notion can be central to epistemology. Second, in his treatment of the lead-in case Wittgenstein seems to have a strongly behaviourist conception, as it were, from the very beginning. He says that we can talk about conventions when considering why holding one's cheek indicates toothache. But no-one would be inclined to say that the relevance of holding one's cheek flows from conventions. Wittgenstein is simply assuming here that the sentence is assigned its role – or use – in terms of applying it if there is cheek holding. Third, given how 'criterion' is explained there seems to be no room for the idea of a defeasible criterion, that is to say, a case where the criterion is satisfied, but the indicated feature is not present. And yet in the tradition that has grown out of Wittgenstein's employment of the talk of criterion the idea of defeasibility has been made central.

The notion of criterion is however central to all Wittgenstein's subsequent discussion of knowledge and language. It figures at crucial stages in the formulation both of arguments and of theses. In the famous private language argument (one of the most discussed parts of the *Philosophical Investigations*), in which Wittgenstein is opposing a traditional philosophical conception of the essentially private nature of sensory experience, his argument against the possibility of a private language rests on the absence of any criterion for correctness of use with a private language. Further, in developing a contrasting conception of sensation language he says that 'an inner process stands in need of outer criteria'. Again, in the rule following discussion he repeatedly raises questions about criteria for claims we make.

The major general questions about Wittgenstein's later epistemology are about what real content this talk of criteria has, and what justification Wittgenstein has for the claims he is making. The suspicion in relation to content is that Wittgenstein is close to endorsing a condition for the intelligibility of language akin to the condition of verifiability. Thus, when he talks of a private language as needing (but necessarily lacking) a criterion for correctness does he mean that the speaker must be able to verify that he or she is using the words correctly? If not, what does he mean? If that is what is meant then it leaves his claims and arguments open to the charge that verificationism is highly implausible. There seem to be many claims I can understand and which may be true, which I cannot verify. For example, I cannot verify that God exists, but I seem to understand the claim. So, a central worry is making sense of talk of criteria without lapsing into verificationism. A second problem is that there seems to be an alternative model of language as theoretical, in which sense is grounded without conclusive tests for truth.

Wittgenstein's talk of criteria was developed in two ways. A representative of the first development is Norman Malcolm. He argued that since meaning required that terms (in particular, psychological terms) are linked to criteria, scepticism about other minds is incoherent. The sceptic understands the claims he is doubtful about, but says that we cannot know whether they are true. But simply in virtue of mastering the criteria he must be able to know in some circumstances that they are true. It seems clear, though, that something close to a verificationist approach to meaning is assumed in this argument. The second development is one according to which expressions are linked to criteria, but it is in principle possible that a claim for which the criteria are satisfied is not true. Criteria are defeasible. But if the criterion is satisfied and the claim happens to be true, then that amounts to the subject's knowing it is true. The satisfaction of (defeasible) criteria in the right circumstances yields knowledge. This conception is developed by Gordon Baker (1974) and Crispin Wright (1982), and it faces the crucial question that John McDowell (1998 [1982]) raised as to how knowledge can be generated on the basis of criteria fulfilment where that is in fact no guarantee of truth. How can that yield knowledge even in the true case? There are then problems with understanding Wittgenstein's general approach and about its subsequent development.

2.2 Wittgenstein on psychological knowledge
In many ways Wittgenstein's focus in relation to knowledge (and the grounds of our claims) is on psychological knowledge.

He wonders about how we ground our psychological ascriptions, especially first-personal ones. Here is a typical remark dealing with backward-looking ascriptions of intention (1953: sec. 635):

'I was going to say . . .' – You remember various details. But not even all of them taken together shew your intention. It is as if a snapshot of a scene had been taken, but only a few scattered details of it were to be seen: here a hand, there a bit of a face, or a hat – the rest is dark. And now it is as if we knew quite certainly what the whole picture represented. As if I could read the darkness.

In relation to this Wittgenstein has, in a way, three general themes. One is the rejection of the traditional model of psychological self knowledge. The old picture was that one self-ascribes in virtue of the recognized presentation within consciousness of the appropriate mental item – say a belief or an intention. By extended probing Wittgenstein reveals this as hopeless. Second, he emphasizes the relevance of circumstances to the grounding of psychological ascriptions. According to him what makes a psychological claim true is, often, elements in the context. Third, he explores the idea that our very propensity for self-ascription contributes to the truth of what we say. Putting it very crudely, it is true that I acted for a certain reason because I answered the question 'Why did you do it?' in that way.

For Wittgenstein an especially interesting case is that of knowledge of sensations – the prime example being pain. When considering this Wittgenstein famously says (1953: sec. 246):

> If we are using the word 'to know' as it is normally used (and how else are we to use it?), then other people very often know when I am in pain. – Yes, but all the same not with the certainty with which I know it myself! – It can't be said of me at all (except perhaps as a joke) that I *know* I am in pain. What is it supposed to mean – except perhaps that I *am* in pain?

In this famous passage in the *Philosophical Investigations* Wittgenstein affirms his anti-sceptical stance, a stance that we, no doubt, endorse. But he combines that with a denial that I can know that I am in pain. On this conception, knowledge of pain belongs to those *not* feeling the pain. This seems implausible. It seems quite clear that a person suffering from a migraine does realize that he or she has a suffering. Further, such a person can also realize that the pain is easing when it does, and so on. People monitor and keep track of their own sensations, and their knowledge of it figures in their practical thinking. Someone can decide to go to the dentist because he knows that he has toothache. We seem to talk of people knowing this kind of thing. Why does Wittgenstein make this rather incredible denial of knowledge? There are, perhaps, two factors. The first is that we do not often remark that someone knows they are in pain. As far as talking is concerned we ascribe pain, and we would rarely add that the subject knows, or so much as raise a question about the subject's knowing. However, the question is what explains this lack of use. Wittgenstein, thinking, as he does, of language use as akin to a game, tends to interpret restrictions on use as reflecting basic rules 'of the game'. There is however a more obvious explanation along lines famously suggested by Paul Grice (1989). We assume that people who are in pain know that they are in pain and so once we have conveyed that someone is in pain, we do not need to add the extra information that they know, since we generally talk in ways that are relevant and efficient. Further, Grice brought out, that the fact that we speak within these constraints itself explains how implications are generated by what we say. If I say to someone that the Provost is not drunk today – a remark which is perfectly true – they would infer that it was worth saying, and hence news, and so infer, quite incorrectly, that he was often drunk. Applying this sort of explanation puts the idea that people know about their own pains in the category of the obvious, rather than the category of the mistaken. Second, Wittgenstein provides a justification for his view in the following remark (1953: sec. 246):

> The truth is: it makes sense to say about other people that they doubt that I am in pain; but not to say it about myself.

We can read into this remark an assumption that the role of knowledge-ascriptions is to rule out something – namely the presence of doubt as to some matter. The general idea is that a term gets its function by ruling out something. The specific assumption is that knowledge-ascriptions rule out doubt. The problem with this justification is that it is not obvious that we should contrast knowledge with doubt. The more obvious candidate would be ignorance. Knowledge ascriptions exclude ignorance. If so then the fact that no one has doubts as to whether they are in pain does not imply that it is inappropriate to talk of knowledge.

Wittgenstein, then, seems to distort how we should think of self knowledge.

3. On Certainty

A repeated feature of Wittgenstein's later writings is that he engages with the thoughts of a great figure, for example, St. Augustine, or

Sigmund Freud, or James Frazer, or Wolfgang Kohler.[2] His approach tends to be that of agreeing with the famous thinker on some important matter, but of disagreeing about why things are the way they are agreed to be. This is the pattern exhibited by *On Certainty*, which is Wittgenstein's most extensive discussion of knowledge. In this book the great thinker who is its stimulus is G. E. Moore.[3] Wittgenstein is, we are told in the preface by the editors, responding to two of Moore's most famous articles – namely, his 'Proof of the external world' (hereafter PEW) and his 'In defence of common sense' (hereafter DCS).[4] Indeed, this is obviously true. *On Certainty* (hereafter OC) is the record of Wittgenstein's response to these papers of Moore.

It needs pointing out that *On Certainty* is simply a collection of notes that Wittgenstein made over a period late in his life.[5] He did not prepare them for publication. It is obvious that they are simply evolving thoughts about a topic. Wittgenstein is uncertain, and repetitive – debating with himself. Here is a characteristic remark (1969: sec. 532):

> [I do philosophy now like an old woman who is always mislaying something and having to look for it again: now her spectacles, now her keys.]

Many remarks are simply questions. We should not, then, treat every remark as if it is part of something we can call Wittgenstein's account of knowledge.[6] The appropriate method here, I think, is to attach most weight to the themes he repeats, rather than to every proposal he sets down or voices. Out of these themes an approach emerges which we are entitled to think of as Wittgenstein's later view about knowledge.[7]

4. The Moorean background

To make sense, then, of Wittgenstein's discussion it is necessary to describe briefly what Moore is up to in those papers. I think that it is fair to say that in these two papers Moore is in the business of constructing his own highly original response to scepticism. This response is not yet properly understood (perhaps because it cannot be), nor evaluated. I shall restrict myself to a very brief and superficial account of Moore's arguments. In 'In defence of common sense' Moore gives a summary of some of his central philosophical convictions. The part of it that stimulated Wittgenstein is section 1. There Moore specifies a series of propositions (which set of propositions he calls (1)) all of which are, in some sense, about himself, and he claims that he knows (with certainty) them all to be true.[8] Among them are such claims as that there is a living body which is his body, and which has remained on or near the surface of the earth, which is in space, along with other bodies; the earth has itself existed for many years before that body; etc. Moore then specifies a class of claims which consists of those claims which say of other human beings what those in (1) say about Moore himself. About this class Moore states that the other human beings know (with certainty) about themselves what Moore knows about himself on the list (1). Moreover, Moore adds that he himself knows with certainty that they do know these things.

Part, then, of Moore's view is that he knows a range of things, and further knows that there are others who know the same range of things about themselves.

Moore himself supports these claims in roughly two ways. The first way is that of pointing out certain supposed oddities, or elements of paradox, in denying these knowledge ascriptions. Second, Moore claims simply that he does know all this, and he adds that he knows it on the basis of evidence or reasons, and hence not directly. He also adds that he cannot, at the time of writing, say in detail what those reasons, or that evidence is.

The second article is Moore's infamous 'Proof of the external world'. In that, Moore's so-called proof comes in the final pages of the paper. Moore argues as follows. He holds up his two hands and asserts that here are two hands. He claims that hands are external objects. He observes that it follows that there are two external objects, and that he has proved it. Moore's suggested proof has always puzzled philosophers. One worry has been that what he presents does not actually amount to a proof of the external world. A second worry has been that, even if it does, it is far from clear what significance it can have for the philosophical engagement with scepticism. If I asked myself what is Moore's purpose in PEW I would say that he is trying to show that the assertion by various philosophers that we cannot prove that there are external objects (or that such a task is remarkably difficult) is simply a mistake. Fundamentally Moore is engaged in correcting what he sees as a common error among philosophers.

I have said that these two papers are part of Moore's response to scepticism. But there is an important question that I want to raise, although not discuss. How are Moore's two papers related? It seems clear that Wittgenstein treats them as a sort of unity, but when reading his discussion we need to be aware that there may be significant differences between them.

I want to divide my presentation into two sections. The first section attempts to convey and partly evaluate what Wittgenstein thinks is wrong with Moore's approach. The second section tries to describe Wittgenstein's positive account of what is special about the claims that Moore thinks we all know.

5. Wittgenstein's criticisms of Moore

As a lead-in to the critical section we can take note of the very first remark in OC. Wittgenstein says (1969: sec. 1): 'If you do know that *here is one hand*, we'll grant you all the rest.'[9] Now, it is of course somewhat incautious to assume this first remark is one he would have maintained throughout, and incautious too to assume we know quite what Wittgenstein means by 'the rest', but it indicates the main direction of Wittgenstein's criticism. He doubts that it is correct to claim that the things that Moore thinks are known are really known, and he seems to think that should Moore be right about *that* there is nothing else to object to.

We can, though, ask how plausible it is to suppose that Moore is wrong about this. For myself I tend to think Moore does possess the knowledge he claims. I suggest, then, that we approach Wittgenstein's discussion with some resistance to the direction of his criticism. Wittgenstein would say that this simply means that I am as confused as Moore. That claim cannot be assessed without considering his reasons, but we do need to retain a sense of how *radical* Wittgenstein's attitude is.

What reasons does Wittgenstein offer for his scepticism?[10] Summarizing Wittgenstein's reasons is, in fact, very hard, and I remain unsure whether the groupings I present here are the best.

(1) At times Wittgenstein seems to think that it is Moore's view that simply saying (sincerely) 'I know that P' itself amounts to a demonstration

that there is knowledge. And he links Moore's so regarding it to Moore's thinking that knowledge is a (mental) state like being in pain where one cannot hold that one is in it without being in it. Thus Wittgenstein says (1969: sec. 178):

> The wrong use made by Moore of the proposition 'I know . . .' lies in his regarding it as an utterance as little subject to doubt as 'I am in pain'. And since from 'I know it is so' there follows 'It is so', then the latter can't be doubted either.[11]

Some philosophers, including the Oxford philosopher John Cook Wilson, may have thought this, and Wittgenstein is obviously right to criticize it. Believing that you know P does not mean that you do know. What is not obvious, though, is that Moore deserves the rebuke. In the first place, in PEW Moore does not rely on the sincere claim that he knows that here are hands. Rather, he thinks that holding up his hands for people to see gives them knowledge that there are hands. That it can do this seems undeniable. It is simply like my holding up a ticket to a ticket inspector to let him know I have one. Does Moore in DCS rely on the mistake that Wittgenstein highlights? The answer I believe is that he does not rely on this at all; he shows no inclination to think that sincerely asserting that one knows means in itself that one knows.

(2) Another theme in Wittgenstein's discussion concerns not the conditions of talking about knowledge, but the idea that the generality of some of the claims, or of the categories in those claims, that Moore considers, renders the propositions unsuitable to be objects of knowledge. Their generality makes them unfit to be facts or information that someone learns. Thus Wittgenstein says (1969: sec. 36):

> 'A is a physical object' is a piece of instruction which we give only to someone who doesn't yet understand either what 'A' means, or what 'physical object' means. Thus it is instruction about the use of words, and 'physical object' is a logical concept. (Like colour, quantity, . . .) And that is why no such proposition as: 'There are physical objects' can be formulated.[12]

Wittgenstein expresses similar worries about some other propositions that Moore focuses on.[13]

But this response goes little beyond mere assertion by Wittgenstein. He has a point in his remark that we are unlikely to say that, for example, tables are physical objects to someone who perfectly well understands the terms 'table' and 'physical object'. The question that is raised, though, is *why* we are unlikely to say that. Wittgenstein's explanation is that it does not express a proposition. An alternative explanation is that once someone understands 'table' and 'physical object', it is completely obvious that tables are physical objects, and so one would never be giving them news by *saying it* to them. Wittgenstein's attitude seems open to some comments that W. V. Quine directed at Rudolf Carnap. Quine neatly observed that the generality of a category is, as he puts it, 'only a difference in degree, and not in kind'. The most general categories in one scheme of thought might not be the most general in another. So, we are under no obligation to adopt Wittgenstein's view that such general claims are not ones we really know.[14]

(3) A recurring theme in the argument is that the cases that Moore claims to be knowledge cannot be knowledge because the subjects fail certain tests for knowledge. Wittgenstein stresses two features. 'To know' requires being able to show the claim to be true, but we cannot show that the claims that Moore lists are true. Further, the claims in question have not been investigated and we cannot really say *how we know them to be true*, which again is something that a claim to know needs backing up with. Here is one expression of this sort of argument (1969: sec. 243):

> One says 'I know' when one is ready to give compelling grounds. 'I know' relates to a possibility of demonstrating the truth. Whether someone knows something can come to light, assuming that he is convinced of it.
>
> But if what he believes is of such a kind that the grounds that he can give are no surer than his assertion, then he cannot say that he knows what he believes.

This is shortly followed by the next passage (1969: sec. 245):

> So if I say 'I know that I have two hands', . . . I must be able to satisfy myself that I am right. But I can't do that, for my having two hands is not less certain before I have looked at them than afterwards.

Now, I think that Wittgenstein's remarks along these lines in *On Certainty* give us rich food for thought. He brings out that in relation to many of the claims that Moore is talking about if we do think they are known, then we cannot infer from that description – that it is knowledge – much in the way of implications about the knower. The knower need not be able to demonstrate them, nor have any sense how he knows (or as one might say, we know), nor be able to give a reason for believing them. This is one respect in which reading *On Certainty* very successfully disturbs some common assumptions about knowledge. The question is how we should react to these observations. We can view it as evidence that Moore is wrong to talk of knowledge, or we can take it as evidence that knowledge does not require such capacities on the part of a knower. It seems more reasonable to me to conclude that knowledge can come apart from these capacities. Thus I do know that water is H_2O, but I do not know how I know it, nor can I prove it, nor can I give reasons to suppose it is. When we track knowledge we are not tracking such capacities. What then are we tracking? Wittgenstein's discussion gives that question real urgency.

(4) Wittgenstein is also impressed by the thought that there is something totally inappropriate in ascribing knowledge in the circumstances in which Moore does it. He expresses this general idea often, one case being this (1969: sec. 423):

> Then why don't I simply say with Moore 'I *know* that I am in England'? Saying this is meaningful *in particular circumstances*, which I can imagine. But when I utter the sentence outside those circumstances, as an example to shew that I can know truths of this kind with certainty, then it at once strikes me as fishy.

He immediately adds: 'Ought it to?' Here is another expression of the same type of point (1969: sec. 464):

> My difficulty can also be shewn like this: I am sitting talking to a friend. Suddenly I say: 'I knew all along that you were so-and-so.' Is that really just a superfluous, though true, remark?
>
> I feel as if these words were like 'Good Morning' said to someone in the middle of a conversation.

It is impossible here to assess this sort of remark which is so central to Wittgenstein's discussion, but it is possible to fill out his thinking. The background is thinking of language as akin to a game in which there are rules as to when to say things; these rules determine the contexts in which the words can be used. Outside those contexts such sentences, although grammatical and proper as sentences in the language, are inappropriate. He thinks that there are circumstances in which assuring someone we know something is appropriate, and where if we pass the related tests, what we say will be true. But outside those contexts such an assurance is not appropriate. Philosophers are prone to use such expressions in the wrong circumstances, and also to think of the role of such sentences in an incorrect way.

What though is Wittgenstein's positive account of what is special about Moorean propositions and what does he think we can learn from investigating them?

6. Wittgenstein's positive account

Wittgenstein puts his approach in the following words (1969: sec. 136):

> When Moore says he *knows* such and such, he is really enumerating a lot of empirical propositions which we affirm without special testing; propositions, that is, which have a peculiar logical role in the system of our empirical propositions.

What is special about them? One aspect is that no one doubts them; as Wittgenstein puts it, they 'stand fast' for us. Wittgenstein, however, thinks that they stand fast, not because we have overwhelming evidence of their truth, but because they are elements in our picture of the world, and so amount to the framework within which we do form doubts and resolve issues about other matters by attending to evidence. As he strikingly says (1969: sec. 210):

> Much seems to be fixed, and it is removed from the traffic. It is so to speak shunted onto an unused siding.

Wittgenstein calls them 'world picture propositions' and also 'hinge' propositions. Wittgenstein links this to how we would regard someone who expressed doubts about such matters or denied them. His view is that we cannot easily understand such a doubt, nor can we happily describe a denier as mistaken. These propositional attitudes are, according to Wittgenstein, restricted in application to beliefs outside the central pictures.

The description that Wittgenstein offers is more complex than that. First, he acknowledges that the system of pictures is not unchanging

(1969: sec. 97): 'the river-bed of thoughts may shift'. So there is a dynamic aspect to this feature of our cognitive lives. Second, Wittgenstein stresses that this process of removing certain claims from doubt or investigation is not based on reasons. A typical remark is this (1969: sec. 148):

> Why do I not satisfy myself that I have two feet when I want to get up from a chair? There is no why. I simply don't. That is how I act.

Wittgenstein emphasizes that our cognitive practices run along certain lines, because we simply process things that way. He talks of us as 'animals', with processes grounded in 'instinct but not ratiocination' (1969: sec. 475).

Standing back somewhat, a way to read Wittgenstein's approach is as opposing an image of human cognition that we tend to adopt when thinking about ourselves. According to this image the claims we accept and count as knowledge are backed by reasons and our acceptance of them reflects our rational response to those reasons. Wittgenstein wishes to undermine what we might call this *rationalist* image. He does so at two levels. First, when we consider many of the things we rely on or assume, they are not linked to reasons. They simply have a role for us. Second, and this can be read as part of what Wittgenstein is getting at in the rule-following debate – our ability to appreciate reasons and to react rationally to content has to be seen as resting on a more primitive level of processing, a level of brute reaction and response. The classic rationalist image overlooks both points.

Intermixed with Wittgenstein's discussion of Moore's claims to knowledge, and his further description of our cognitive nature with its attendant rejection of what I have called the rationalist image, there are remarks about scepticism. These remarks agree with Moore in rejecting scepticism, and so their discussions provide contrasting approaches to its rejection. Wittgenstein makes many remarks which are relevant, but among the most important themes are the following. He claims that any cognitive process, including the generation of doubt, requires a context of claims that are not at issue, so we cannot be universal sceptics. He says (1969: sec. 341):

> the *questions* that we raise and our *doubts* depend on the fact that some propositions are exempt from doubt, are as it were like hinges on which those turn.

He adds (1969: sec. 342):

> it belongs to the logic of our scientific investigations that certain things are *in deed* not doubted.

This is part of the point of Neurath's famous metaphor of our beliefs as a raft. There has to be something we rely on if there be any raft at all. Wittgenstein also stresses that it is impossible to separate understanding a language from assenting to empirical claims. If general scepticism is coherent then we can maintain understanding without assent, but Wittgenstein alleges we cannot do this. Thus, he says (1969: sec. 369):

> If I wanted to doubt whether this was my hand, how could I avoid doubting whether the word 'hand' has any meaning? So that is something I seem to *know* after all.

Wittgenstein also criticizes some of the pro-sceptical arguments, most notably those appealing to the possibility of dreaming. He claims that 'I cannot seriously suppose that I am at this moment dreaming.'[15] This is a claim that Malcolm developed in his discussion of dreaming and scepticism.

Now, although, as Anthony Kenny once remarked, OC is a three-cornered dialogue between Moore, Wittgenstein and scepticism, it seems to me that Wittgenstein and Moore are the major players, with the sceptic following a poor third. Wittgenstein does not really focus seriously on pro-sceptical arguments.

Space does not allow any thorough evaluation of Wittgenstein's vision of cognition. I have already expressed some doubts about his denial that we can be said to know the Moorean claims. There are two points that I wish to raise. The first is that Wittgenstein is not very clear about what exactly is special about the so-called world picture propositions. Of course we currently all assume that we have not been to Mars, but it can hardly be said that is definitive of my world picture. As I follow developments in space travel, which are, naturally, slow, I stand quite prepared to accept that someone has been to Mars, and I also stand quite prepared to believe it of myself, given suitable developments. So I feel like asking what is supposed to be special about it.

Wittgenstein does not really tell us. Second, and relatedly, Wittgenstein does not explain why the claims that are sidelined are sidelined. He gives the impression of thinking that their exclusion is somehow involved in the very practice of judgement that we acquire. But he needs to say more if we are to properly understand the model he is offering. Thus one might be inclined to suggest that my conviction that humans have two hands is simply confirmed so thoroughly that it has ceased to be a live question in the community, although individual members have to relearn it. It is not so much sidelined as simply deposited in the episte-mological bank.

There are, then mysterious aspects to Wittgenstein's epistemology, as he developed it in his later period. Perhaps, as I have suggested, he wraps a brilliant and insightful opposition to what I have called rational-ism inside some questionable and unclear claims. Perhaps more of his positive vision is sound than that. Either way, reading *On Certainty* is an intellectually disturbing experience which anyone seriously interested in epistemology should not avoid.

Notes

1 For a more developed and complicated presentation of Wittgenstein's later phi-losophy as fundamentally negative see Snowdon (2011).
2 The *Investigations* opens with a consideration of Augustine, and the 'seeing as' sections in it, perhaps, deal with the Gestalt psychologist Kohler.
3 G. E. Moore was a Cambridge philosopher, who became professor of philosophy there in 1925, and retired in 1939, to be followed by Wittgenstein. He wrote about ethics and value, notably in *Principia Ethica* (1903), introducing the idea of the naturalistic fallacy, and developing a conception of ethics in which the consequences of action determine its rightness given a pluralist conception of value. This conception influenced the Bloomsbury group, and has been debated in ethics ever since. But he was also fascinated by issues in the philosophy of per-ception and epistemology. He opposed what might be called revisionary meta-physics, such as idealism, and defended the common sense conception of the world. This aspect of Moore's thought has always puzzled readers, but it is fair to say that recently there has been a resurgence of interest in his views. Moore's and Wittgenstein's lives were closely entwined. Moore was one of the examin-ers of Wittgenstein's when he was awarded his doctorate by Cambridge, and he attended and wrote about Wittgenstein's classes.

4   These two articles can be found in Moore (1959). The 'Defence' paper dates
    from 1925, and the 'Proof' paper from 1939. The editors of *On Certainty*, G. E.
    M. Anscombe and G. H. von Wright, pick these articles out in their preface.
5   There is an interesting question which can be raised at this point. *On Certainty*
    is a sequence of notes. However, some notes are simply made by the writer as
    aides to himself or herself. But other note makers evidently have in mind the
    idea that there will be readers. Such notes are, to some extent, *for* readers. To
    which group do these notes belong? It seems to me that Wittgenstein did envis-
    age these notes as notes for others. So, although not each note can be regarded
    as a settled opinion of Wittgenstein's, they are for us to read.
6   I want in this footnote to record my impression that there is in the course of
    OC a change in the mood of the discussion. Towards the end Wittgenstein's
    writings are more concentrated on themes that are developed at length, fewer
    remarks critical of Moore are thrown out. It is as if in the course of writing the
    notes Wittgenstein has at last achieved a focus on what he felt he most needed
    to investigate.
7   The fact that some of the entries are dated very close to Wittgenstein's death
    make reading this a very poignant experience.
8   Moore does not remark explicitly on the first-person character of the proposi-
    tions. Moreover, on the list there are propositions which are, as formulated,
    not first-personal. However, Moore does describe them as about himself, and
    describes the extended list that he then constructs as ones which are about
    other people. So, he in effect treats them as first-personal.
9   Oddly Wittgenstein ignores the fact that Moore's example in PEW talks of
    hands – in the plural. Clearly, this modification does not affect the suspicion
    that he is voicing. It is also perhaps worth remarking that Moore himself never
    explains why he makes his proof rest on a claim about a pair of hands!
10 McGinn (1989: ch. 6) contains a very helpful discussion of what Wittgenstein's
    arguments are.
11 I have cited one exposition of this criticism, but it recurs a number of times in
    OC. Here are some other cases where Wittgenstein seems to be advancing more
    or less the same criticism: OC: sections 6, 15, 137.
12 Wittgenstein (1969: sec. 36). This doubt relates to the conclusion of the proof in
    PEW.
13 Section 4 of OC queries the meaning of 'I am a human being,' and section 258
    is sceptical about the meaning or significance of 'I have a body.' These are the
    kinds of things that Moore lists as known in DCS.
14 For Quine's view see 'On Carnap's views on ontology' (Quine, 1966). To adopt
    Quine's thought that the involvement of high generality does not in itself induce
    a change in the nature of the claim is not to adopt everything that he says
    against Carnap. For Carnap's famous exposition of his own view, see Carnap
    (1950).
15 Wittgenstein (1969: sec. 676) – this is the final section in OC.

Further reading

The most important texts of Wittgenstein's to read for his views on epistemology are the *Philosophical Investigations* (1953) and *On Certainty* (1969). A very good introductory book on Wittgenstein, with some discussion of his views on knowledge, is Anthony Kenny's *Wittgenstein* (Cambridge, MA: Harvard University Press, 1973), and one that introduces in particular the *Philosophical Investigations* is Marie McGinn's *Routledge Philosophy Guidebook to Wittgenstein and the Philosophical Investigations* (London: Routledge, 1997). In approaching *On Certainty* the two articles by Moore have to be read (see Moore, 1959). An excellent guide to *On Certainty* is McGinn (1989). For the attempt to defeat scepticism based on the idea that terms are linked to criteria see Malcolm (1966). For two powerful discussions of Wittgenstein's notion of criterion, see Charles. S. Chihara and J. A. Fodor's 'Operationalism and ordinary language: A critique of Wittgenstein', in Pitcher (1966), and Rogers Albritton's 'On Wittgenstein's use of the term "criterion"', also in Pitcher (1966). John McDowell (1998 [1982]) presents and discusses the approach which allows defeasible criteria. For some of Grice's ideas about meaning and implication, which are plausible and do not fit well with Wittgenstein's conception, see Grice (1989: especially chs. 2 and 3).

References

Baker, G. P. (1974), 'Criteria: A new foundation for semantics', *Ratio*, 16, 156–89.

Carnap, R. (1950), 'Empiricism, semantics, and ontology', *Revue Internationale de Philosophie*, 4, 20–40.

Grice, P. (1989), *Studies in the Way of Words*. Cambridge, MA: Harvard University Press.

Malcolm, N. (1966), 'Knowledge of other minds', in Pitcher (1966), pp. 371–83.

McDowell, J. (1998 [1982]), 'Criteria, defeasibility and knowledge', in *Meaning, Knowledge, and Reality*. Cambridge, MA: Harvard University Press, pp. 369–94.

McGinn, M. (1989), *Sense and Certainty: A Dissolution of Scepticism*. Oxford: Blackwell.

Moore, G. E. (1903), *Principia Ethica*. Cambridge: Cambridge University Press.

—(1959), *Philosophical Papers*. London: George Allen & Unwin.

Pitcher, G. (ed.) (1966), *Wittgenstein: The Philosophical Investigations*. Garden City, NY: Anchor Books.

Quine, W. V. (1966), *The Ways of Paradox and Other Essays*. New York: Random House.

Snowdon, P. F. (forthcoming 2011), 'Wittgenstein on sense data and experience', in E. Kuusela and M. McGinn (eds), *The Oxford Handbook of Wittgenstein*. Oxford: Oxford University Press.

Wittgenstein, L. (1953), *Philosophical Investigations*, (trans.) G. E. M. Anscombe. Oxford: Blackwell.

—(1958), *The Blue and Brown Books*. Oxford: Blackwell.

—(1969), *On Certainty*, (eds) G. E. M. Anscombe and G. H. Von Wright. Oxford: Blackwell.

Wright, C. (1982), 'Anti-realist semantics: The role of *criteria*', *Royal Institute of Philosophy Lecture Series*, 13, 225–48.

CHAPTER 10

QUINE, GOLDMAN AND TWO WAYS OF NATURALIZING EPISTEMOLOGY

Ram Neta

Throughout much of its post-Reformation history, at least in Western Europe, prominent contributions to philosophy were made almost exclusively by people who also made prominent contributions to the natural sciences, and their contributions to each informed their contributions to the other. But why is this? Is it because the information that we get from the natural sciences is highly relevant to answering philosophical questions? Or is it because the findings of philosophers, such as they are, are highly relevant to answering the empirical questions raised by the natural sciences? In the century-long tradition that began with Gottlob Frege's seminal writings in the 1870s, and ran through much of the philosophy written in English in the 1950s and 1960s – the tradition that has come to be known as 'analytic philosophy' – the prevailing answer to both of these last two questions was: no. According to this analytic tradition, the findings of the natural sciences were of virtually no relevance to philosophy, and vice-versa. Natural science was engaged in the enterprise of constructing a rational, coherent and true understanding of how the world works, using the materials furnished by sensory experience. Philosophy, in contrast, was engaged in the enterprise of trying to delineate the rules by virtue of which any particular state or event would count as *rational, coherent, true* or *understanding*, at all, and it did so independently of the materials furnished by sensory experience, and relying only on reasoning. Philosophy and natural science were not simply distinct, but neither could supply much useful information to the other.

For instance, in his *Logisch-Philosophische Abhandlung* (1921), the great Austrian philosopher Ludwig Wittgenstein wrote:

> 4.111 Philosophy is not one of the natural sciences.
>
> . . . .
>
> 4.1121 Psychology is no more closely related to philosophy than any other natural science . . .
>
> 4.1122 Darwin's theory has no more to do with philosophy than any other hypothesis in natural science.

The idea present in these passages was one shared by Gottlob Frege, Rudolf Carnap, A. J. Ayer, P. F. Strawson and other prominent analytic philosophers in the century roughly spanning 1870 to 1970. These analytic philosophers thought of the philosophical enterprise as one of discovery – by means of reflection alone, and without any essential dependence upon empirical information – of those rules by virtue of which something was good or bad, right or wrong, valid or invalid, true or false, rational or irrational.

How might this sort of philosophical enterprise proceed? Gottlob Frege's work in the foundations of arithmetic provided the paradigm. By the 1870s, a great deal was known about arithmetic, and Frege, a professor of mathematics at the University of Jena, was quite familiar with this vast body of knowledge. But Frege was interested not so much in extending the body of arithmetical knowledge as he was in discovering what it was, fundamentally, that made all of these known arithmetical facts true, and what it was, fundamentally, that made the proof of an arithmetical claim a valid proof. In order to discover these two things, Frege set about, in his 1884 *Die Grundlagen der Arithmetik*, trying to find the smallest and simplest possible set of axioms, and the smallest and simplest set of rules of derivation, such that those rules, when applied to those axioms, would result in proofs of all known arithmetical truths and no known arithmetical falsehoods.

Around 1910, Bertrand Russell and Alfred North Whitehead extended Frege's efforts, and attempted to axiomatize all of mathematics (in their three-volume *Principia Mathematica*, the volumes of which were published in 1910, 1912 and 1913). Soon after, Russell attempted something even more ambitious (in his 1914 *Our Knowledge of the External World*): to find the smallest and simplest set of axioms, and the smallest and simplest set of rules of derivation, such that those rules, when applied to those axioms, would result in proofs of all known truths concerning physical objects. This latter program was most fully executed by Rudolf Carnap in his work *Der Logische Aufbau der Welt*, published in 1928. In this program, natural science was relevant at only one point, and that was in determining which statements concerning physical objects were true, and so needed to be derived within the axiom system that Carnap was attempting to formulate. But once the truths concerning physical objects are fixed, Carnap thought that the information provided by the natural sciences could have no further relevance to philosophy.

One way of understanding the late twentieth-century movement to 'naturalize epistemology' is as a reaction against the idea that the natural sciences have such limited relevance to epistemology. Epistemological naturalists take the findings of the natural sciences to be relevant to the epistemological enterprise of discovering those rules by virtue of which a cognitive state is rational or not, knowledge or not, or, more generally, correct or not. Many such epistemologists take the findings of psychology to be so relevant, and some of them also take Darwin's theory to be relevant. But there are many different ways in which one can take the findings of the natural sciences to be relevant to epistemology, and consequently, many different forms of naturalism in epistemology. In this essay, I discuss two very different versions of naturalized epistemology: one version due to W.V. Quine, and the other due to Alvin Goldman. I then mention, very briefly, a few other forms of naturalism in epistemology.

1. Quine

In contrast to many contemporary epistemologists, Quine takes epistemology to be a particular branch of the study of a particular kind of animal behaviour. To understand his conception of epistemology, we need to begin by understanding how he conceives of the study of animal behaviour in general, and of linguistic behaviour in particular.

All animals engage in goal-directed behaviour in order to satisfy their needs in a challenging environment. At any given point in time, we can think of an animal's behavioural repertoire at that time as a function from sensory stimuli to motor response. Animals can change their behavioural repertoire over time as a result of conditioning, but different animals are susceptible to different sorts of conditioning. For instance, dogs can be conditioned to salivate in response to noises that human beings cannot be conditioned to respond to at all. And, to take another example, human beings can be conditioned to respond to certain complicated patterns of noises, gestures or inscriptions by producing other complicated patterns of noises, gestures or inscriptions; but other, non-human animals cannot be conditioned to respond in this same way to such stimuli. In other words, human beings, unlike other animals, can be conditioned to respond to human language by producing human language themselves.

An animal's susceptibility to conditioning can itself be adaptively beneficial to the animal, or its species. For instance, when a dog is conditioned to salivate in response to a particular noise that has, in the past, been perceptually associated with feeding, the dog's salivation makes it easier for the dog to chew and digest the food that it may be about to receive. Again, when a dog is conditioned to respond to the sound 'sit!' by sitting, that response makes it easier for the dog to acquire the desirable reward that has been associated with this response in the past. And when a human being is conditioned to respond to the perception of human language by the production of human language, then the human being acquires a whole new mechanism for altering its behavioural repertoire: communication. The person who hides in fear when she sees the Aurora Borealis can learn to stay and calmly gaze at the sight once she learns through communication that there is no basis for her fear. The leader who speaks in a frightened tone of voice to her followers can learn to speak in a calm and reassuring tone of voice once she learns through communication that this is more likely to produce the desired submissiveness in her followers. And finally, the scientist who describes a fire as the shedding of phlogiston can learn to describe it as the consumption of oxygen once she learns through communication what the mechanisms of combustion are.

So, because humans can be conditioned to respond to human language by producing human language, they can be conditioned to communicate, and communication provides them with a new mechanism for altering their behavioural repertoire, including their linguistic behavioural repertoire. Now, so far, I have described communication simply as a process of responding to certain complicated patterns of noises, gestures or inscriptions by producing other complicated patterns of noises, gestures or inscriptions. But because human beings can be conditioned to respond differentially to patterns of enormous complexity, the patterns of which we speak here can be extremely complex. And, as it happens, over the course of human linguistic history, these patterns have actually become extremely complex, and are now multi-layered. We can describe one layer of patterns by segmenting the gestures, noises and inscriptions into a certain set of units that we call 'words'; we can describe another layer of patterns by segmenting the gestures, noises and inscriptions into a set of larger and more inclusive units that we call 'sentences'; and we can describe yet another layer of patterns by segmenting the gestures, noises and inscriptions into a set of still larger and still more inclusive units that we call 'theories'.

We said above that human beings can alter their linguistic behavioural repertoire either as a result of conditioning or as a result of communication. But when they alter their linguistic behavioural repertoire, they can alter any or all of these layers of patterns in the noises, gestures and inscriptions they make. Sometimes, the only part of their behavioural repertoire that they alter is their tone of voice (as in the case of the leader who learns to speak to her followers in a calm and reassuring tone of voice). Sometimes, the only part of their behavioural repertoire that they alter is their words (as when someone learns to call someone else by a particular name). But sometimes, they alter very large scale units in their gestures, noises and inscriptions – they alter their theories. This process, whether it is brought about by conditioning or by communication, is what we will call 'theory change'. And epistemology, for Quine, is a branch of the study of theory change.

Of course, the study of theory change includes many different branches. Which of these branches is the one that Quine identifies as epistemology? Here is how Quine himself (1990: 1–2) puts the point:

From impacts on our sensory surfaces, we in our collective and cumulative creativity down the generations have projected our systematic theory of the external world. Our system is proving successful in predicting subsequent sensory input. How have we done it?

Neurology is opening strange new vistas into what goes on between stimulation and perception. Psychology and more particularly psycholinguistics may be looked to for something to say about the passage from perception to expectation, generalization, and systematization. Evolutionary genetics throws further light on the latter matters, accounting for the standards of similarity that underlie our generalizations and hence our expectations. The heuristic of scientific creativity is illuminated also, anecdotally, by the history of science.

Within this baffling tangle of relations between our sensory stimulation and our scientific theory of the world, there is a segment that we can gratefully separate out and clarify without pursuing neurology, psychology, psycholinguistics, genetics, or history. It is the part where theory is tested by prediction. It is the relation of evidential support, and its essentials can be schematized by means of little more than logical analysis.

The segment of which Quine speaks in the preceding paragraph – the segment that can be clarified without pursuing neurology, psychology, psycholinguistics, genetics or history; the segment that involves the relation of evidential support – is that segment the study of which constitutes epistemology. In short, epistemology, for Quine, is the study of evidential support.

This characterization of epistemology is completely unremarkable for an analytic philosopher: Carnap, Ayer or Russell could easily have offered just the same characterization. So what is distinctively naturalistic about Quine's conception of epistemology then? And in what sense does epistemology, for Quine, become a 'chapter of psychology', as he repeatedly says?

The answer to these questions is strongly suggested by the context in which Quine situates naturalistic epistemology throughout his writings. For Quine, the effort to naturalize epistemology is a response to the failure of a particular program that Carnap undertook. Recall that Carnap initially attempted to construct a so-called 'phenomenalistic' language into which (along with the terms of logic and set theory) all our talk of material things and events could be translated. (A 'phenomenalistic' language is one in which there are no expressions that refer to material things and events, and all reference is directed towards features of our subjective experience.) This program failed, even by Carnap's own lights: Carnap was never able to specify a language that was both phenomenalistic and also adequate for translating all our talk of material things and events. Carnap concluded, as did most other philosophers, that our talk of material objects and events is not simply a means for stating facts that could be more elaborately stated using phenomenalistic language. But Carnap still thought that he could at least use his phenomenalistic language as a device for stating *the evidential basis* for all our talk of material things and events. In attempting to naturalize epistemology, Quine was simply calling into question the central presupposition of this latter program, viz., that there is a phenomenalistic language in which the evidential basis for all our talk of material things and events could be stated. If our talk of material things and events is not itself phenomenalistically statable (which it isn't, given the failure of the earlier program), then why suppose that the evidential basis for our talk of material things and events is phenomenalistically statable? To naturalize epistemology is to give up the presupposition that our evidential basis is phenomenalistically statable, and to treat the question of what our evidential basis is as itself an empirical question – one to be answered by looking and seeing what our evidential basis is. That is what is distinctively naturalistic about Quine's epistemology.

This interpretation of Quine's naturalistic program can help us to understand the otherwise puzzling paragraph of 'Epistemology naturalized' in which Quine (1969) first explicitly introduces the idea of a naturalized epistemology. The paragraph that I have in mind here is the third paragraph of the following famous passage (1969: 75–6):

> Two cardinal tenets of empiricism remained unassailable . . . and so remain to this day. One is that whatever evidence there *is* for science *is* sensory evidence. The other, to which I shall recur, is that all inculcation of meanings of words must rest ultimately on sensory evidence. Hence the continuing attractiveness of the idea of a *logischer Aufbau* in which the sensory content of discourse would stand forth explicitly.

> If Carnap had successfully carried such a construction through, how could he have told whether it was the right one? The question would have had no point. He was seeking what he called a *rational reconstruction*. Any construction of physicalistic discourse in terms of sense experience, logic, and set theory would have been seen as satisfactory if it made the physicalistic discourse come out right. If there is one way there are many, but any would be a great achievement.

> But why all this creative reconstruction, all this make-believe? The stimulation of his sensory receptors is all the evidence anybody has had to go on, ultimately, in

arriving at his picture of the world. Why not just see how this construction really proceeds? Why not settle for psychology? Such a surrender of the epistemological burden to psychology is a move that was disallowed in earlier times as circular reasoning. If the epistemologist's goal is validation of the grounds of empirical science, he defeats his purpose by using psychology or other empirical science in the validation. However, such scruples against circularity have little point once we have stopped dreaming of deducing science from observations. If we are out simply to understand the link between observation and science, we are well advised to use any available information, including that provided by the very science whose link with observation we are seeking to understand.

Many philosophers have wondered what Quine could have in mind here when he invites epistemologists to 'see how this construction [of one's theory of the world] really proceeds', to 'settle for psychology', and to 'understand the link between observation and science'. These claims seem to suggest that Quine wants epistemology to cease studying how we *ought* to think, and confine itself to studying how we actually *do* think – and this is just how some philosophers have interpreted Quine's program (e.g. see Jaegwon Kim's widely influential interpretation of Quine: 1988). But this interpretation of Quine has two problems. First, it makes his view look very unattractive: clearly, there is some worthwhile project of studying how we ought to think, and if epistemology isn't the study of how we ought to think, then what is? And second, this interpretation of Quine is very hard to square with the passage quoted above from *Pursuit of Truth*, in which Quine (1990) says that we can clarify relations of evidential support 'without pursuing psychology'. Isn't this latter claim simply inconsistent with Quine's claim that epistemology – the study of evidential support – can become a chapter of psychology?

The interpretation that I have offered dissolves the apparent inconsistency, and also helps us to understand why Quine is not rejecting the epistemologist's effort to understand how we ought to think. I'll take up each of these points in turn.

When Quine says that we can clarify relations of evidential support without pursuing psychology, what he has in mind is this: relations of evidential support are, broadly speaking, logical or statistical, and we can understand what those relations are by doing logic or statistics, not by doing psychology. But when Quine says that epistemology can become a chapter of psychology, what he has in mind is this: in order to understand what evidence supports our theories, and to what extent, what we need to do is to locate our actual evidential bases, and determine to what extent those evidential bases do stand in the relevant logical or statistical relations to our theories. Of course, in figuring out what our actual evidential bases are, or even in figuring out what our theories are, we may apply a principle of charity, and allow our determination of those bases or those theories to be partly guided by consideration of which evidential bases would successfully support which theories. This is a way in which logic and statistics can themselves help to guide the empirical study of psychology. But still, the attempt to figure out what our actual evidential bases are, and what our theories are, is a thoroughly empirical enterprise, and this is the sense in which epistemology – the study of evidential support relations – is a chapter of psychology.

But, to say that epistemology is a chapter of psychology is *not* to deny that epistemology has a normative dimension, i.e., that it concerns how we *ought* to think. As Quine writes (1990: 19):

> To emphasize my dissociation from the Cartesian dream, I have written of neural receptors and their stimulation rather than of sense or sensibilia. I call the pursuit naturalized epistemology, but I have no quarrel with traditionalists who protest my retention of the latter word. I agree with them that repudiation of the Cartesian dream is no minor deviation.

> But they are wrong in protesting that the normative element, so characteristic of epistemology, goes by the board. Insofar as theoretical epistemology gets naturalized into a chapter of theoretical science, so normative epistemology gets naturalized into a chapter of engineering: the technology of anticipating sensory stimulation.

So there is theoretical epistemology, which is the study of what evidence we actually have for whatever theories we actually hold. And there is normative epistemology, which is the study of how to adjust our theories in order most effectively to anticipate sensory stimulation. And both of these pursuits can be guided by logic and statistics, though both of them are heavily empirical. In this respect, the different branches of epistemology are like the different branches of the study of human action: we can study the reasons for which people do what they do, and we can also study what sort of action proves most successful in achieving its goals. But both of these branches of empirical study are guided by our theory of what it is to act rationally (or what is typically called 'rational choice theory').

For Quine, then, epistemology is the study of evidential support, and this study has three branches. First, there is the empirical, psychological study of what evidence we actually have, and what theories we actually hold. Second, there is the empirical, normative study of what strategies of theory change we should employ, in order to optimize or at least improve our ability to anticipate future sensory stimulation. And third, there is the logical and statistical study of evidential support relations, i.e., of the logical or statistical relations that obtain between the sentences our assent to which is most directly and universally keyed to particular sensory stimulations ('observation sentences', as Quine calls them) and our theories. The first two of these branches are obviously empirical, and the second of those two empirical branches is obviously normative. In describing only the first two of these branches as obviously empirical, I do not mean to suggest that the third branch is non-empirical. But empiricality is a matter of degree for Quine. Our beliefs about logic and statistics are less immediately or directly impacted by our sensory stimulations than our beliefs about psychology are. Or, to put the same point using Quine's famous metaphor, logic and statistics are farther from the sensory periphery of our web of belief than psychology is. (An accessible discussion of this metaphor is in Quine and Joseph Ullian's 1970 co-authored book *The Web of Belief.*)

Quine himself devotes most of his efforts in epistemology to the second of these three enterprises. Specifically, he outlines a number of principles that should (and, he thinks, for the most part do) guide our theory change so that it can successfully anticipate future sensory stimulation. There is, for instance, the principle of simplicity, according to which we should hold to the simplest theory that predicts and explains all our evidence. And there is the principle of minimum mutilation, according to which we should change our theories as slightly as possible in order to predict and explain all our evidence. (Again, see *The Web of Belief* for discussion of these principles of theory revision, as well as others.) These principles can conflict with each other, and sometimes conflict with other principles that guide our efforts to change our theories so as most successfully to anticipate future sensory stimulation. In case of such conflict, we must simply strive to do the best we can, and there is no recipe for that. All we have are principles to guide our theory choice, and good judgement to guide us in cases in which the principles conflict.

I have so far ignored a complication in Quine's account of evidence and of evidential support. For Quine, the logical or statistical relations involved in evidential support must be relations among sentences; some sentences imply or probabilify other sentences. But when Quine describes our evidence, he frequently speaks of sensory stimulations. How do the sensory stimulations that Quine takes to constitute our evidence relate to the sentences that Quine takes to stand in relations of evidential support (e.g. implication or probabilification) with our theories? For Quine, this relation is causal. The sentences that Quine takes to stand in relations of evidential support with our theories are what Quine calls 'observation sentences'. Observation sentences are those sentences which, for each person in a given community, have the following property: no matter what else that person believes, when she receives a sensory stimulation of a particular kind, then she will assent to that sentence. Assent to observation sentences is causally keyed to the occurrence of a particular kind of sensory stimulation within a given community. This makes observationality relative to a community of speakers, but it also insures that the same evidence can be had by multiple speakers within that community. In short, it insures the publicity of evidence, at the cost of making it community-relative.

Two things remained constant throughout Quine's writings in epistemology. The first is that he held steadfastly to the conception of epistemology that I have outlined above: I see no sign of his deviating from this conception – at least at the level of abstraction described above – at any point in his career. Quine changed his mind about a number of things in philosophy, but he did not change his mind about the points mentioned above. The second is that, at no point in his career did Quine have anything to say in response to some of the questions that form the focus of so much epistemological attention since the 1963 publication of Edmund Gettier's agenda-setting paper 'Is knowledge justified true belief?', e.g., what is knowledge? What is it for a belief to be justified? What is it for someone to be justified in believing a proposition? Does knowledge require justification? Does knowledge require some especially strong relation between the believer and the world? It is these questions to which Alvin Goldman has devoted most of his attention in epistemology over the past four decades, and it is to the history of his various views that I now turn.

2. Goldman

Unlike Quine, Goldman did not begin his career in epistemology by attempting to develop a comprehensive account of how epistemology fits into the study of human behaviour. Rather Goldman began by addressing himself to a very local epistemological issue to which Quine never addressed himself. Specifically, Goldman began work in epistemology by trying to solve the Gettier problem, i.e., by trying to explain what must be added to an account of empirical knowledge as justified, true belief in order to offer non-circular conditions for knowledge that are both necessary and sufficient. The Gettier problem can be briefly illustrated by means of the following example (but for more detailed discussion of the problem and some proposed solutions, see Chapter 11 in this volume):

> Jones believes, on the basis of very compelling evidence that his co-worker Smith owns a Ford. And so Jones has a justified belief that Smith owns a Ford. But this belief is false: despite all the evidence to the contrary, Smith does not in fact own a Ford. Nonetheless, Jones' co-worker Brown owns a Ford. And so, when Jones infers from his belief that Smith owns a Ford to the conclusion that one of his coworkers owns a Ford, Jones comes to believe something true. Furthermore, this latter true belief is justified, since it is deduced (by means of an obviously valid deduction) from something else that Jones justifiably believes. So Jones has a justified and true belief that one of his co-workers owns a Ford. But Jones does not know that one of his co-workers owns a Ford. So justified true belief is not sufficient for knowledge.

It is possible to multiply such examples *ad infinitum* for cases of empirical belief, but it is not clear that such cases can be constructed for non-empirical belief. In fact, Goldman took the traditional analysis of knowledge as justified true belief to be correct for non-empirical knowledge, but he wanted to find an adequate analysis of empirical knowledge.

Roughly, on Goldman's earliest published view (1967), S has empirical knowledge that p if and only if S's true belief that p is causally connected in an appropriate way with the fact that p, where what counts as an appropriate causal connection is to be specified simply by appeal to an open list of examples (e.g. perception, memory, testimony from someone who perceives or remembers, and good inference from something perceived or remembered). Gettier cases fail to qualify as knowledge because they do not involve the appropriate sort of causal connection between the fact believed and the believer's belief.

While Goldman gave up this causal account of knowledge nine years later, he never gave up its central contention that, whether or not S knows that p (in the particular sense of 'know' that interests epistemologists, Goldman now adds) depends upon the *causal origination* or *causal sustenance* of S's true belief that p. In fact, it was Goldman's insistence upon this point, and his way of developing the point, that put his epistemology in contact with empirical science, and thereby made him a kind of 'naturalist' in epistemology. For Goldman, knowing is a matter of having the right kind of causal history. Epistemology is supposed to tell us what very general sort of causal history is the 'right' kind for knowing, but cognitive science is supposed to spell out the details, and tell us specifically which of our cognitive faculties or methods of belief-formation provide this right kind of causal history, and under what conditions. Thus, epistemology and cognitive science work together, on Goldman's view, to provide us with a detailed account of what it is to know something, which is just an account of the causal history that constitutes knowledge.

In his 1976 essay 'Discrimination and perceptual knowledge', Goldman presented what is generally regarded as a counterexample to his 1967 causal theory of knowledge, and attempted to accommodate the example by appeal to a view that he would eventually call 'reliabilism', which is itself a version of the general idea that whether or not S knows that p depends upon the causal formation or causal sustenance of S's true belief that p. Here is the example that Goldman presented (and which he credits to Carl Ginet): Henry is driving through the countryside looking at a barn. His vision is normal, and he sees the barn clearly, and thereby forms the belief 'there's a barn there'. Unbeknownst to Henry, however, this is fake barn country, and almost all of the apparent barns in this region happen to be mere barn facades; Henry just happened to be looking at one of the only real barns in the area. While Henry has a justified true belief that there's a barn there, he does not know that there's a barn there. But notice that, in a normal situation in which Henry is driving through the countryside and sees a barn, he can come thereby to know that there's a barn there, even though the causal relation between his belief and the fact that there's a barn there is no different in the barn facade case than it is in the normal case. So Henry's failure to know, in the barn facade case, that there's a barn there, cannot be due to any lack of an appropriate causal connection between his belief that there's a barn there and the fact that there's a barn there. His failure to know must be due to something else. But what could it be due to? Goldman claims that it is due to the fact that Henry cannot reliably discriminate real barns from barn facades (at least not by looking at them from the distance and angle that he actually occupies), and that the exercise of this discriminatory ability is required for knowledge that there's a barn there when Henry is in barn facade country, but it is not required for such knowledge when Henry is normally situated. In short, knowing that *p* requires an ability reliably to discriminate between its being the case that *p* and its being the case that some relevant alternative to *p* obtains, where which alternatives count as 'relevant' varies from context to context.

Goldman leaves it open whether the context that fixes the range of alternatives that are relevant to whether or not someone knows something is the context of the putative knower, or is rather the context of someone who is thinking about the putative knower. But, no matter how this issue is resolved, Goldman's reliabilism involves the claim that knowing involves the exercise of a discriminative ability. And this is just one way of spelling out the very general claim that, for *S* to know that *p*, *S*'s true belief that *p* must have the right kind of causal history.

The 1976 view that I just described is a view about the requirements for perceptual knowledge, and it is a view according to which, as Goldman originally presented it, perceptual knowledge does not require that one's perceptual belief be justified. But by the time of his 1979 paper 'What is justified belief?' Goldman reversed himself on this last point, and claimed that perceptual knowledge, like non-empirical knowledge, does require something that epistemologists call 'doxastic justification': in other words, it requires that the belief that constitutes knowledge is itself a justified belief. (For someone to have a justified belief is different from her having a justification to believe something: you can have a justification to believe something whether or not you actually believe it.) But doxastic justification, on Goldman's view, itself requires a certain kind of causal reliability. On Goldman's view, for a belief to be justified involves its being formed by a *reliable process*. A reliable process is one that tends to produce a high ratio of true beliefs. It is empirically obvious that such processes include at least normal forms of perception, memory, inference and testimony: this is why these processes are sources of doxastic justification, and so of knowledge.

Goldman elaborates the view just mentioned in much greater detail in his 1986 book *Epistemology and Cognition*. That book contains a detailed account of knowledge, as well as of doxastic justification. And the book also elaborates the relationship that Goldman takes epistemology to have to the empirical sciences of cognition. I'll start by explaining Goldman's account of knowledge, then proceed to his account of justification, and finally say something about how he conceives of the relation between epistemology and cognitive science.

Goldman's 1986 account of knowledge and of justification, like his earlier accounts, is a causal reliabilist account. According to this account (1986: 63):

> S's believing p at t is justified if and only if (a) S's believing p at t is permitted by a right system of J-rules, and (b) this permission is not undermined by S's cognitive state at t.

This requires a bit of gloss: J-rules are rules according to which some beliefs are permitted and others are not. A system of J-rules is 'right' just in case its dictates concerning which beliefs are permitted and which are not are correct (and such correctness may, for all we say here, be independent of whether or not anyone takes such dictates to be correct). Finally, there are a couple of ways in which a permission may be 'undermined' by the believer's cognitive state. One way in which such undermining can occur is for the believer to have reason to believe that her belief that *p* is not justified. Another way in which such undermining can occur is for the believer simply to believe that her belief that *p* is not justified. In either case, *S*'s belief that *p* is not justified.

Goldman fleshes out this schematic account of doxastic justification by imposing conditions on the rightness of a system of J-rules. A right system of J-rules must make the permissibility of a belief depend upon the process by which the belief is formed or sustained. More specifically, a right system of J-rules must make the permissibility of a belief depend upon the extent to which the processes by which the belief is formed or sustained tend to result in valuable consequences. And more specifically still, a right system of J-rules must make the permissibility of a belief depend upon the extent to which the processes by which the belief is formed or sustained tend to result in a high ratio of true to false beliefs. While a number of different accounts of J-rule rightness satisfy these conditions, Goldman favours the following schematic account (1986: 106):

> A J-rule system R is right if and only if R permits certain (basic) psychological processes, and the instantiation of these processes would result in a truth ratio of beliefs that meets some specified high threshold (greater than 0.50).

When Goldman speaks of a 'basic' psychological process, he means a process that is not acquired as a result of learning: it is either unacquired, or else acquired simply through maturation. And when Goldman speaks of the truth ratio that would result from the instantiation of such a process, he means the truth ratio that would result in normal worlds, i.e., in worlds that work in roughly the way that we take the actual world to work (whether or not the actual world does, in fact, work that way). Finally, the normal worlds in question, whether or not they include the actual world, will include a wide range of counterfactual worlds.

This, then, is Goldman's 1986 account of doxastic justification. What is his account of knowledge? For Goldman, knowledge involves true belief that is doxastically justified, and is formed by a process that is *locally* reliable, i.e., reliable specifically in the kind of setting in which the belief is actually formed, whether that kind of setting obtains in a world in which the belief is true, or in a world in which some relevant alternative to the belief is true.

Since knowledge and doxastic justification both involve reliability of one kind or another, and questions concerning the identity and reliability of our psychological processes are empirical questions, Goldman sees a close relationship between epistemology, on the one hand, and empirical questions concerning the identity and reliability of our psychological processes, on the other. What we know and what we're justified in believing depends upon how we form our beliefs and how reliable those belief-forming processes are.

While Goldman has continued to refine a few details of his views concerning knowledge and justification, much of his work over the past quarter century has involved applications of his reliabilist account of knowledge and of justification to questions concerning how to organize social institutions so as to improve the production and dissemination of knowledge. Thus, in his 1999 book *Knowledge in a Social World*, Goldman discusses how the institutions of science, law, politics, education and communication can be organized so as to maximize our acquisition of true belief, and minimize our acquisition of false belief. This book was seminal in creating the now very professionally active field of social epistemology.

Clearly, Quine and Goldman conceive of epistemology, and its connection to the empirical findings of psychology and cognitive science, very differently. Goldman devotes much of his epistemological work to addressing questions such as 'what is knowledge?' or 'what is it for a belief to be justified?'; these are questions that he takes to be answerable simply by a priori reflection. He also devotes much of his epistemological work to addressing questions such as 'what are our sources of knowledge?' or 'which sorts of beliefs are justified?'; these are questions that he takes to be answerable empirically, largely by means of cognitive science. Quine, in contrast, has nothing to say about any of these questions. For Quine, epistemology is simply the study of evidential support: what evidence do we have? How does evidence support theory? What principles guide proper theory choice given a body of evidence? These are the epistemological questions to which Quine devotes all of his attention. Goldman has very little to say about any of these questions. In fact, perhaps the only place in his corpus in which Goldman discusses any of these questions about evidence is in his 2010 paper 'Williamson on knowledge and evidence', in which he proposes that a person's evidence set at a given time t consists of all and only those propositions that the person is noninferentially propositionally justified in believing at t. But this proposal is offered not on the basis of any empirical considerations, but solely on the basis of its plausibility to reflection. In short, the epistemological question that Quine took to be an empirical question is one that Goldman barely treats at all, and when he does treat it, he treats it as an a priori question. And the epistemological questions that Goldman took to be empirical questions are questions that Quine simply never addressed.

3. Other forms of naturalism in contemporary analytic epistemology

Although Quine and Goldman are the two most influential naturalistic epistemologists, the past two decades have witnessed a number of other important efforts to naturalize epistemology. In this concluding section, I'll mention three of these, and then conclude with a brief remark about how the term 'naturalism' has come to be extended in recent epistemological theorizing.

In a number of papers, and in his 2002 book *Knowledge and its Place in Nature*, Hilary Kornblith argues that, contrary to what Goldman and most other epistemologists suppose, the question 'what is knowledge?' is like the question 'what is water?' or 'what is soil?' in being an *empirical* question, i.e., a question the answer to which can be discovered only on the basis of sensory evidence. More specifically, on Kornblith's view, empirical findings from cognitive ethology can furnish us with an answer to the question of what knowledge is. According to these findings, knowledge is reliably formed true belief. Of course, Kornblith concedes, our intuitive judgements about hypothetical cases can also lead us – as they lead Goldman – to the view that knowledge is (at least something like) reliably formed true belief. But, while most philosophers take such intuitive judgements to be a priori evidence for a hypothesis concerning the nature of knowledge, Kornblith takes these intuitive judgements to be formed on the basis of a great deal of background empirical knowledge that we have. For Kornblith, to the extent that our intuitive judgements are a good guide to the nature of knowledge, this is because they embody a great deal of empirical knowledge.

Second, in the past decade, a number of epistemologists (including Jonathan Weinberg, Shaun Nichols, Stephen Stich, Stacy Swain and Joshua Alexander) have begun to engage in the empirical study of our intuitive judgements about hypothetical cases. Rather than attempting to answer epistemological questions by consulting their own intuitive judgements about hypothetical cases, these epistemologists survey a large sample of people, under a large variety of conditions, in order to study the conditions that influence our intuitive judgements. By understanding what these conditions are and how they operate, these epistemologists hope to be able to factor out the influence of irrelevant factors (e.g. cultural bias, order effects) on our theorizing about epistemological matters. Even if epistemological questions are a priori, these epistemologists insist that it is an empirical matter to figure out which a priori considerations are worthy of our trust and which ones are not. (Influential papers in this tradition include Weinberg, Stich and Nichols'

2001 paper 'Normativity and epistemic intuitions', as well as Swain, Alexander and Weinberg's 2008 paper 'The instability of philosophical intuitions'.)

Third, since the publication of Christopher Cherniak's 1986 book *Minimal Rationality*, a number of epistemologists, impressed both by the dictum that 'ought' implies 'can', as well as by the empirically demonstrable limits and failures of human rationality, have attempted to specify epistemic norms that can be followed by creatures whose rational powers are as feeble as ours are. Such epistemologists (e.g. Michael Bishop and J. D. Trout, in their 2005 book *Epistemology and the Psychology of Human Judgment*) have tended to reject, for instance, the claim that our beliefs ought to be logically consistent (and that our degrees of belief ought to be probabilistically coherent) on the grounds that it is, as a matter of empirically demonstrable fact, impossible for any normal human being to have fully consistent or coherent beliefs. On their view, epistemology has to begin with the empirical findings of cognitive science, for the issue of how we ought to think is constrained by the issue of how it is possible for creatures like us to think, and the latter issue can only be settled by cognitive science.

I have now surveyed the various forms of naturalized epistemology that are influential in the world of contemporary English-speaking philosophy. But I should mention that the term 'naturalism' is sometimes used to describe a kind of epistemological theorizing that does not make close contact with the empirical findings of the natural sciences. Consider the following passage from Bernard Williams' book *Truth and Truthfulness* (2002: 22–3):

> Naturalism is a general outlook which, in relation to human beings, is traditionally, if very vaguely, expressed in the idea that they are 'part of nature' – in particular, that they are so in respects, such as their ethical life, in which this is not obviously true. . . .
>
> Questions about naturalism . . . are questions not about reduction but about explanation. . . . The questions concern what we are prepared to regard, at each level, as an explanation. Moreover, we have no reason to think that what is to count as an explanation, from bits of nature describable only in terms of physics to human beings and their cultures, is at each level the same kind of thing. The question for naturalism is always: can we explain, by some appropriate and relevant criteria of explanation, the phenomenon in question in terms of the *rest* of nature?

To naturalize epistemology, on this conception, is not necessarily to put epistemology into contact with empirical science, but rather to explain epistemic facts by appeal to the natural, non-epistemic facts, whatever exactly those are, and however *a priori* or unscientific may be our knowledge of them. On this broader conception of naturalism, any attempt to explain the epistemic facts without appeal to anything over and above nature (e.g. a Cartesian god, or a Kantian thing-in-itself) and without appeal to other epistemic facts (e.g. brute support relations between mental states and propositions) counts as naturalizing epistemology.

Further reading

Bishop, M. and Trout, J. D. (2005a), 'The pathologies of standard analytic epistemology', *Noûs*, 39, 696–714.

BonJour, L. (1994), 'Against naturalized epistemology', *Midwest Studies in Philosophy*, 19, 283–300.

Feldman, R. (1999), 'Methodological naturalism in epistemology', in J. Greco and E. Sosa (eds), *The Blackwell Guide to Epistemology*. Malden, MA: Blackwell, pp. 170–86.

Foley, R. (1994), 'Quine and naturalized epistemology', *Midwest Studies in Philosophy*, 19, 243–60.

Fumerton, R. (1994), 'Skepticism and naturalistic epistemology', *Midwest Studies in Philosophy*, 19, 321–40.

Goldman, A. I. (1994), 'Naturalistic epistemology and reliabilism', *Midwest Studies in Philosophy*, 19, 301–20.

—(2005), 'Kornblith's naturalistic epistemology', *Philosophy and Phenomenological Research*, 71, 403–10.

Grandy, R. (1994), 'Epistemology naturalized and "Epistemology naturalized"', *Midwest Studies in Philosophy*, 19, 341–9.

Hylton, P. (1994), 'Quine's naturalism', *Midwest Studies in Philosophy*, 19, 261–82.

Johnsen, B. (2005), 'How to read "Epistemology naturalized"', *The Journal of Philosophy*, 102, 78–93.

Kaplan, M. (1994), 'Epistemology denatured', *Midwest Studies in Philosophy*, 19, 350–65.

Kappel, K. (2011), 'Naturalistic epistemology', in S. Bernecker and D. Pritchard (eds), *The Routledge Companion to Epistemology*. New York: Routledge, pp. 836–47.

Kitcher, P. (1992), 'The Naturalists' Return', *The Philosophical Review*, 101, 53–114.

Kornblith, H. (1994), 'Naturalism: Both metaphysical and epistemological', *Midwest Studies in Philosophy*, 19, 39–52.

Maffie, J. (1990), 'Recent work on naturalized epistemology', *American Philosophical Quarterly*, 27, 281–93.

References

Bishop, M. and Trout, J. D. (2005), *Epistemology and the Psychology of Human Judgment*. New York: Oxford University Press.

Carnap, R. (1928), *Der Logische Aufbau der Welt*. Translated as *The Logical Structure of the World*, and included in *The Logical Structure of the World and Pseudoproblems in Philosophy* (1967) (ed. and trans.) R. A. George. Berkeley: University of California Press.

Cherniak, C. (1986), *Minimal Rationality*. Cambridge, MA: The MIT Press.

Frege, G. (1884), *Die Grundlagen der Arithmetik*. Translated as *The Foundations of Arithmetic* (1950), (trans.) J. L. Austin. Oxford: Blackwell.

Gettier, E. L. (1963), 'Is knowledge justified true belief?', *Analysis*, 23, 121–3.

Goldman, A. I. (1967), 'A causal theory of knowing', *The Journal of Philosophy*, 64, 355–72.

—(1976), 'Discrimination and perceptual knowledge', *The Journal of Philosophy*, 73, 771–91.

—(1979), 'What is justified belief?', in G. S. Pappas (ed.), *Justification and Knowledge: New Studies in Epistemology*. Dordrecht: D. Reidel, 1–23.

—(1986), *Epistemology and Cognition*. Cambridge, MA: Harvard University Press.

—(1999), *Knowledge in a Social World*. Oxford: Clarendon Press.

Kim, J. (1988), 'What is "naturalized epistemology"?', *Philosophical Perspectives*, 2, 381–405.

Kornblith, H. (2002), *Knowledge and its Place in Nature*. Oxford: Clarendon Press.

Quine, W. V. (1969), 'Epistemology naturalized', in his *Ontological Relativity and Other Essays*. New York: Columbia University Press, pp. 69–90.

—(1990), *Pursuit of Truth*. Cambridge, MA: Harvard University Press.

Quine, W. V. and Ullian, J. S. (1970), *The Web of Belief*. New York: Random House.

Russell, B. (1914), *Our Knowledge of the External World as a Field for Scientific Method in Philosophy*. Chicago: Open Court.

Russell, B. and Whitehead, A. N. (1910, 1912, 1913). *Principia Mathematica* (three volumes). Cambridge: Cambridge University Press.

Swain, S., Alexander, J. and Weinberg, J. M. (2008), 'The instability of philosophical intuitions: Running hot and cold on Truetemp', *Philosophy and Phenomenological Research*, 76, 138–55.

Weinberg, J. M., Nichols, S. and Stich, S. (2001), 'Normativity and epistemic intuitions', *Philosophical Topics*, 29, 429–60.

Williams, B. (2002), *Truth and Truthfulness: An Essay in Genealogy*. Princeton: Princeton University Press.

Wittgenstein, L. (1921), *Logisch-Philosophische Abhandlung*. Translated as *Tractatus Logico-Philosophicus*. For revised edn (1974), see (trans.) D. F. Pears and B. F. McGuiness. London: Routledge & Kegan Paul.

CHAPTER 11

IN GETTIER'S WAKE

John Turri

1. Introduction

One main goal of epistemology is to define knowledge. Legend has it that the 'traditional' or 'standard' view of knowledge is justified true belief (K = JTB) and that this traditional view reigned supreme for decades, centuries even. As one leading epistemology textbook puts it (BonJour, 2001: 43),

> It is reasonable to say [that] some version or other of the traditional conception of knowledge was taken for granted . . . by virtually all philosophers seriously concerned with knowledge in the period from the time of Descartes until the middle of the twentieth century.

But that all changed in 1963 when an unheralded young philosopher at Wayne State University in Detroit, Edmund Gettier, published a paper as short as it has been influential: 'Is justified true belief knowledge?'. Gettier's paper has since engendered a half-century's worth of responses. If you added up the number of times that this article has been discussed or cited in the literature (thousands of times), and divided that by the number of words in the article (approximately 930), the resulting quotient would be larger than the quotient for any other work of philosophy ever published. Now *if* we call this the 'citation **per** word formula' for calculating a publication's influence, then it is safe to say that Gettier's article is the greatest philosophical caper of all time.

2. Gettier cases and their structure

Chapter 10 of this volume already introduced us to Gettier's discussion. But let's expand on what was said there.

Gettier presented two cases that he thought were clear counterexamples to the JTB theory. In particular, Gettier contended that his cases showed that having a justified true belief was *insufficient* for knowledge, from which it follows trivially that K ≠ JTB. A case of this sort is called a *Gettier case*. The *Gettier problem* is the problem of identifying why the subject in a Gettier case lacks knowledge. It is widely assumed that unless we solve the Gettier problem, we'll be unable to adequately define knowledge. Interestingly, Gettier wasn't the first to come up with what we now call Gettier cases. According to Bimal Matilal (1986: 135–7), the classical Indian philosopher Sriharsa constructed similar examples in the 1100s to confound his opponents, and Roderick Chisholm (1989) reminds us that Bertrand Russell and Alexius Meinong also constructed such cases decades earlier than Gettier. But still it is customary to call them 'Gettier cases'.

Gettier cases are easy to construct, once you get the feel for them. Here are two prototypical examples (not Gettier's originals).

> (LAMB) One of Dr. Lamb's students, Linus, tells her that he owns a Lamborghini. Linus has the title in hand. Dr. Lamb saw Linus arrive on campus in the Lamborghini each day this week. Linus even gave Dr. Lamb the keys and let her take it for a drive. Dr. Lamb believes that Linus owns a Lamborghini, and as a result concludes, 'At least one of my students owns a Lamborghini.' As it turns out, Linus doesn't own a Lamborghini. He's borrowing it from his cousin, who happens to have the same name and birthday. Dr. Lamb has no evidence of any of this deception, though. And yet it's still true that at least one of her students owns a Lamborghini: a modest young woman who sits in the back row owns one. She doesn't like to boast, though, so she doesn't call attention to the fact that she owns a Lamborghini. (Vaguely modelled after Lehrer, 1965: 169–70)

Most philosophers who consider this case say that (a) Dr. Lamb does *not* know that at least one of her students owns a Lamborghini, even though (b) she has a justified true belief that at least one of her students owns a Lamborghini.

(SHEEP) Shep is trekking through a pasture. He gazes down across the field and notices an animal. Viewing conditions are optimal. It appears to be an unremarkable sheep, so he believes, 'That's a sheep in this field,' from which he concludes, 'There's at least one sheep in this field.' As it turns out, Shep isn't looking at a sheep, but rather a dog dressed up to look just like a sheep – a very cleverly disguised dog! Shep has no evidence of this deception. The thought that it was a disguised dog never even occurs to him. And yet it is still true that there is a sheep in the field. It's directly behind the dog, hidden from Shep's view. (Adapted from Chisholm, 1989: 93.)

Most philosophers who consider this case say that (a) Shep does not know that there is a sheep in the field, even though (b) he has a justified true belief that there is a sheep in the field.

Gettier claimed that the success of these cases as counterexamples to the JTB theory depends on two principles. First, that justification isn't factive. This means that it is possible to have a false justified belief. Second, that justification is closed under deductive entailment. This means that if you're justified in believing some proposition P, and P entails some other proposition Q, and you deduce Q from P, and believe Q based on that deduction, then you're justified in believing Q too.

In light of these two points, here is one way to understand the 'recipe' for generating Gettier cases (Feldman, 2003: 28). Begin with a justified false belief that P (which is possible, if justification isn't factive). Then have the protagonist deduce a true consequence, Q, of the justified belief that P, and have the protagonist believe Q on the basis of this deduction (surely this is possible). The resulting belief in Q will be justified (by the assumption that justification is closed under deductive entailment). And the overall result will be a justified true belief that Q, without knowledge that Q.

Here is another way of understanding the Gettier recipe (Zagzebski, 1996). Start with a belief sufficiently justified to meet the justification requirement for knowledge. Then add an element of bad luck that would normally prevent the justified belief from being true. Lastly add a dose of good luck that 'cancels out the bad', so the belief ends up true anyhow. The justification of the justified true belief appears oddly disconnected from the truth, and the overall result will be a justified true belief, one which doesn't amount to knowledge.

3. Some proposed solutions to the Gettier problem

Attempted solutions to the Gettier problem are legion. Some responses are conservative, in that they hew closely to the original JTB theory, introducing as little change as possible to handle the cases. Some responses are radical, in that they break decisively with the spirit of the JTB account, either dramatically refashioning the justification requirement, or even eliminating it entirely. Here I'll review some of the most influential and interesting responses to the Gettier problem (see Shope, 1983, for details on other approaches).

Some philosophers looked at Gettier cases and thought that the problem amounts to this: the subject has a justified true belief, but the belief is essentially based on a false premise. In LAMB the false premise is Dr. Lamb's belief, 'My student Linus owns a Lamborghini,' and in SHEEP it is Shep's belief, 'This animal in the field is a sheep' (where 'this' refers to the cleverly disguised dog). This suggests the *no essential false basis theory of knowledge* (NFB): You know that P just in case (i) P is true, (ii) you believe that P, (iii) your belief that P is justified and (iv) your belief that P isn't essentially based on any falsehood. (For examples of this idea, see Clark, 1963, and Harman, 1973.)

One problem with NFB is that it can't handle simple variants of Gettier cases. Consider this variant of LAMB.

> (LUCKY LAMB): The case is the same as LAMB, except that unbeknownst to Linus he has just inherited a Lamborghini. His cousin died and left it to him.

In this case Dr. Lamb's belief 'My student Linus owns a Lamborghini' is true, so NFB can't handle LUCKY LAMB, because in this case it is true that Linus owns the Lamborghini in question. Another problem with NFB is that it appears to give the wrong verdict in cases like this:

> (BLUE DRESS) Bill awaits Monica's arrival. He wonders whether she'll wear a scarlet dress. He hears a step on the staircase and swings around to see Monica enter the room. 'What a dazzling indigo dress!' he thinks, and concludes, 'Monica's dress isn't scarlet.' And he's right: her dress isn't scarlet. But it isn't indigo either. It's ultramarine.

Intuitively Bill knows that Monica's dress isn't scarlet. But his belief is based on the falsehood that her dress is indigo, so NFB rules that he doesn't know that Monica's dress isn't scarlet. (For examples of this line of thought, see Saunders and Champawat, 1964 and Warfield, 2005.)

Other philosophers looked at Gettier cases and thought that the problem is this: the subject has a justified true belief, but the justification is defeated (see, for example, Lehrer and Paxson, 1969 and Klein, 1976). In LAMB Dr. Lamb's justification is defeated by the fact that Linus is deceiving her (or, in LUCKY LAMB, that LINUS is trying hard to deceive her). In SHEEP Shep's justification is defeated by the fact that he's being deceived by a cleverly disguised dog. This suggests the *simple defeasibility theory of knowledge* (SDT): you know that P just in case (i) P is true, (ii) you believe that P, (iii) your belief that P is justified, and (iv) your justification for believing P is undefeated. Some fact F defeats your justification for believing P just in case (i) you believe P based on evidence E, (ii) E justifies belief in P, but (iii) the combination (E + F) *fails* to justify belief in P. In LAMB the defeater is the fact that Linus is deceiving Dr. Lamb about owning a Lamborghini (or, in LUCKY LAMB, is earnestly trying to deceive Dr. Lamb). In SHEEP the defeater is the fact that Shep is looking at a cleverly disguised dog.

One problem with SDT is that it seems to rule out too much. Consider:

> (INSANE) You were just tenured! Excitedly you phone to tell your best friend Sophia the wonderful news. Naturally Sophia believes and congratulates you. However, unbeknownst to either of you, your dean just went insane – succumbed to the pressures of profit-driven university governance – and is absolutely certain you were not tenured.

It is a fact that your dean is absolutely certain that you were not tenured, and that fact combined with your testimony fails to support Sophia's belief that you were tenured, technically defeating her justification. Thus SDT rules that Sophia doesn't. But intuitively she does know.

In response it has been suggested that knowledge is *ultimately* undefeated justified true belief. Call this the *modified defeasibility theory*: (MDT) you know that P just in case (i) P is true, (ii) you believe P based on evidence E, (iii) E justifies belief in P and (iv) E is ultimately undefeated. E is ultimately undefeated just in case there is no fact F such that (E + F) fails to justify belief in P; or if there is such a fact, then there is some further fact F* such that (E + F + F*) does justify belief in P.[1] In such a case F* is a defeater defeater. In INSANE, F* is the fact that your dean's conviction is borne of insanity. The main problem with MDT, however, is that the very device it introduces to give the intuitively correct verdict in INSANITY also deprives it of the ability to handle the original Gettier cases. Consider LAMB. The fact that Linus is deceiving Dr. Lamb is a defeater (= F). But the fact that the modest female student does own a Lamborghini is a defeater defeater (= F*). This last fact is a defeater defeater because this combination,

> E: My student Linus has possession of this Lamborghini, drives it frequently, and has a title to the Lamborghini with his name and birthdate on it; and
>
> F: My student Linus does not own this Lamborghini; and
>
> F*: That young female student of mine owns a Lamborghini,

justifies Dr. Lamb's belief that at least one of her students owns a Lamborghini. It does this because F* obviously entails that at least one of her students owns a Lamborghini. And it would do so, no matter how many of Dr. Lamb's other students don't own a Lamborghini.

The responses we've looked at so far have been conservative. They respond to Gettier cases by adding a fourth condition to the three conditions featured in the traditional JTB account. But there were more radical responses. Some philosophers looked at Gettier cases and thought that the problem amounts to this: the fact that P doesn't cause the subject to believe that P (Goldman, 1967). In LAMB it is a fact that one of Dr. Lamb's students owns a Lamborghini, but it isn't this fact (namely, the fact that the female student owns one) that causes Dr. Lamb to believe that one of her students owns a Lamborghini. In SHEEP it is a fact that there is a sheep in the field, but it isn't this fact that causes Shep to believe it. This observation led to *the causal theory of knowledge* (CTK): you know that P just in case (i) P is true, (ii) you believe that P and (iii) the fact that P is true causes you to believe that P. CTK gives up on justification entirely as a condition on knowledge. The problem with CTK is that it is easy to introduce deviant causal chains into the description of any Gettier case, which would make it true that the relevant fact causes the subject to believe that P. For example, suppose that we add the following background to SHEEP. A clever farmer dressed up the cleverly disguised dog to fool Shep. The farmer was caused to do this, oddly enough, by the fact that there is at least one sheep in the field as Shep treks by. So the fact that there is at least one sheep in this field (= P) caused the farmer to dress up the dog, which caused Shep to believe that there is at least one sheep in this field. So the fact that P caused Shep to believe that P. CTK thus rules that Shep knows that P. But intuitively this is the wrong verdict.

Another problem with CTK is that if we impose a causal requirement on knowledge, then it becomes difficult to avoid sceptical consequences for beliefs about abstract matters, such as mathematical and logical truths, because it isn't clear that, say, the fact that $2 + 2 = 4$ can cause anything. It also becomes difficult to explain how we know things about the future, because it doesn't seem possible for future facts to cause our beliefs now. Strategies for overcoming these problems have been proposed, but not to the satisfaction of many.

A descendant of CTK is reliabilism about justification and knowledge.[2] Rather than give up entirely on justification as a condition on knowledge, some argued that we can understand justified belief as belief produced by a reliable cognitive process (Goldman, 1979), and then understand knowledge as roughly justified true belief, where 'justification' is given the relevant reliabilist reading. The result is *process reliabilism*: (PR) you know that P just in case (i) P is true, (ii) you believe that P and (iii) your belief that P is produced by a reliable cognitive process (i.e. your belief is 'justified'). PR might handle Gettier cases by pointing out that in LAMB, for example, Dr. Lamb's belief is produced by making deductions based on the testimony of someone who is trying to deceive her, which plausibly isn't a reliable process. And in SHEEP Shep's belief is produced by making deductions based on mistaken appearance, which plausibly isn't reliable either.

The main criticism of PR is that it has no principled way of *individuating* cognitive processes, and so no principled way of deciding whether any given true belief amounts to knowledge (Conee and Feldman, 1998). For example, why say that Shep is basing his deductions on misleading appearances, rather than on perceptual experience? Perceptual experience is reliable. But then why doesn't Shep know? Another problem with PR is that it can't handle simple variants of Gettier cases. Consider this variant of SHEEP:

(SPECIAL DOG) The case is the same as SHEEP, except that the disguised dog is very special. It tracks Shep and appears to him *only* when at least one sheep is nearby. It wouldn't appear to him unless there were a nearby sheep. It also prevents him from encountering any other non-sheep sheep-lookalike that would mislead him into concluding that there is at least one sheep nearby.

In SPECIAL DOG the following method seems perfectly reliable for Shep: from the fact that something looks like a sheep nearby, conclude that there is at least one sheep nearby. So PR rules that in SPECIAL DOG Shep knows that there is at least one sheep nearby. But it would be very surprising if Shep knew in SPECIAL DOG but not in SHEEP.

Other philosophers looked at Gettier cases and thought that the problem is this: it is just an accident that the subject's belief is true (e.g. Unger, 1968). In LAMB it is just an accident that Dr. Lamb ended up being right that at least one of her students owned a Lamborghini. And in SHEEP it is just an accident that Shep ended up being right that there's at least one sheep in the field. This suggests the *no-accident theory of knowledge* (NAT): you know that P just in case (i) P is true, (ii) you believe that P and (iii) it is not at all an accident that your belief that P is true. NAT omits justification from its definition of knowledge, which leaves open the possibility that there can be 'unreasonable' knowledge, that is, knowledge which the subject is unjustified in believing is true (Unger, 164). For example, if an epistemic guardian angel watched over you and ensured that your every wish came true, then wishful thinking would be a way for you to gain knowledge, since it would be no accident that your wishful beliefs turned out to be true. Many judge this to be an absurd consequence of the view – surely believing something because you want it to be true isn't a way of gaining knowledge! Another potential problem with NAT is that it is very difficult to explain what clause (iii) amounts to.

A related family of views propose a *safety condition* on knowledge (Sosa, 1999; Pritchard, 2005), which is intended to give content to the idea that knowledge can't be 'accidental' or 'lucky'. The most conservative version of a safety-based view simply appends a safety condition to the traditional analysis, yielding the *safe justified true belief theory of knowledge* (SJTB): you know that P just in case (i) P is true, (ii) you believe that P, (iii) your belief that P is justified and (iv) your belief that P is safe. A true belief is safe just in case it wouldn't easily have been false. What does it mean to say that a true belief 'wouldn't easily have been false'? There's no precise way to define this, but the intuitive idea is that *something significant* would have had to change in order to have made the belief false. One problem with this view is that it fails to handle simple variants of Gettier cases, such as SPECIAL DOG, because the Gettiered belief is not only justified and true, but also safe. To see why, recall that in SPECIAL DOG the cleverly disguised special dog wouldn't appear to Shep unless there were a nearby sheep, and also prevents Shep from encountering any other non-sheep sheep-lookalike that would mislead him into concluding that there is at least one sheep nearby. In effect, the special dog acts as a sort of epistemic guardian angel for Shep on such matters, which ensures that his beliefs about nearby sheep are not only true but also safely formed.

Another family of views proposes a *sensitivity condition* on knowledge (Dretske, 1970; 2005; Nozick, 1981). A conservative sensitivity-based view might simply append a sensitivity condition to the JTB analysis, but sensitivity theorists typically dispense with justification altogether. Your belief that P is sensitive just in case the following conditional is true: if P were false, then you wouldn't believe that P. A sensitivity condition on knowledge handles standard Gettier cases. In LAMB if it were false that at least one of the students owned a Lamborghini, then Dr. Lamb would still believe that at least one student did (because Linus would still have deceived her). In SHEEP if it were false that there was at least one sheep in the field, then Shep would still believe that there was (because the cleverly disguised dog would still have tricked him). One problem facing this diagnosis is that it can't handle simple variants of the cases. For example, it can't handle SPECIAL DOG because the special cleverly disguised dog wouldn't have tricked Shep if there were no sheep nearby; and the special cleverly disguised dog would prevent anything else from tricking Shep; so if there weren't a nearby sheep, Shep wouldn't believe that there was one. Another serious problem facing this view is that it implies that knowledge isn't closed under some trivial, known deductive entailments. (We'll soon return to closure and how counterintuitive it can be to deny it, in the next paragraph and again in Section 4. See also Vogel, 1990, and Hawthorne, 2005, for a defence of closure.)

Related to the sensitivity-based account of knowledge, Fred Dretske (2005) has also argued for a sensitivity-based account of reasons or justification. On this view, justification isn't closed under deductive entailment, and even fails to transmit across some simple, known deductive entailments. Generally speaking, a justification to believe P is an indication that P is true. Indications carry information. Information comes from sources. Consider a thermometer, which is a source of information. The thermometer indicates the ambient temperature in the room. Its readout provides a reason for believing that it is twenty-one degrees in here. The readout carries information about the ambient temperature, in this case that it is twenty-one degrees. 'That it is twenty-one degrees' entails 'that it is not eighteen degrees being misrepresented as twenty-one degrees'. But the latter claim is *not* part of the readout's content – it doesn't carry that information. And yet the readout's content entails it. So your reason for believing that it is twenty-one degrees needn't also be a reason for you to believe the obvious deductive consequences of the claim that it is twenty-one degrees. It might be easier to grasp how potentially counterintuitive this is by considering the matter more schematically. According to Dretske, the following is possible: reason R justifies you in believing P, and you *know* that the truth of P *guarantees* the truth of Q, but still, R does *not* justify you in believing Q. If Dretske is right about this, then one of the key assumptions of Gettier's original discussion – namely, that justification is closed under deductive entailment – is thrown into doubt.[3]

A more recent approach to the Gettier problem is to argue that knowledge can be defined as true belief for which the subject *earns credit* for believing the truth, but a Gettier subject doesn't earn credit for believing the truth, which explains why she doesn't know (e.g. Greco, 2003; Zagzebski, 2009). For example, in SHEEP Shep doesn't earn credit for believing the truth about whether there's a sheep in the field. Rather, we would credit a confluence of odd circumstances for the fact that Shep ends up believing correctly. It is an open question whether the operative notion of *credit* can ultimately sustain this treatment of the Gettier problem. A related view defines knowledge as follows: you know that P just in case you have a true belief that P *because* you believed competently; however, it is argued, although the Gettier subject has a true belief, and believes competently, he doesn't have a true belief because he believes competently, which explains why he doesn't know (Sosa, 2007). Another related view defines knowledge as follows: you know that P just in case the fact that you have a true belief that P is a manifestation of your cognitive powers; however, it is argued, although the Gettier subject has a true belief, and exercises her cognitive powers, the fact that she has a true belief isn't a manifestation of her cognitive powers, which explains why she doesn't know (Turri, 2011; forthcoming). The jury is still out on this family of approaches.

Some have argued that Gettier's intuition about his cases was wrong: Gettier cases *are* cases of knowledge. Stephen Hetherington (1998; 1999; 2011) argues that a Gettier subject knows despite coming perilously close to not knowing, and supplements this by diagnosing intuitions to the contrary. Whereas safety theorists would claim that the unsafety of a Gettier subject's belief disqualifies it as a case of knowledge, Hetherington contends that its unsafety misleads us into thinking that the Gettier subject doesn't know. The Gettier subject's belief might very easily have been false, and we mistake this *near failure* for an actual failure. Gettier subjects straddle the divide between *just barely knowing* and *not knowing*. Although ingenious, Hetherington's view remains a minority position (Lycan, 2006; Turri, forthcoming).

Many philosophers have taken Gettier cases to show that justified true belief isn't sufficient for knowledge, even though it still is necessary. And as we've already seen, some have tried to replace justification with something else entirely, such as an appropriate casual relation, a safety condition or a sensitivity condition. But at least one philosopher has argued that they're all wrong because knowledge is simpler than any of them had imagined: knowledge is mere true belief (Sartwell, 1991; 1992). Crispin Sartwell's argument for this position is simple: knowledge is the goal of inquiry; the goal of inquiry is true belief; so knowledge is true belief. Inquiry just is the procedure of generating beliefs about particular propositions, and when we ask whether some claim is true, what we want is to *know* whether it is true. In other words, knowledge is the goal of inquiry. But most philosophers will object that we also want our true beliefs to be *justified*, well supported by evidence, so Sartwell has left out an important aspect of our goal. Sartwell accepts that we want justified beliefs, but argues that this is only because justification is a good sign that we've got what we really want, namely, true belief. Justification is instrumentally good because it is a good sign that we do know, but isn't an essential part of knowledge.

4. The Scylla and Charybdis of post-Gettier epistemology: or, teetering between fallibilism and scepticism

Nearly all epistemologists think that Sartwell is wrong, and that knowledge requires something more than true belief. Most epistemologists still think that justification is a necessary condition on knowledge, even if justified true belief isn't sufficient for knowledge. And most epistemologists still agree with Gettier that justification isn't factive (Sutton, 2007, dissents). Having a justified belief that P doesn't guarantee that P is true: you could be justified in believing P even though P is false. Moreover, it is widely held that the minimum level of justification required for knowledge is also non-factive: having knowledge-grade justification for believing that P doesn't guarantee that P is true. To put it differently, the conventional wisdom in contemporary epistemology is that knowledge-grade justification is *fallible*: you could be wrong even though you have it.

But fallibilism has struck many as deeply problematic. What follows is one way of explaining why fallibilism can seem both attractive and deeply puzzling (BonJour, 2001).

Suppose you have a true belief. In order for it to be knowledge, how much justification must be added to it? Think of justification for a belief as measured by *how probable* the belief is given the reasons or evidence you have. We can measure probability any way we like, but one convenient way to measure it is to use the decimals in the interval [0, 1] on the number line. A probability of 0 means that the claim is guaranteed to be false. A probability of 1 means that the claim is guaranteed to be true. A probability of 0.5 means that the claim is just as likely to be true as it is to be false. The question then becomes: how probable, relative to your evidence, must your belief be for it to be knowledge?

Obviously it must be greater than 0.5 – after all, if it were less than 0.5, then it would be more probable that your belief was false, given your evidence! But how much greater than 0.5? Suppose we say that knowledge requires a probability of 1 – that is, knowledge requires justification that *guarantees* the truth of the belief. Call this *infallible justification. The infallibilist conception of knowledge* says that knowledge requires infallible justification. We can motivate the infallibilist conception as follows. If the aim of belief is truth, then it makes sense that knowledge would require infallible justification, because it guarantees that belief's aim is achieved. Clearly it is a good thing to have such a guarantee.

But all is not well with the infallibilist conception. It seems to entail that we know nothing at all about the material world outside of our own minds, or about the (contingent) future, or about the (contingent) past. For it seems that we could have had the same justification that we do in fact have, even if the world around us (or the past, or the future) had been radically different. Our justification doesn't guarantee that a material world exists. (Think of Descartes' evil genius: see Chapter 5.) Neither does it guarantee that there is a past or future. This dramatic sceptical consequence conflicts with commonsense and counts against the infallibilist conception of knowledge. This is presumably part of the motivation for the widespread agreement that justification isn't factive.

We seem compelled to conclude that knowledge requires justification that makes the belief very likely true, but needn't guarantee it. This is the *fallibilist conception of knowledge*. But a question about this view immediately arises: what level of justification does it require? Any point short of 1 would seem *arbitrary*. Why should we pick that point exactly? The same could be said for a vague range that includes points short of 1 – why, exactly, should the vague range extend that far but not further? This might not seem so troubling in itself, but as Laurence BonJour (2001) points out, it suggests an even deeper problem for the weak conception. It brings into doubt the value of knowledge. Can knowledge really be valuable if it is arbitrarily defined? It would count heavily against the fallibilist conception of knowledge if it implied that knowledge wasn't valuable. (Kaplan, 1985, raises related worries about knowledge's value in light of the Gettier problem.)

A related problem for the fallibilist conception of knowledge presents itself, which relates to the second of Gettier's assumptions. Suppose for the sake of argument that we settle on 0.9 as the required level of probability. Suppose further that you believe Q and you believe R, that Q and R are both true, and that you have reached the 0.9 threshold for each. Thus the fallibilist conception entails that you know Q, and it entails that you know R. Intuitively, if you know Q and you also know R, then you know the conjunction (Q & R), just by simple deduction. But, surprisingly, the weak conception of knowledge can't sustain this judgement! To see why, consider that the probability of the conjunction of two independent claims, such as Q and R, equals the product of their probabilities. (This is the special conjunction rule from probability theory.) In this case, the probability of Q = 0.9 and the probability of R = 0.9. So the probability of the conjunction (Q & R) = 0.9 × 0.9 = 0.81, which falls short of the required 0.9. So the weak conception of knowledge along with a law of probability entail that you *don't know* the conjunction (Q & R), because you aren't well enough justified in believing the conjunction. Can we tolerate this result?

So we are faced with a choice between two views, fallibilism and infallibilism, each of which has seemingly unpalatable consequences. If we accept fallibilism, then we seem poised to surrender the intuitive claim that (knowledge-grade) justification is closed under simple, known deductive entailments, and also the intuitive claim that knowledge is valuable. And if we accept infallibilism, then we seem poised to surrender the intuitive claim that we are in a position to know lots of things about the material world, the past and the future.

Notice how Gettier's two assumptions relate to these unpalatable consequences. In setting up his problem, Gettier assumed that (1) justification isn't factive, and (2) justification is closed under deductive entailment. Infallibilism threatens to falsify something in the ballpark of (1), whereas fallibilism threatens to falsify something in the ballpark of (2). Gettier's lasting legacy might well be to force us to choose between these two claims. Are we forced to choose between them, or can we find some way to have our epistemological cake and eat it too?

Notes

1 This is an oversimplification, since there might be defeaters for a defeater defeater. But still, the point is clear enough: whenever justification is defeated (or a defeater defeater is defeated) there's always at least one other fact to defeat the defeater (or to defeat the defeater defeater).
2 Both reliabilism and the CTK were discussed also in Chapter 10 of this volume.

3 The denial of closure has significant implications for epistemology, beyond the Gettier problem. It would also enable a direct and powerful response to many influential sceptical arguments. In fact, this is precisely how the idea of denying closure entered the contemporary discussion. See Dretske (1970), Nozick (1981), and also Pritchard (2008) for a helpful overview.

Further reading

Hetherington, S. (2011), 'The Gettier problem', in S. Bernecker and D. Pritchard (eds), *The Routledge Companion to Epistemology*. New York: Routledge, pp. 119–30.

Shope, R. K. (2002), 'Conditions and analyses of knowing', in P. K. Moser (ed.), *The Oxford Handbook of Epistemology*. New York: Oxford University Press, pp. 25–70.

Zagzebski, L. (1999), 'What is knowledge?', in J. Greco and E. Sosa (eds), *The Blackwell Guide to Epistemology*. Malden, MA: Blackwell, pp. 92–116.

References

BonJour, L. (2001), *Epistemology: Classical Problems and Contemporary Responses*. Lanham, MD: Rowman and Littlefield.

Chisholm, R. M. (1989), *Theory of Knowledge*, 3rd edn. Englewood Cliffs, NJ: Prentice Hall.

Clark, M. (1963), 'Knowledge and grounds: A comment on Mr. Gettier's paper', *Analysis*, 24, 46–8.

Conee, E. and Feldman, R. (1998), 'The generality problem for reliabilism', *Philosophical Studies*, 89, 1–29.

Dretske, F. (1970), 'Epistemic operators', *The Journal of Philosophy*, 67, 1007–23.

—(2005), 'The case against closure', in M. Steup and E. Sosa (eds), *Contemporary Debates in Epistemology*. Malden, MA: Blackwell, pp. 13–26.

Feldman, R. (2003), *Epistemology*. Upper Saddle River, NJ: Prentice Hall.

Gettier, E. L. (1963), 'Is justified true belief knowledge?', *Analysis*, 23, 121–3.

Goldman, A. I. (1979), 'What is justified belief?', in G. S. Pappas (ed.), *Justification and Knowledge: New Studies in Epistemology*. Dordrecht: D. Reidel, pp. 1–23.

Greco, J. (2003), 'Knowledge as credit for true belief', in M. DePaul and L. Zagzebski (eds), *Intellectual Virtue: Perspectives from Ethics and Epistemology*. Oxford: Clarendon Press, pp. 111–34.

Harman, G. (1973), *Thought*. Princeton: Princeton University Press.

Hawthorne, J. (2005), 'The case for closure', in M. Steup and E. Sosa (eds), *Contemporary Debates in Epistemology*. Malden, MA: Blackwell, pp. 26–43.

Hetherington, S. (1998), 'Actually knowing', *The Philosophical Quarterly*, 48, 453–69.

—(1999), 'Knowing failably', *The Journal of Philosophy*, 96, 565–87.

—(2011), *How to Know: A Practicalist Conception of Knowledge*. Malden, MA: Wiley-Blackwell.

Kaplan, M. (1985), 'It's not what you know that counts', *The Journal of Philosophy*, 82, 350–63.

Klein, P. (1976), 'Knowledge, causality, and defeasibility', *The Journal of Philosophy*, 73, 792–812.

Lehrer, K. (1965), 'Knowledge, truth and evidence', *Analysis*, 25, 168–75.

Lehrer, K. and Paxson Jr., T. D. (1969), 'Knowledge: Undefeated justified true belief', *The Journal of Philosophy*, 66, 225–37.

Lycan, W. G. (2006), 'On the Gettier Problem problem', in S. Hetherington (ed.), *Epistemology Futures*. Oxford: Clarendon Press, 148–68.

Matilal, B. K. (1986), *Perception: An Essay on Classical Indian Theories of Knowledge*. Oxford: Clarendon Press.

Nozick, R. (1981), *Philosophical Explorations*. Cambridge, MA: Harvard University Press.

Pritchard, D. (2005), *Epistemic Luck*. Oxford: Clarendon Press.

—(2008), 'Sensitivity, safety, and anti-luck epistemology', in J. Greco (ed.), *The Oxford Handbook of Skepticism*. New York: Oxford University Press, pp. 437–55.

Sartwell, C. (1991), 'Knowledge is merely true belief', *American Philosophical Quarterly*, 28, 157–65.

—(1992), 'Why knowledge is merely true belief', *The Journal of Philosophy*, 89, 167–80.

Saunders, J. T. and Champawat, N. (1964), 'Mr Clark's definition of "knowledge"', *Analysis*, 25, 8–9.

Shope, R. K. (1983), *The Analysis of Knowledge: A Decade of Research*. Princeton: Princeton University Press.

Sosa, E. (1999), 'How to defeat opposition to Moore', *Philosophical Perspectives*, 13, 141–53.

—(2007), *A Virtue Epistemology: Apt Belief and Reflective Knowledge*, Vol. 1. Oxford: Clarendon Press.

Sutton, J. (2007), *Without Justification*. Cambridge, MA: MIT Press.

Turri, J. (2011), 'Manifest failure: The Gettier problem solved', *Philosophers' Imprint*, 11, 1–11.

—(forthcoming), 'Is knowledge justified true belief?', *Synthese*.

Unger, P. (1968), 'An analysis of factual knowledge', *The Journal of Philosophy*, 65, 157–70.

Vogel, J. (1990), 'Are there counterexamples to the closure principle?', in M. D. Roth and G. Ross (eds), *Doubting: Contemporary Perspectives on Skepticism*. Dordrecht: Kluwer, pp. 13–27.

Warfield, T. (2005), 'Knowledge from falsehood', *Philosophical Perspectives*, 19, 405–16.

Zagzebski, L. T. (1996), *Virtues of the Mind: An Inquiry into the Nature of Virtue and the Ethical Foundations of Knowledge*. Cambridge: Cambridge University Press.

—(2009), *On Epistemology*. Belmont, CA: Wadsworth.

CHAPTER 12

EPISTEMOLOGY'S FUTURE HERE AND NOW
Stephen Hetherington

1. Looking to the future

Epistemology has given us ideas, controversies, challenges – this book. What next should we expect, or at least want, from epistemology? Given what it is and has been, what might it become, well into the future? What wholly new ideas could epistemologists be pondering two hundred years from now? *That*, we cannot say. But here is a more manageable question. Might some of what is happening *now* within epistemology matter to forthcoming generations of epistemologists?

Many ideas are presently being proposed within epistemology, a lively part of philosophy at the moment. The rest of this chapter will mention several of those ideas. Some, all, *or* none of them may prosper sufficiently to be included in any updating of this book two hundred years hence.

2. Some current epistemological ideas

2.1 Proper functioning
In Chapter 10, we met the epistemological idea of reliability: does a belief's being produced reliably (so that its being true was likely) make it justified, even knowledge? One potentially significant extension of that

idea is Alvin Plantinga's (1993a; 1993b). According to his theory, knowledge is a belief produced as a result of what he calls proper functioning: the belief will have arisen through a properly functioning truth-directed aspect of a person (such as a cognitive faculty). What does this mean? Reliability will be involved, with there having been a high likelihood of the true belief's sprouting forth. But the influence of *design* will also have permeated the moment. Proper function is the implementation of a faculty, for example, whose *purpose* is to deliver true beliefs, within some apt range of circumstances, regarding a more or less determinate range of topics. It satisfies this purpose when functioning as it *should*, given the kind of aspect it is of the person. In at least that sense, there will have been a design plan behind the knowing.

2.2 Virtue epistemology

And so some epistemology blends with some metaphysics. But Plantinga's has not been the only attempt at understanding knowledge's nature by placing people within a more expansive philosophical story about the world. For instance, is knowing a matter of our somehow functioning *virtuously*? Should epistemology, when seeking to understand knowledge, embrace *that* metaphysical dimension of ourselves? Indeed so, say advocates of what is called virtue epistemology. Ernest Sosa (1980) began such talk among contemporary epistemologists, when urging us to conceive of reliable belief-forming faculties as virtuous because of their reliability.

More recently, there have been two main developments of that idea.

(i) Maybe the *believer* as a whole – not merely a faculty within her – is what is being virtuous. That sounds like a more traditionally congruent way to apply the concept of virtue as such. But how can we then understand a specific piece of knowledge within the believer as present due to that 'larger' virtuousness? Linda Zagzebski has given us the most sustained answer to that question, in *Virtues of the Mind* (1996). She looks to a believer's having been *motivated* virtuously in forming his belief, with the belief's thereby being knowledge.

(ii) Independently of the success or otherwise of Zagzebski's form of theory, virtue epistemology has begun expanding its ambit, seeking further enrichments of epistemology through the idea of an epistemic virtue. Are epistemically virtuous people epistemologically interesting in their own right? Perhaps; and we might study them so as to *emulate* them. They could be epistemic exemplars – epistemic role models. Think of such potentially epistemic – but definitely personal – qualities as open-mindedness, fair-mindedness, emotional calmness and clarity, a love of knowledge. Might an understanding of these even help us to live more happily and decently?

2.3 Knowledge and practice

Here is another way for epistemology possibly to encompass more of our human potential. We could focus upon people as agents – not only people acting virtuously, but people acting at all. Can we enlarge epistemology by finding links between action *per se* and a traditional epistemic phenomenon such as knowledge?

(i) *Normativity.* Might knowledge's presence have normative ramifications for the knower, considered as an agent? Does knowledge's presence or absence constrain when it is, and when it is not, *apt* for a person to act in this way or that? Thus, perhaps knowledge is what renders *assertions* in particular normatively apt. Williamson (2000: ch. 11), especially, has argued that an assertion is appropriate only when expressing knowledge on the speaker's part.

(ii) *Pragmatic encroachment.* Might it even be that a belief is knowledge, or not, partly because of how its being knowledge would fit significantly into the believer's life of action? This is the idea of pragmatic encroachment, notably argued for by Jeremy Fantl and Matthew McGrath in *Knowledge in an Uncertain World* (2009). Maybe knowing has a nature which is somewhat practical.

(iii) *Knowledge-how.* Many actions seem purposeful. Often we call them thoughtful or intelligent, even when the agent was not consciously thinking about how to perform them. Might any such action nonetheless be *implicitly guided* by some of the agent's knowledge (with the knowledge thereby *making* the action purposeful)? This idea was highlighted by Gilbert Ryle (1949; 1971). He distinguished knowledge-that (knowledge of a truth) from knowledge-how (to do an action). And he argued influentially – an influence beginning to be more marked – that knowledge-how's manifestations are not always guided by knowledge-that. Ryle's reasoning has been questioned by Stanley and Williamson (2001), who counter-argue that any case of knowledge-how is really a case of knowledge-that. (To know how to ride a bicycle is to know relevant truths, presented in practical ways to the knower.) Theirs is an *intellectualism* about knowledge-*how*'s nature. (Another way to discard Ryle's view of knowledge-that and knowledge-how as fundamentally different is to regard knowledge-that as a kind of knowledge-how – knowledge how to assert accurately, question accurately, answer accurately, act accurately, reason accurately, etc. This is a *practicalism* about knowledge-*that*'s nature. Practicalism is a further way of conceiving of knowledge's nature as somewhat practical.)

2.4 Contextualism

There has been much recent epistemological talk about how people talk about knowledge. In general, what makes a knowledge-ascription or knowledge-denial true? Here is a traditional form of answer to that question:

> An ascription of knowledge to a person is true if and only if she has the knowl-edge. And she has this knowledge in virtue of aspects of herself and the world – *not* aspects of whoever is making the ascription. (The same sort of point applies to knowledge-denials.)

However, is that form of answer sensitive to all relevant linguistic data? Consider how we react to *sceptical* knowledge-denials. I-while-applying-a-high-standard-for-knowledge may say 'She doesn't really know it' – agreeing with a sceptical verdict. But you-while-applying-a-lower-standard-for-knowledge may say, 'She does know it' – disagreeing with the sceptical verdict. Which of our assertions is correct – absolutely correct, literally true? *Each* can be true (say many epistemologists), rela-tive to its respective context of utterance-while-applying-a-particular-standard-for-knowing. In practice, this is how we tend to talk about knowledge.

That is the basic motivation for what has come to be called *con-textualism* about the semantics of knowledge-ascriptions and -denials. Variants upon that idea are being debated at present. It is a debate, moreover, which concerns epistemological methodology. Some episte-mologists view contextualism as telling us about 'knowledge talk' but not about knowledge as such – a view which could well be taken as describing a substantive limitation upon contextualism's potential epistemological significance. Or, alternatively, does contextualism's focus on 'knowledge talk' bring us as close to accurately ascertaining knowledge's nature (when it is present and when it is not) as is realistically possible?

2.5 Knowledge-first

That depends; can we think directly about knowledge, perhaps by philosophically scrutinizing our shared *concept* of knowledge? Chapter 11 showed us how, most manifestly during the past fifty or so years, epistemologists have sought *conceptual analyses* of knowledge:

> List other aspects of ourselves and the world, ones we understand well and independently (such as truth, belief, and justification). Then say how these are to be combined if knowledge is to be present. Do this so as to describe what it is to know, for *any* conceivable case of knowledge. The result – this description – is an informative articulation of the concept of knowledge.

Yet Chapter 11 also explained how complex and possibly unhelpful that process soon became. And now the methodology of seeking a conceptual analysis at all is being questioned forcefully. In *Knowledge and its Limits* (2000: ch. 1), Timothy Williamson argues that this is not how epistemology should aim to understand knowledge. He propounds this alternative strategy: We should place knowledge *first* in the conceptual order. Do not try to define knowledge in terms of truth, belief and justification, for instance. Consider knowledge itself, directly; possibly use this reflection to understand aspects of these other epistemic phenomena, in turn.

Williamson proceeds to defend several striking (and now much-discussed) theses. Here are some of them:

> Knowledge is a state of mind, entire unto itself. (It is not a composite of a belief – a state of mind – and further features, such as truth, from the world beyond.)
>
> Evidence is only ever knowledge, and knowledge is always evidence. ('E = K', says Williamson.)
>
> A person's knowledge can sometimes explain – in a way belief need not – why she acted as she did.

Knowledge is a normative constraint upon assertion: the latter is only ever apt as an expression of the former. (Section 2.3 noted this thesis.)

Knowledge's presence is not always knowable by the knower. (It is not 'luminous', says Williamson.)

There is more besides in Williamson's densely argued book. Will it prove to have been a significant symbol of epistemology's move from the twentieth century into the twenty-first? Some epistemologists believe so.

3. Forward to the past – sometimes

As epistemology continues doing its doings and taking its shapes, we may wonder where these should end. Are there limits to how far it can travel? Are there only so many shapes it can take, before ceasing to be insightful, even ceasing to be epistemological?

That sort of question arises about epistemology as about any area of philosophy. Suppose that only a small number of fundamental forms of question are genuinely philosophical. One candidate is this: 'Is there a *difference between appearance and reality* regarding phenomenon X?' Another is the question, 'Is there an *ultimate or final possible account, reason, or explanation* regarding X?' I dare not speculate on how many such question-types – jointly comprising the ultimate package of philosophical question-forms – there might be. Time and again, however, one can recognize the recurrence of a form of philosophical questioning or (more generally) a form of philosophical thinking. Could philosophy ever exhaust this underlying supply? Might a specific area of philosophy, such as epistemology, do so – before beginning to repeat itself?

I raise that meta-philosophical question non-judgementally. Some ideas may *deserve* to be repeated. Refining and reinvigorating of them could occur, too. The meta-philosophical question also arises because when pondering (in Section 2) various epistemological ideas which could, for all we yet know to the contrary, become influential in later years, we may have been reminded of a few older philosophical thoughts.

(i)   Zagzebski's version of virtue epistemology (Section 2.2) links episte-
      mology with some ancient philosophy. She draws upon Aristotle's
      account of personal virtues. In effect, she is saying, epistemology
      supplies extra reasons why philosophy should not lose sight of
      Aristotle's account. For him, these are aspects of a person's char-
      acter which embody a genuine record of success. (Good intentions
      are not enough.) Virtue epistemology in general may also be recre-
      ating a mediaeval philosophical sensitivity to such matters (Wood,
      1998: 17).
(ii) Practicalism (Section 2.3) conceives of all cases of knowledge-that as
      instances of appropriate kinds of knowledge-how – as abilities or skills,
      say. This interpretation could be regarded as returning us to Plato's idea
      of knowledge as a power (an idea explained in Chapter 2).
(iii) Williamson's conception of knowledge (Section 2.5) as an unana-
      lysable mental state might remind us of another ancient idea. It is
      not so unlike thinking of knowledge as a state of direct apprehen-
      sion – a comparison explained by Gerson (2009: 158–63). The com-
      parison is not perfect, since Williamson allows that when a person
      knows a particular truth she also believes it. But there is something
      striking about even the partial return of that ancient conception of
      knowledge – a conception otherwise seemingly at odds with much
      contemporary epistemology.

Nor should we overlook the possibility of some *sceptical* ideas regaining
an epistemological centrality – a status which, time and again over the
centuries, has been theirs. I did not mention these in Section 2 because
at the moment such ideas are not front and centre within epistemology.
This could easily change, though.

4. Epistemology's future

I am not saying that epistemology must eventually, in a way which would
render it a *failure*, run out of ideas. Let us ask Section 3's initial question
again, more optimistically this time. Could there ever be a welcomely
Final Epistemology, an aptly and helpfully Completed Epistemology? We
may imagine attaining a listing of all and only epistemological truths. Is
it *that* for which epistemologists are striving?

Even if so, and even if it is possible, we are not there yet. Epistemology currently seems to contain some new ideas. But newness as such is not a virtue in an idea. We should always ask where a specific philosophical idea – new or renewed – can best be leading us. Michael Dummett (2010: 21) says that 'philosophy does not advance knowledge; it clarifies what we already know.' If he is right, then epistemology only clarifies what we already know about knowledge and related phenomena. Without epistemology, we would believe only murkily about knowledge, say. With epistemology, clarity can dawn over the whole epistemic landscape.

Surely not, though. Epistemology clarifies *and* puzzles. It enlightens *and* darkens. It confirms *and* challenges. Even outstanding epistemology might do any of this. Epistemology's most mind-catching thinkers calm us *and* surprise us. This book is evidence of that. Epistemology may be revisionary, even of favoured claims to know. We can relinquish previously firm commitments when epistemology advises us to do so; which, sometimes, it does.

With what would we be left, then, if epistemology could ever be completed? Maybe with at least some of the ideas in this book; which ones, though?

Further reading

General. Hetherington (2006) gathers together papers intended to stimulate future epistemological research in several different possible directions.

Proper functioning. For critical discussions of Plantinga's (1993a; 1993b) theory, along with his responses, see Kvanvig (1996).

Virtue epistemology. Sosa (2007; 2009) has continued developing his virtue epistemology. Baehr (2006) provides a sympathetic yet critical analysis of Zagzebski's (1996) approach to understanding knowledge. For a more recent virtue epistemology, see Greco (2010). On the idea of an epistemic exemplar, see Zagzebski (2006). For an attempt to combine traditional epistemology with reflection upon intellectual virtues, see Wood (1998). An extended epistemological account just of intellectual virtues is provided by Roberts and Wood (2007).

Knowledge and practice. The idea of knowledge's presence being what renders actions normatively apt is defended by Hawthorne and Stanley (2008), as well as by Fantl and McGrath (2009). For a practicalism about knowledge, see Hetherington (2011: ch. 2). There is also increasing epistemological interest in knowledge-how independently of whether one of intellectualism and practical-ism is true: see Bengson and Moffett (forthcoming).

Contextualism. The seeds of contextualism were planted by Dretske (1970) and Lewis (1979). Cohen (1986; 1991) began developing it more fully, particularly in response to sceptical claims. For recent versions and defences of contextualism, see Lewis (1996) and DeRose (2009). Hawthorne (2004) and Stanley (2005) dis-cuss associated conceptual options. (Note that there is an older use of the word 'contextualism'; as to which, see Hetherington [1996: ch. 24]. It reflects some of Wittgenstein's views on knowledge; as to which, see Chapter 9 of this book.)

Knowledge-first. Greenough's and Pritchard's collection (2009) includes criti-cal responses to Williamson (2000), followed by his replies. Williamson (2007) presents some related views.

References

Baehr, J. S. (2006), 'Character in epistemology', *Philosophical Studies*, 128, 479–514.

Bengson, J. and Moffett, M. (eds) (forthcoming), *Knowing How: Essays on Knowledge, Mind, and Action*. Oxford: Clarendon Press.

Cohen, S. (1986), 'Knowledge and context', *The Journal of Philosophy*, 83, 574–85.

—(1991), 'Skepticism, relevance, and relativity', in B. P. McLaughlin (ed.), *Dretske and His Critics*. Cambridge, MA: Blackwell, pp. 17–37.

DeRose, K. (2009), *The Case For Contextualism: Knowledge, Skepticism, and Context, Vol. 1*. Oxford: Clarendon Press.

Dretske, F. I. (1970), 'Epistemic operators', *The Journal of Philosophy*, 67, 1007–23.

Dummett, M. (2010 [2001]), *The Nature and Future of Philosophy*. New York: Columbia University Press.

Fantl, J. and McGrath, M. (2009), *Knowledge in an Uncertain World*. New York: Oxford University Press.

Gerson, L. P. (2009), *Ancient Epistemology*. Cambridge: Cambridge University Press.

Greco, J. (2010), *Achieving Knowledge: A Virtue-Theoretic Account of Epistemic Normativity*. Cambridge: Cambridge University Press.

Greenough, P. and Pritchard, D. (eds) (2009), *Williamson on Knowledge*. Oxford: Clarendon Press.

Hawthorne, J. (2004), *Knowledge and Lotteries*. Oxford: Clarendon Press.

Hawthorne, J. and Stanley, J. (2008), 'Knowledge and action', *The Journal of Philosophy*, 105, 571–90.

Hetherington, S. (1996), *Knowledge Puzzles: An Introduction to Epistemology*. Boulder, Colo.: Westview Press.

— (ed.) (2006), *Epistemology Futures*. Oxford: Clarendon Press.

—(2011), *How To Know: A Practicalist Conception of Knowledge*. Malden, MA: Wiley-Blackwell.

Kvanvig, J. L. (ed.) (1996), *Warrant in Contemporary Epistemology: Essays in Honor of Plantinga's Theory of Knowledge*. Lanham, MD: Rowman & Littlefield.

Lewis, D. (1979), 'Scorekeeping in a language game', *Journal of Philosophical Logic*, 8, 339–59.

—(1996), 'Elusive knowledge', *Australasian Journal of Philosophy*, 74, 549–67.

Plantinga, A. (1993a), *Warrant: The Current Debate*. New York: Oxford University Press.

—(1993b), *Warrant and Proper Function*. New York: Oxford University Press.

Roberts, R. C. and Wood, W. J. (2007), *Intellectual Virtues: An Essay in Regulative Epistemology*. Oxford: Clarendon Press.

Ryle, G. (1949), *The Concept of Mind*. London: Hutchinson.

—(1971 [1946]), 'Knowing how and knowing that', in his *Collected Papers*, Vol. II. London: Hutchinson, pp. 212–25.

Sosa, E. (1980), 'The raft and the pyramid: coherence versus foundations in the theory of knowledge', *Midwest Studies in Philosophy*, 5, 3–25.

—(2007), *A Virtue Epistemology: Apt Belief and Reflective Knowledge, Vol. I*. Oxford: Clarendon Press.

—(2009), *Reflective Knowledge: Apt Belief and Reflective Knowledge, Vol. II*. Oxford: Clarendon Press.

Stanley, J. (2005), *Knowledge and Practical Interests*. Oxford: Clarendon Press.

Stanley, J. and Williamson, T. (2001), 'Knowing how', *The Journal of Philosophy*, 98, 411–44.

Williamson, T. (2000), *Knowledge and Its Limits*. Oxford: Clarendon Press.

—(2007), *The Philosophy of Philosophy*. Malden, MA: Blackwell.

Wood, W. J. (1998), *Epistemology: Becoming Intellectually Virtuous*. Downers Grove, IL: IVP Academic.

Zagzebski, L. T. (1996), *Virtues of the Mind: An Inquiry Into the Nature of Virtue and the Ethical Foundations of Knowledge*. Cambridge: Cambridge University Press.

—(2006), 'Ideal agents and ideal observers in epistemology', in Hetherington (2006), pp. 131–47.

Index

Goodman's 'new' Problem of induction vs Hume

Scepticism of external world knowledge - can it be refuted?

Gettier's Criticism of Justified True Belief analysis of knowledge
Significance of Kripke's distinction between rigid - non-rigid designat
Hume's analysis of causation: compared with counterfactory theory

Ali Alexander Nouredinne
Balkan
♡